Revolution in the Bleachers

Revolution in the Bleachers

How Parents Can Take Back Family Life
in a World Gone Crazy over Youth Sports

Regan McMahon

GOTHAM
BOOKS

GOTHAM BOOKS
Published by Penguin Group (USA) Inc.
375 Hudson Street, New York, New York 10014, U.S.A.

Penguin Group (Canada), 90 Eglinton Avenue East, Suite 700, Toronto, Ontario M4P 2Y3, Canada (a division of Pearson Penguin Canada Inc.); Penguin Books Ltd, 80 Strand, London WC2R 0RL, England; Penguin Ireland, 25 St Stephen's Green, Dublin 2, Ireland (a division of Penguin Books Ltd); Penguin Group (Australia), 250 Camberwell Road, Camberwell, Victoria 3124, Australia (a division of Pearson Australia Group Pty Ltd); Penguin Books India Pvt Ltd, 11 Community Centre, Panchsheel Park, New Delhi – 110 017, India; Penguin Group (NZ), 67 Apollo Drive, Mairangi Bay, Auckland 1311, New Zealand (a division of Pearson New Zealand Ltd); Penguin Books (South Africa) (Pty) Ltd, 24 Sturdee Avenue, Rosebank, Johannesburg 2196, South Africa

Penguin Books Ltd, Registered Offices: 80 Strand, London WC2R 0RL, England

Published by Gotham Books, a division of Penguin Group (USA) Inc.

First printing, May 2007
10   9   8   7   6   5   4   3   2   1

Portions of the text previously appeared in Regan McMahon's article "How Much Is Too Much?" published March 6, 2005, in the *San Francisco Chronicle Magazine*.

Gotham Books and the skyscraper logo are trademarks of Penguin Group (USA) Inc.

LIBRARY OF CONGRESS CATALOGING-IN-PUBLICATION DATA
McMahon, Regan.
    Revolution in the bleachers : how parents can take back family life in a world gone crazy over youth sports / by Regan McMahon.
        p. cm.
    ISBN 978-1-592-40284-7 (hardcover)
    1. Sports for children—United States. 2. Sports for children—Social aspects—United States. 3. Children—Family relationships—United States. 4. Parent and child—United States. I. Title.
    GV709.2.M356 2007
    796.083—dc22   2006027873

Printed in the United States of America
Set in Adobe Garamond
Designed by Spring Hoteling

While the author has made every effort to provide accurate telephone numbers and Internet addresses at the time of publication, neither the publisher nor the author assumes any responsibility for errors, or for changes that occur after publication. Further, the publisher does not have any control over and does not assume any responsibility for author or third-party Web sites or their content.

For Blair, Kyle and Hayley

CONTENTS

FOREWORD BY BILL WALTON

x

INTRODUCTION

xiii

CHAPTER 1

The Rise of Girls' Sports and Its Impact on the Family

1

CHAPTER 2

How Soccer Changed Everything

22

CHAPTER 3

The Rise of Elite Clubs

32

CHAPTER 4

The Risks to Young Bodies

66

CHAPTER 5
Child's Play
98

CHAPTER 6
Growing Up Stressed Out
126

CHAPTER 7
Guess Who's Not Coming to Dinner
154

CHAPTER 8
Are Parents Driving the Craziness?
177

CHAPTER 9
When Coaches Have All the Power
210

CHAPTER 10
Start a Revolution
239

ACKNOWLEDGMENTS
259

RESOURCES
263

BIBLIOGRAPHY
265

INDEX
267

Foreword

Bill Walton

I grew up in the most unathletic family imaginable. I never shot a single basket with my dad, although I did see him run one time at a church picnic and nearly fell over laughing. My parents knew nothing of this world of sports that has become my life. In fact, when I go to visit them these days in our family home of 55 years, the first words out of their mouths are usually, "So, Billy, did you ever get a job????" And I'm now 54 years old.

What my parents taught us was life itself: love, friendship, cooperation, the value of education and, mostly, hard work. They also taught us balance, and that the choices that we would make regarding our course in life were our own. They were always supportive, positive and constructive, but well aware that sports were just a part of a much bigger world that included education (at the top of the list), art, literature, music, social awareness and involvement, family and friends. Most important, my parents came out to support the dreams that we were chasing: Whatever they were, Mom and Dad were there for us—in the bleachers.

There is no stronger motivation in parents' lives than the drive to create a better world with more opportunities for our own children. Sadly, this overpowering emotion has gotten so warped and out of kilter that Regan McMahon decided to write a book calling for a "Revolution in the Bleachers." She has succinctly captured all that has gone wrong, including overzealous parents determined to make their child the next "great one" at any cost. But her book is not a compendium of complaints. It is a proud parent's plea to bring a level of reason and sanity to the most important issue of the day: our future and the culture that we want our children to grow up in.

Like Regan, I am a proud parent myself. I always encouraged our four children to play sports for fun, for their health, and to learn life's greatest lessons along the way. The invaluable experiences that a youngster absorbs from being involved in competitive athletics as a member of a team can go a long way toward determining his or her ultimate level of success, happiness and achievement. But in our house, it was always their choice: from whether to play at all, to what sports, to the amount of time dedicated to their dreams. It's their lives. Our children are not living for us. And we should not be trying to live through them. No matter how hard we try and how desperately we want the best for our children, the only way that someone is going to be truly great at anything is if they want to get there themselves. The worst things you can do for the ones you love are the things that they could and should do for themselves.

The master teachers in my own life have always stressed the need for balance in everything. Balance in athletics can be defined as keeping the head directly over the mid-point between your two feet so that you can quickly get to what is next. The balance needed to become proficient at anything also requires relentless attention to your emotional, psychological and spiritual balance. As part of that desired balance, never discount the power and importance of free time—the time necessary to dream, to rest, to reflect, to ponder, to choose; time when and where it's very quiet, so that when you come back around you're ready for whatever's next.

Regan has done a remarkable job of bringing together all these aspects of this complex issue and offering workable solutions that challenge us to be better as parents, as human beings, and to be a better member of the most special of all teams: your family.

As our children were growing up, I told them that I wanted, first and foremost, to be their dad. I didn't want to be their coach; that is a different relationship, one that requires a tougher personal bond than I want with my children. I tried to always be there for them. But I warned them that if they wanted me as their coach, I can be a tough coach. It has taken me a lifetime to understand that there is nothing on earth stronger than gentleness.

I have learned almost everything I know through my lifelong association with the most perfect of games, basketball—things like teamwork, preparation, dealing with adversity and how to deliver peak performance on command. As I have moved through life's stages—from child to parent, from student to teacher—I have come to fully comprehend the most fundamental aspect of being a dad and a teacher. It's not what or how you teach, it's who the teachers are themselves.

I am profoundly grateful to Regan McMahon for this magnificent book. *Revolution in the Bleachers* is the perfect guide to ensure that our greatest and most important dreams really do come true. By being in those bleachers when your child is out there on the fields of life, hopefully you'll be able to experience that life-changing moment when your son or daughter comes up to you after the game is over, and, looking up with those most beautiful eyes, says, "Dad—thanks for coming."

Introduction

I remember the day it happened. It was yet another jam-packed Saturday morning, and my husband, Blair, and I were facing a logistical challenge to the space-time continuum sufficient to qualify us for the rally at Monte Carlo. We had to get two kids to three games in two cities all before lunchtime. Hayley, then 11, had a soccer game at 9 in Alameda on Bay Farm Island, a lush, green soccer paradise on the eastern shore of San Francisco Bay 20 minutes from our home near downtown Oakland. Kyle, then 14, had a soccer game at 10 in the Oakland Hills, 20 minutes in the opposite direction, at a junior college field surrounded by redwoods, laurel and eucalyptus, where just before turning into the parking lot you can catch spectacular views across the bay to the Golden Gate Bridge. I stuffed Hayley in the minivan, and Blair whisked Kyle into the Honda. Gentlemen, start your engines.

When Hayley's game was finished we zoomed up to catch the rest of Kyle's game and then switch cars so Hayley could change out of her soccer clothes into her volleyball uniform while her dad drove her to her Catholic Youth Organization (CYO) game in East Oakland, 15 minutes in yet another direction. En route she'd wolf down a sandwich I'd packed as she exchanged her shin guards for knee pads, while I dropped Kyle back home (luckily his baseball season was still three months away) and then rushed to her game, hoping to get there before the ref's whistle.

Somewhere between the girls' post-game snack on the island and the handoff in the hills, it hit me: This is nuts.

Then I started pondering: How did we get here? And can we maintain this pace? Why do seasons for different sports have to overlap? Why does everyone I know spend so much of their time in the car, shuttling kids to practices and games? And if it's this hard for me, with a husband to carry 50 percent of the load, what must it be like for single parents, or families with more than two kids, or kids in split-custody situations who have to keep track of their uniforms and equipment between two houses? And however hectic our life had become, being the working parents of two athletic kids, it was nothing compared with the lives of families with kids playing elite club sports, who have more practices per week and play games an hour or more away from home every Saturday and Sunday—except when they're traveling to a tournament multi-hours and sometimes several states away, six, eight or more times a year, where they stay in a motel and play up to six games in a weekend.

Is this really the best version of childhood we can offer our kids? Or is everyone giving up too much? Too many weekends, too many summers. Too much family time. Too much downtime. Too many meals together at home. I wondered if there was a way to get some balance back. Team sports are great—kids can get good, healthy exercise, have fun and learn values like sportsmanship, courage, discipline and focus that will serve them later in life. But has something gotten distorted in recent years? Winning has superseded fun, learning and development while youth sports have been transformed into a star system modeled on professional sports, with all its greed and excess and glorification of attitude and individualism.

I figured it was time to step back and take a look at the evolution of youth sports and find out how parents are navigating the changed landscape. I began with a cover story in the *San Francisco Chronicle Magazine*, the Sunday supplement of the newspaper where I am an editor. I raised the issues busy sports families are facing and I explored the angles of elite club sports, the dramatic rise in overuse injuries among young athletes, the increased stress in players' lives and the lack of downtime they now have. I interviewed coaches, parents, psychotherapists and parenting experts. I asked lots of questions that have no easy answers, like how much is too much (which ended up being the title of my article) and is it fair to limit a child to one sport per season to reduce stress for the whole family?

The response I got from readers was overwhelming. "Until your article appeared, I thought I was the only parent feeling this way," wrote Roy Cardozo. "Please write more about this subject because our society is stealing childhood from children and that certainly is a crime," wrote Joe Breuer, the dad of a club volleyball player in Marin County who has to drive his daughter an hour and a half each way up a crowded commute corridor to her club practice in Sonoma County two or three days a week, and goes to a tournament "at least once a month that's usually 100 to 2,700 miles away."

I got an e-mail from Fred Cesano, who was coach of the No. 1 Boys Under 18 team in the country in 2000. "I recently gave up club soccer because of many of the things you wrote about," he said. "I'm just going to concentrate on high school ball now because it comes with a different attitude and pride." Paul Gordon wrote, "We have two kids in grade school and experience much of what you have written about. It's really out of control at the expense of the family." The e-mails started pouring in before I'd even had my coffee on Sunday morning, and they continued all day. Then when I was driving the kids to school on Monday, discussion of my article was all over the morning talk shows. By week's end I'd been invited to take the mike on a sports radio call-in show in Santa Cruz, two hours away, to talk about the issues it had stirred up.

Clearly I had struck a nerve. And I was surprised at how many coaches responded positively. One e-mailed to ask if he could post the article on his soccer league's Web site. Another soccer league cited it in their next season's enrollment letter, assuring parents they supported a more balanced approach to youth sports. I even got a request for permission to reprint the article from a soccer magazine in England—the country that *invented* soccer!

Still, I knew I'd only scratched the surface. When I got an opportunity to continue investigating the topic for this book, I was able to broaden my research to a national scope. I tuned in to a coast-to-coast discussion on the problems in youth sports that's going on every day in the sports sections and editorial pages of America's newspapers. I listened in on elite soccer parent Internet chat rooms. I talked to hockey dads in Vermont and baseball nuts in San Diego. I interviewed athletes in middle school, high school and college, and even some pros. I grilled coaches from the rec level to Division I university teams. I turned to psychologists to learn what young athletes are telling them about their stressed-out lives. I got the medical perspective on intense year-round play from orthopedic surgeons and sports medicine specialists. I read a shelf full of books on the state of youth sports and childhood in new millennium America. And I tried to sort out how we got here, where we're going and what we can do to make things better for kids and families. Practical suggestions of "What You Can Do Now" appear at the end of most chapters.

It should be noted that I interviewed athletes, parents and coaches during the academic year of 2005–2006. So when I identify someone as a sophomore, it's because she was when I spoke to her. By publication time, she'll be a junior. The experiences my interview subjects recounted and the feelings they expressed provide a window on their world as it existed in that moment, on that team, with that coach, as it felt to them at that age. Circumstances may have changed by now, but what they said then was their truth at that time.

I'm not an expert, I'm a concerned parent. I'm not anti-sports; I love sports, having been a hard-core child athlete myself: Competitive figure skating took up much of my life from ages 8 to 16. In middle school I would skate from 6 to 8 in the morning before school and return after school and skate into the night, eating dinner from the snack bar alone while I did my homework between the afternoon and evening sessions. I was on the basketball and swim teams in high school. And my adult life has been filled with ocean sports— bodyboarding and, recently, surfing—and winter sports: cross-country and downhill skiing, and occasionally my first love, ice skating.

The focus of this book is team sports in particular. I understand there will always be prodigies in individual sports who give up any semblance of normal life to train and excel. My interest lies in the societal shift in the United States whereby organized sports have become the primary way children socialize and increasingly the only way they play outdoors, and in how team sports have invaded and transformed family life. There are unique pressures on team players. In an individual sport, you're not expected to show up for practice even when you're sick and sit on the sidelines to show your commitment to the team, for example.

We all know the many benefits of youth sports. But as youth sports have escalated in intensity, competitiveness, time commitment and parent involvement, certain risks are beginning to surface as well, from overuse injuries, stress and depression to inappropriate sideline behavior and fractured family patterns.

Things have gotten out of whack, and it's time to regain our balance. It's time for a revolution in the bleachers.

Regan McMahon
Oakland, California
June 2006

Revolution in the Bleachers

CHAPTER 1

*The Rise of Girls' Sports and
Its Impact on the Family*

When I started to think about why we parents are running around so much more than our parents did, I realized that the biggest factor is the rise of sports programs for girls. When I was a kid growing up in the '60s, girls might pursue individual sports like ice skating, gymnastics or horseback riding, but they usually didn't get into team sports until high school, if at all. In my family, I was a figure skater from 2nd through 10th grades, when I quit partially because I wanted to participate on my school's basketball and swim teams. My older sister, Brigid, and I went to Catholic school, and there was always league play with other private and parochial schools. It never occurred to me that there were schools where girls had no opportunity to play sports. (See the box about Margo Freistadt on page 5.) Brigid was a competitive equestrian from 3rd grade until college, and picked up riding and jumping again as an adult. But in our sports, competitions were few and far between within a given year. We weren't going to tournaments every weekend like many of today's young athletes.

Some boys got into team sports like Little League baseball, Pop Warner football or hockey by age 8 or 10, but participation wasn't universal and didn't start in kindergarten, as is the case with contemporary soccer. Sports were played seasonally, with breaks between the seasons. Intense time commitment generally didn't kick in until high school.

Parenting styles and the parental fear factor were different then, too. Parents would drop kids off for lessons, usually didn't attend their kids' practices and—horror of horrors to today's parents—didn't feel they had to attend every game. A boy might ride his bike to the local park for baseball, or walk to and from a practice or game at his school—in an era when most kids attended the school nearest their house—while Mom and his sister stayed home.

Today, parents are more involved on every level, from chauffeuring to cheering. And if they have a boy and a girl, they have double the commitment, double the time expenditure, double the miles to travel. Parents believe their towns and cities aren't as safe as they were in previous generations, so many don't feel comfortable letting their kids get to games and practices on their own. City streets are more dangerous, gang members and criminals are more often armed and the sensationalizing of child abductions, starting in the 1980s, has scared parents silly. (In fact, research shows that most abductions are done by family members, as in a custody dispute, but parents continue to believe in the high risk of strangers harming and/or snatching their children.)

The places kids pursue athletics are often far from home these days. Many no longer attend their neighborhood schools. They go to private or charter schools or transfer to a better public school outside their district, and belong to elite sports clubs that may practice an hour or more from home and play games several counties or even states away. Parents now scramble to get their son to his game on one side of town (or the state) and their daughter to hers many miles in the opposite direction. In the old days, the daughter wouldn't have had a game to get to.

What changed things for girls—and made logistics more complicated for parents—is Title IX, which was passed in 1972 as an Education Amendment to the Civil Rights Act of 1964 to end gender discrimination in federally funded school programs. But the explosion in girls' sports affected parents in more ways than having more kids to shuttle to more places. The dramatic increase in women's collegiate sports programs meant athletic elementary and high school girls had an opportunity for college sports scholarships. Universities suddenly had rosters to fill in women's teams they hadn't had before. That was one special moment in time, but the legacy of Title IX is intrinsically related to the parental frenzy over youth sports today for both boys and girls. Parents' lust for college scholarships is driving much of the craziness that has infected youth sports, and has influenced decisions about early participation, early specialization and membership on elite club teams.

J. T. Hanley, coach of the women's varsity soccer team at Bishop O'Dowd High School in Oakland, California, says, "I think the perception is that Title IX created $8 billon of scholarship money, and that every Division I college football program like Notre Dame got their equivalency by having an equal number of Division I women's soccer scholarships. When in fact that's not how it works. A lot of parents think that every year the scholarship tree blooms and full-ride fruit drops to the ground. And it's just not reality."

Most people know Title IX made a big difference, but few know the history of its passage, the struggles endured on the way to full compliance and the effect Title IX continues to have on youth sports.

Sports as a Civil Right

It all started with the civil rights movement, whose great achievement, with the Civil Rights Act of 1964, was that the United States government acknowledged that discrimination based on a person's color or ethnicity was unfair, un-American and illegal. As the '70s dawned, women in Congress and across the country began to press the point that discrimination against women for no other reason than that they were female was equally repugnant and intolerable. Particularly concerned that women were being denied access to university, law and medical school admission, a committee of female U.S. representatives drew up language that would bar discrimination in any federally funded school program. The drafters of Title IX, and many who would ultimately vote for its passage, may not have had girls' sports programs on their minds at the time, but the amendment's impact in that area was colossal.

Title IX said simply:

No person in the United States shall, on the basis of sex, be excluded from participation in, be denied the benefits of, or be subjected to discrimination under any educational program or activity receiving Federal financial assistance.

Those 37 words changed everything. Signed into law by President Nixon in June 1972, the Educational Amendments of 1972 were the first legislation to ensure equal access to education for both sexes. It was clearly a victory for women, whose applications soon flooded college admissions offices, but the government dragged its feet in clarifying what schools were actually required to do under Title IX, which officially went into effect in June 1973. In November 1973, the National Collegiate Athletic Association (NCAA) caught wind of the idea that the new law would affect college sports and feared it would ruin them. Would schools have to field a women's football team? Would men and women have to share shower facilities? Many colleges had no budget at all for women's sports. How would they go from zero to matching the million-dollar men's sports budgets?

Health, Education, and Welfare Secretary Caspar Weinberger finally issued Title IX rules in June 1974. Males and females would have an equal opportunity to play sports, though schools didn't have to spend money on them in equal numbers. And each sex would be entitled to the same quality of coaches and locker rooms, travel and

Player Profile

Margo Freistadt

Margo Freistadt, a journalism colleague of mine, has seen the difference Title IX made when she compares her own experience with her daughter's. Margo grew up in various small towns in Colorado and moved to California at 14. A strong basketball player, she had no team to play for because her high school in the rural community of Manteca had no sports for girls. But her college did: She played varsity all four years for Oberlin, a Division III school in Ohio, and briefly played in France after college, when there was no opportunity for women to play pro basketball in the United States. Margo got to know her future husband playing pickup games at public rec centers and outdoor playgrounds in San Francisco. And their daughter, Kenny Ludlow, grew up playing for recreational and traveling teams, and now, as a freshman, plays on the junior varsity basketball team for San Francisco's Lowell High School. Margo likes to say that Kenny has been playing basketball since she was in the womb, because Margo didn't break off her twice-weekly games until she was six months pregnant, and then only because "I was usually playing with all men, and nobody wanted to be the one that hit the pregnant lady."

*What was it like being an athletic girl in
an era before Title IX really took hold?*

I was what was called then a tomboy. They don't really use that term anymore. I played at recess with boys, whatever was in season: basketball, football, baseball, track, marbles. I started focusing on basketball, because I liked it more, when I was maybe 6 or 7.

But there weren't any girls' teams. At recess we always just picked teams, and I always got picked maybe third or fourth. So I was the third or fourth best football player in my grade. I was a pass receiver, and I could catch the ball and run like very few of the other kids. And then all the other kids who were as good as I was got picked up on Pop Warner teams. And everybody knew girls can't do that. Some of my friends and I talked about how maybe I could just wear a helmet so they couldn't tell I was a girl. But then how would I get around my parents and the teachers, who all knew I was a girl? My friends wanted me to be on their team because they knew I could catch. I remember knowing that it was unfair, but not knowing you could fight against it.

Later on, when I was in late high school, I realized there were lawsuits about that kind of thing. My mom was in the feminist movement at that point. And I realize, looking back on it, that if I had explained the situation to my mom, I might have been one of those early lawsuits. But that mind-set just didn't exist. It was just like, this is how it is. It didn't occur to me or any of my friends that it could be different. I graduated from high school in 1974, and Title IX passed in '72, but it didn't hit us in high school.

Even my senior year of high school we didn't have girls' sports. There was GAA—Girls Athletic Association—which was a club you could join if you were athletic, and the girls from the different schools would get together once a year for each sport and play the other school. But you just had one chance to do that. And they had this weird girl thing where you voted for who was going to be on the team, so the popular people got to represent the school instead of girls who could have been on a varsity team.

Years later, when my daughter made it onto on a traveling team for 10-year-olds, one of the first tournaments we played in was in Manteca, at my high school. The only time I remember even being in that gym, there was once at a required-attendance pep rally where everybody had to cheer for the boys' team.

I graduated in '74, so this was 25 years later, and I go with my daughter, a 10-year-old, who has uniforms, three referees—I didn't have a real referee until I was in college! I mean, it was an amazing feeling to me, just how far we've come. This is what my daughter can do that I could never have done. And it was my high school gym, which girls didn't even go in except to cheer for the boys. It was an amazing experience.

She's an exceptional athlete, so when she was in 6th and 7th grade, people started inviting her to be on their teams, like soccer and volleyball. She played basketball for her middle school, but just during the season. And now she made the junior varsity basketball team as a freshman. But she doesn't want to play basketball all the time. She's finding her own path. It was hard to watch for a while, because I was thinking, "If I had that opportunity, I would have been at the gym every day all day, I would have been wearing my uniform to school, I would have been wearing my uniform for *pajamas*!" But she has a lot of other things she's interested in.

equipment. The rules weren't signed by President Gerald Ford till May 1975. Title IX still faced opposition and legal challenges, and the final guidelines were not laid down until 1979, during the Jimmy Carter administration. As Karen Blumenthal explains in her excellent book *Let Me Play: The Story of Title IX, the Law That Changed the Future of Girls in America,* to comply, a school must do one of these three things:

- Offer males and females approximately equal opportunities to play sports. So if three-quarters of the student body were male and one-third female, one third of the varsity athletic spots should go to females.
- Show a history of improving opportunities for girls and women.
- Show that it is meeting the demands and interests of its female students. Money spent on each gender does not have to be the same, but scholarship money has to be dealt out in equal proportion. For example, if half the athletes are girls, they should get half the scholarship money.

Those basic guidelines are still in place today, but Title IX has continued to come under attack. In 1983, the Justice Department under the Reagan administration reinterpreted Title IX to mean it applied only to the specific programs that got federal funding. In 1984, the Supreme Court sided with a Christian college that had sued that it shouldn't have to abide by Title IX rules throughout the school just because the admissions office received federal funding for tuition assistance. It took a new law, passed in 1988 after overriding a presidential veto, to restore fully the provisions and spirit of Title IX. Still, the amendment would face two more big hurdles.

The landmark 1992 case that ushered in the new era of women's sports (and fueled the mid-'90s explosion that produced the U.S. Women's National Soccer Team featuring Mia Hamm, Brandi Chastain and Julie Foudy, which won the Women's World Cup in 1999) was a suit brought by gymnast Amy Cohen. She and her teammates filed a class-action lawsuit against their school, Brown University, after it eliminated the women's gymnastics team as a cost-cutting measure. Told they could compete if they financed the team themselves, Cohen and her teammates went into a fund-raising frenzy but were ultimately barred from competing as a varsity team and denied access to the varsity locker room and weight room. A lower court ruled that Brown's action was in violation of Title IX. The school hadn't met any of the three tests set out in the guidelines. Regarding the first test, nearly half of Brown's students were women, yet just over one-third were athletes, and women received only a quarter of the money spent on varsity sports. As for the second test, Brown hadn't added or expanded a women's team in 10 years. For the third, the court concluded that female Brown students' lack of participation in sports was affected by Brown's not offering or cutting women's teams in various sports. The court rejected Brown's argument that women just weren't interested.

When the Supreme Court refused to hear Brown's appeal in 1996, the university had to reinstate the gymnastics program, and other schools began to examine their own programs. That's when opportunity really opened up and the stampede began. The women who competed for the United States in the 1996 Olympics in Atlanta were referred to as "the Title IX babies" because they had gotten college athletic scholarships or even gotten to play on college teams, something many of their mothers could only have dreamed of. They brought home the gold in gymnastics, softball, basketball, soccer and synchronized swimming.

Despite the success of the U.S. women at the 1996 Olympics, their victory in the 1999 Women's World Cup and the glories of U.S.

women in the 2000 Olympics in Australia, the amendment came under attack on the occasion of its 30th anniversary in 2002. Most colleges had added women's sports programs without cutting men's teams, but in the first decade of the new millennium, in a tough economy, some schools began to cut so-called minor men's sports, such as wrestling, water polo and gymnastics, and blamed the cuts on Title IX. The word went out that men's programs were being eliminated to comply with Title IX rules. A complaint from the National Wrestling Coaches Association prompted President George W. Bush's secretary of education, Rod Paige, to appoint a presidential commission to review "opportunity in athletics" and present recommendations.

The commission—heavily stacked with Division I universities with big football programs—released a report containing recommendations that would have seriously watered down the amendment's effectiveness. Two panel members, Olympic swimmer Donna de Varona and soccer star Julie Foudy, refused to sign the report and instead issued their own minority report and held a press conference to stress that chipping away at Title IX would be disastrous for women's sports. "You can't negotiate equality," said Foudy. The problem wasn't Title IX, they and many sportswriters and observers pointed out. It was the enormous cost of college football programs. Maybe that's where things were out of balance. In the end, the education secretary rejected his own commission's report and accepted only a few uncontroversial proposals. Title IX remained as it had been, the law of the land.

So how does it work today?

J. T. Hanley, who played soccer in college and has been a soccer coach for 23 years, at the elementary, middle school and elite club levels, in the Olympic Development Program (ODP) and, for the past 11 years, at Bishop O'Dowd, explains: "There has to be equity of opportunity across the board. So your equivalency can be met in lots of different ways. If you have like sports—girls' basketball and boys' basketball, for example—then those scholarships have to be the same. But if you have a sport that's a gender-only sport, you can take those scholarships and spread them across the breadth of your women's programs. So you could take the equivalent number of football scholarships and give a few to women's gymnastics, a few to women's lacrosse, etc."

Brandi Chastain saw firsthand the difference in opportunity that Title IX made. As she writes in her 2004 memoir, *It's Not About the Bra: Play Hard, Play Fair, and Put the Fun Back into Competitive Sports*, "of the seventy-five universities that had women's soccer programs when I was in college, few had a full complement of scholarships. Although I was the country's college freshman player of the year, I didn't get a full scholarship until my senior year. Today, thanks in part to Title IX, there are 894 NCAA women's soccer programs (294 for Division 1), and there are more women's teams playing college soccer than any other college sport. Those programs, at least in Division 1, can have up to twelve full scholarships per year to be divided among their players."

Soccer Boom

"Title IX is what created this boom in women's soccer, hands down," says Coach Hanley. "But it was like the Gold Rush. The first people who got there—the Michelle Akers, the Mia Hamms, the Christine Lillys, the Brandi Chastains—those elite players were able to benefit the most in terms of the depth of the number of people who really got something from it. These folks who have been coming in the last 10 or so years are like the people who showed up in the Gold Country after all the gold had been taken out. They're out there every day waitin' for that big nugget that's gonna come up, and the odds against that happening are extreme."

How extreme? Only 1 percent or fewer of athletes involved in

PLAYER PROFILE

BRANDI CHASTAIN

When I arrived at her home in a genteel part of San Jose, California, the first thing I had to do after walking up the rose-lined brick path to the front door of her two-story Colonial was duck into the bathroom off the kitchen, where there was no mistaking whom I was visiting: There on the wall, right above the toilet, was a framed copy of the *Sports Illustrated* cover with Brandi Chastain on her knees, shirtless and exulting in triumph after making the winning penalty shot in the 1999 Women's World Cup, accompanied by the one-word headline "Yes!" That victory, many people believe, is what kicked American youth soccer into overdrive, especially for girls. Chastain went on to win a silver and a gold Olympic medal, be a founding player of WUSA, America's first professional women's soccer league, and captain of the pro team the San Jose CyberRays. Her engaging book, *It's Not About the Bra: Play Hard, Play Fair, and Put the Fun Back into Competitive Sports*, written with Gloria Averbuch, was published in 2004. Since 2005 she has worked as a sideline reporter for Major League Soccer on ESPN2. And in 2005 she and former U.S. Women's National Team member Julie Foudy and former CyberRays general manager Marlene Bjornsrud founded the nonprofit Bay Area Women's Sports Initiative to promote women's sports. They call it BAWSI, pronounced "bossy," "because we both are," Chastain told my San Francisco *Chronicle* colleague Michelle Smith. A major project of BAWSI is bringing an after-school fitness and nutrition program to at-risk girls in Bay Area elementary schools. Using curriculum provided by the Women's Sports Foundation's program Go-

GirlGo!, collegiate and former collegiate female athletes work one-on-one with girls to educate them about exercise, obesity and nutrition as well as to do physical activity. Many of these girls from disadvantaged families have never had a coach, get as little as 20 minutes of P.E. a week in school and have previously had no female athletic role models in their lives.

Chastain's home is near her alma mater, Santa Clara University, where her husband, Jerry Smith, coaches the women's soccer team and her 17-year-old stepson, Cameron, is headed in a few months as a freshman. At the time of our interview in May 2006, Chastain was just a few weeks away from delivering her first child. (Son Jaden Chastain Smith was born June 8, less than 12 hours before the start of the first 2006 World Cup game.)

What do you think of the decline of P.E. in American schools, as if it's not important?

It's astonishing. It's astonishing that we don't have leadership that sees the importance of it. We can find billions of dollars to fight a war, but we can't continue to educate and keep our kids healthy. It's really astounding. So that's why I think programs like ours need to exist. And we have to find ways to make them grow and expand, because if the schools are not given the resources necessary to make it happen, we have to help them. Even before BAWSI became an idea, parents would come up to me and my teammates with the national team and say, "It's amazing what has happened to my daughter once she started playing sports. She was shy and quiet and never would raise her hand in class; the teachers always tried to get her involved. Once she started playing sports, her personality has just blossomed, she's more willing to get involved in things, she asks more questions." So just for that reason alone it's imperative that our program exist.

The other side to what Marlene and I are doing is to educate theses kids about their own health care and about how they're really in charge of it. We explain that their brains function better when they eat healthy food, get good sleep and exercise, and that their relationships will benefit when they feel good about themselves. This is a huge problem in America. We've got to be the fattest country in the world. The obesity rates for kids are staggering. So if we can even get one kid to change her habits or understand exercise better, we're winning already. But we have an uphill battle.

With the rise of the club teams, a lot of kids are specializing in one sport at a very young age.

I'm a living example that it's not necessary to just play one sport to be successful in that sport. I played everything from softball to basketball to baseball. I played everything. Granted, the time was different, and girls' sports was semi-new and soccer was just getting started in my area. But I caution parents when they ask, "What's the best advice you can give me?" I say, "Let your kids try everything. Allow them to explore ballet and dance and computer and reading and science and tennis and volleyball and baseball." Because ultimately, when they find what they love, whether they know it or not, all those things that they learned in all those other places are going to help in whatever it is they choose.

It seems as if a lot of parents are focused on their kid getting a scholarship to college.

We've created this machine, kind of on the girls' side, too. Now with Title IX and the opportunity to participate, there are tens of thousands of girls who never would have played sports before, which is incredible. Before Title IX it was something like 1 out of 10 girls were participating in sports. Now it's 1 out of 3. But as Billie Jean King always says, how about the other two? What she's getting at is: We want to get them engaged as well because of the other things that sports gives them. So we are a part of the machine that's creating the whole scholarship situation. I've heard time and time again from parents: "My child's getting a scholarship to *this place*," or, "We *need* a scholarship." So I say, "I think you're barking up the wrong tree." Because putting that pressure on this 11-year-old girl to get a scholarship, perhaps to an institution that she's not really interested in going to but because they're offering the most money you're going to tell her that's the best place for her, is also not healthy.

So I'm a part of the problem, too, but I'm trying to find solutions. And by creating BAWSI, by using GoGirlGo!, by helping parents keep in perspective what sports adds to their kids' lives as opposed to what can we get back from it in terms of the rewards—a scholarship, for example—I'm hoping to counterbalance that cultural shift that we see happening.

Why do you think parents have gone a little nuts over youth sports?

I think it's media-driven, and parents are susceptible to what they see on television as much as kids are. When they watch a baseball game and they see "Now up to bat, Barry Bonds. Now up to bat, Alex Rodriguez" making over $20 million to *play baseball,* that gets your attention. I don't blame parents for that. What I blame them for is not being realistic about that and saying, "OK, maybe not us," and just giving the child the opportunity to participate. If they have aptitude and passion, OK, support them. But don't force them into trying to be that superstar and put pressure on them to be that person, when that most likely will not be them.

What do you think about today's travel teams, which start at Under 10, meaning kids as young as 8 are doing it?

The first traveling I did was to Petaluma [about an hour and a half away], which seemed like a hundred states away from San Jose, California. I didn't do much traveling when I was younger, because it was just neighborhood soccer, on a team coached by my dad, who learned it out of a book. He was a marine, so we did a lot of pushups and ran a lot of laps!

I have mixed emotions about the traveling. Because I've seen how wonderful it is to play in your neighborhood, to stay with your own team. The girls on my team were in a two-mile radius of each other. The parents all got along, we went to each other's houses on the weekend. But then when I got older and I started expanding my soccer and got on to the state team at the 16-year-old level and I did go out of state, and then I did go out of the country, a lot of things were offered to me that, if I didn't have soccer, I never would have experienced. I never would have heard Japanese or Chinese, or had Portuguese food or flown on an airplane across the Atlantic Ocean. I loved the benefits of both opportunities. I think it's maybe a little bit much for young kids to travel that far, because the experience is semi-lost on them. They don't grasp how much it costs, how hard their parents have to work for the money, the time commitment. And they don't get it yet. So I would like to see it more localized, staying home until they get a little bit older. Late middle school and up, maybe that's the right time.

There were a lot of things I didn't do as a teenager because I was involved in soccer. But then there were a lot of things I got to do that my friends never got to do because of soccer.

Do you think that things will balance out? It seems like things have gotten kind of crazy in one direction.

I don't know. But what we're trying to achieve in BAWSI and what I try to achieve on my own, when I represent myself or Santa Clara University or the U.S. Women's National Soccer Team or standing on the sideline for Major League Soccer, is to stress what great things sports have to offer and why they're really important. Like I told the kids yesterday when we gave out their uniforms, their T-shirts for the first day, about the pride and the respect and the commitment and the responsibility that goes along with being part of a team. And how your teachers can give you information, your coaches can coach you and give you information, but if you ever want anything in life, it's up to you to take that information and make something of it. And I want those kids to walk away with that empowerment.

Because that's what sports did for me. I tell them I was never perfect. I made a lot of mistakes. And I make a mistake every day, if not many mistakes. But getting up and fighting and finding better solutions is a part of the process. And that's why, for me, sports can't die for kids. And we have to make sure we find a way to continue that message, because they don't get it anywhere else. I've been through school, I've gone to college, I've worked in the workforce, and there's no other place I've experienced that gives me all of those things at one time.

youth sports will get college scholarships. Yet somehow those numbers don't discourage parents from believing their kid will be in that 1 percent, especially if they start off as early as possible, get the kid on a select team and play year-round.

Dean Koski, coach of the men's varsity soccer team at Lehigh University, a Division I school in Pennsylvania, says, "A lot of parents think that just being on a competitive club team is going to bring them scholarship money. I can't tell you how often we get parents who say, 'Our kid plays on one of the best club teams in the country; they're international champs.' But the kid doesn't play, he's on the bench. I mean, they get hung up on the idea that the most important thing is what team their kid is on, as opposed to how their son or daughter is being developed within that club.

"Parents say, 'I want our son to get a scholarship because college is so expensive.' From a mathematical standpoint," Koski says, "I tell them, just on the men's side, there are probably 20,000 or 30,000 kids coming out of high school every year, and easily half of them are playing soccer. There are only 200 Division I teams, and each year, each program at most can offer three scholarships, and only half of them offer scholarships. So you're really looking at only 300 scholarships for every kid in this country. There's a better chance of getting academic money than athletic money. There's a lot of misinformation out there for parents. So I think they're chasing dreams for their kids that just aren't there."

"Every year I get e-mails from kids who didn't make their college team or got put on as a red shirt, asking me what they should do," says Hanley. "And I always want to tell them, 'Call your parents and tell them you just got your first lesson in reality.'

"Your daughter could be a starting player for the most intense elite club team, but there are no guarantees that that's going to mean anything. She'll probably play in college if she chooses to. But it's going to be, show up on the first day of tryouts with her boots and her shin guards and take her chances with all of the other walk-ons. Because those walk-ons are the same kids: They all played Class I. They all played Premier [a higher all-star level of Class I players]. Some of them might have even played ODP at the state level. A lot of players, not a lot of scholarhips. A lot of players, and not a lot of spots. They don't turn over a dozen kids every year. You're talking, even in a big program, maybe eight would be a huge turnover. Take those big programs and the recruited players, there's going to be half of that number that are kids that have been invited in, so you're talking about three or four slots out of eight that you're competing for with kids who are as good as you."

Hanley thinks the scholarship frenzy on the women's side will subside when the first wave of Title IX babies become mothers and have the perspective that not everybody makes it. "When they're moms," says Hanley, "I think you're going to see a paradigm shift, because they'll have experienced what the reality of it is and they'll be able to add a dimension of experiential wisdom to it. They'll be able to tell their son or daughter, 'You know, honey, I played high-level soccer from 8 on and ended up playing walk-on at a Division III school,' just as today a father may tell his son, 'When I was 8, I wanted to play in the NFL, and I played on my high school team, but by 10th grade I realized it wasn't gonna happen for me.' Of course it's good to encourage your kids, but it's also good to keep it real."

And once you do, says Hanley, "you can redirect the energy into enjoying the experience," rather than having the entire emphasis be on winning, with an underlying goal of getting a college scholarship that the odds are against you getting.

Yet that voracious hunger for scholarships is what's driving parents' mania. And it all starts in kindergarten, with soccer.

THE BENEFITS OF SPORTS FOR GIRLS

Research shows that playing sports helps boost girls' self-esteem, increases their academic performance and helps them perform better in the workplace as adults, since they've learned focus, discipline and ambition and how to work as part of a team. Teenage girls who play sports tend to get better grades and are less likely to get pregnant or get involved with drugs and alcohol.

"I have seen a lot of positive effects in their socialization skills for being involved in it," says high school soccer coach J. T. Hanley. "They tend to be much more supportive of one another than some of their nonathletic female peers. And they tend to be less swayed by other people's views of them; particularly they don't worry about what boys think about them as much as some of their nonathletic sisters do. And I like the long-range positive effects of that."

Tess Amato is the mother of three star athletes in Pasadena, California. Her oldest child, Ashley, was a competitive figure skater until 9th grade, played club soccer and was a four-year starter on her varsity high school team, then switched to rugby when she went to Boston College, and played all four years. Now she plays in an adult soccer league. Amato's son, Jamen, played baseball and club soccer, was a four-year varsity starter in high school soccer and earned a 50 percent scholarship to play soccer for Boston College. Youngest daughter Mary, a high school sophomore, plays club soccer and has been a starter on the varsity team since freshman year.

Amato is well aware of the benefits of athletics for girls.

"The kids are really fit, and they're really health-conscious," she says. "They drink skim milk, which I find disgusting, and if I don't buy low-fat yogurt, they have a fit. They're not an-orexic; they're just really health-conscious. Nobody drinks soda. None of them has ever smoked a cigarette. There are these ancillary benefits you really can't argue with.

"And with girls, you don't want them to start obsessing about themselves. One of the things I really liked about Ashley playing sports in high school is I used to love to watch the kids come on the field. These pretty girls with their ponytails walking across the field, lugging their equipment bags and sitting down and taping their ankles and talking to each other . . . I really felt they saw themselves as athletes, which to me was a really nice self-image when high school girls can be so prone to image issues. I loved the way they viewed themselves and the way they encouraged each other, saying 'Nice hit' or whatever. I found that incredibly healthy and rewarding, and it made me very proud of the girls.

"Now Ashley's 22 and she comes home from work and watches reality shows. When they were in high school and had soccer, they certainly didn't watch any TV. Obviously, it's a double-edged sword."

CHAPTER 2

How Soccer Changed Everything

Believe it or not, there was a time not so long ago that families spent Saturday mornings together at home or someplace other than a soccer field. As I have said, when I was growing up, youth sports were dominated by boys, and kids generally didn't get started in team sports until 3rd grade at the earliest, joining seasonal teams like football, baseball and basketball, with some kids not getting involved until middle school and almost no one getting serious till high school. Soccer changed all that, becoming the universal sport of grade school, with programs starting in kindergarten and close to 50 percent participation by girls.

Soccer—known in other countries as football—has been the premier sport worldwide for generations (rules of the modern game were codified in England in the late 1800s). As Jim Haner explains in his entertaining book *Soccerhead: An Accidental Journey into the Heart of the American Game*, it has deep roots here, as well. Immigrant communities played it on the East Coast of the United States in the 19th century during the heyday of the textile industry, when mills sponsored soccer teams and workers provided the talent and fandom. Participation took a dive when mills relocated to the South in the second half of the century and nearly dried up completely when the Depression caused mill closures in the Northeast. Ethnic social clubs in the Northeast and Midwest kept the sport alive with waves of European immigrants who brought their love of the sport along with their hopes for a better life in America. Clubs in places like Boston, Philadelphia, New Jersey, Baltimore and St. Louis continued to vie for national championships, but by 1950, the sport was largely forgotten or ignored in most of the country.

Soccer didn't get a toehold nationally until the mid-'60s. The American Youth Soccer Organization (AYSO) began in Torrance, California, in 1964, started a girls' program in 1971, and by the mid-'90s had grown to nearly 40,000 teams with 570,000 children in 46 states. And that is only one of a host of soccer organizations across the country. United States Youth Soccer Association (USYSA) came on the scene in 1974, and by 2002 had 3 million participants, ages 5 to 19, playing in 6,000 leagues. USYSA is the youth division of the United States Soccer Federation, which governs soccer in our country, and is a member of the global Fédération Internationale de Football Association (FIFA), which staged its first Under 16 World Youth Tournament in 1985.

The big boom here came in the '80s and inspired the rise of elite club teams, which have come to dominate the sport (more on this in Chapter 3). Many adults raised on baseball and football thought soccer would never catch on nationally, that it was too foreign and not high-scoring enough. But the skeptics were wrong. Soccer had too much going for it. And much of it was parent- as well as kid-friendly. It was a safer alternative to football as a fall sport. It's inexpensive at the recreational level. It doesn't require a lot of special equipment or a specific facility, like hockey. You don't have to be particularly big, as most do in football. You don't have to be especially tall, as in basketball. The more athletic you are, the better you can be, but you don't need to be a certain body type or height. It offers almost nonstop action from a squad that fields more than twice as many players as basketball. And at the beginning stages, it doesn't require a special skill set to succeed, the way a sport like baseball does. All it asks of the youngest players is to do what comes naturally them: run around and chase and kick a ball. What could be more fun?

"Soccer embodies everything that is right about youth sports," writes Scott B. Lancaster in his 2002 book *Fair Play: Making Organized Sports a Great Experience for Your Kids.* "Everyone plays, positions are interchangeable, and there is plenty of continuous movement and action. The low-key nature and lack of pressure that accompanies the sport appeals to kids, and soccer has grown quickly in popularity.

"In any given soccer match, even among the top players in the world, dozens of errors are committed. The very nature of continuous uninterrupted play creates these errors, yet the flow of the game allows all to forget the past sequence as players move on immediately to the next series of touches on the ball."

So there's a lot less pressure on kids during a game than there is, say, on young Little Leaguers who have to suffer the humiliation of striking out or missing a ball that comes right to them in the outfield, or a Pop Warner player who misses a field goal or fumbles with all eyes in the stands on him.

Lancaster, now director of National Football League Youth Programs, is a former amateur women's soccer coach and was director of the marketing arm of the United States Soccer Federation in the 1980s. He later founded and directed his own company, City Block Sports, through which he marketed the U.S. Women's National Soccer Team and represented superstar Mia Hamm. He also created City Block Soccer, an inner-city player development program for girls and boys 5 to 14 in the early to mid-'90s. Lancaster notes that soccer's development benefited from the fact that, in the beginning, "it was foreign to most adults. Rather than a group of parents showing up every weekend to disrupt the game with negative comments and actions, youth soccer became more of a community outing than any organized youth sports program. Moms in lawn chairs and dads on the sidelines spent time observing but also caught up with neighbors and friends while their kids had fun entertaining themselves. As a result of all the positive experiences people were having, the sport thrived, and the number of participants today dwarfs that of most other organized sports."

Soccer of the Suburbs

A quirky aspect of the soccer boom in the United States is that it developed in an opposite fashion from how it developed and continues to grow in the rest of the world: from the suburbs in, rather than from the city out. Women's varsity soccer coach J. T. Hanley explains:

"Everywhere else in the world, soccer is for the most part a working-class sport. It's much more analogous to what inner-city youths here experience in basketball, in that they develop their game independent of a club. They develop their technique and skills on a playground or somewhere, and at a certain point somebody notices them and they get brought into an AAU [Amateur Athletic Union] club or a Boys Club and they begin to learn the tactical parts of the game.

"That's the way soccer is everywhere else in the world. Here, it's all about the club. And with a few notable exceptions around the country, all established clubs are suburban, particularly on the women's side."

Soccer in America today is a highly structured experience rather than a street experience. It's played almost exclusively in an organized manner, set up and regulated by adults.

"It's so unlike anything you would see anywhere else," says Hanley. "I have friends in the U.K. who laugh when I tell them about the system here or when they come over here to watch. They just howl at how we do things. You have kids over there who may be phenomenal soccer players, but they're also encouraged in track, in cricket, in rugby, in other activities. And more important, they're allowed to be kids.

"Here in this country, if there aren't bibs, cones and a ball bag, there is no soccer going on, for the most part. There's got to be structure to it. There, the majority of it is the other way around. You might train with your club team twice a week, but you play soccer every day."

The newfound attraction to soccer as an organized team sport has dramatically changed how children play, how families spend their weekends and how children relate in their peer groups. Previously, kids didn't tend to get involved in team sports till 3rd grade or later. So they had all that time in toddlerhood, preschool and the first few years of grade school to enjoy free play by themselves or in small groups, in the backyard, the park or the school playground before pursuing a sport with uniforms, practices and games scored and refereed by adult officials. Sometimes kids would invent their own game, with or without a ball, make up their own rules and scoring, and settle their own disputes over what's in or out of bounds, what's fair and what's cheating, how long a game lasts, etc. Their athletic abilities weren't being judged or ranked. They didn't face a draft or cuts. They had weekends and afternoons free and summers off. They traveled on vacation for fun, not to tournaments for interleague competitions. They tried out new sports one by one as their bodies matured enough to be able to play those sports. They didn't specialize in one sport beginning at age 6 or 8.

But once soccer began being offered in kindergarten, parents flocked to the registration tables in droves. They were excited to sign their kids up for all the right reasons: so they could run around and get healthy exercise, have fun with their friends, make new friends from a wider circle, learn sportsmanship and how to be a team players, learn discipline and focus and gain self-esteem as well as experience the highs and lows of competition, which builds character and teaches life lessons.

What's unique about the soccer phenomenon is that this "new" American sport went from being practically unknown to universally embraced within 10 or 15 years. Before soccer took hold, it was understood that there were some kids who played sports and some who didn't. A parent might watch for signs of athleticism when she threw the ball around with her child at a park when he was little and think, "I can see he's got a good arm. Maybe he'll be a good baseball player when he gets old enough for Little League."

But soccer programs inspired such a lemming-like response that a majority of middle- and upper-middle-class parents sign their kids up for soccer at age 5, whether they are athletic or not. To not do it makes you or your child the odd person out. So now it's not just a sport, it's a tool of socialization.

Recreational soccer also fills a gap created by grade school budget constraints and academic priorities that led to the cutting of physical education programs. In times past, kids got exercise, gained skills and learned individual sports in P.E. class. At one time, everything from croquet and badminton to baseball and basketball were taught as part of the regular school curriculum. Students would discover at school if they had a certain aptitude or passion for a sport, and might build their skills in class before ever going out for a team at school or in a recreational league.

Soccer's role as a safe environment for kids to play in can't be underestimated, either. The sport's popularity explosion in the '80s came at a time when parents were increasingly worried about their children's safety in day care centers (around the time of the McMartin Preschool case; the owners were indicted in 1984 for sexually abusing the children in their care but acquitted at their 1990 trial) and in their neighborhoods, where there was great concern about child abductions, fueled by the media and a few high-profile incidents. Parents began to believe that it wasn't safe to let their children play in their front yard or even their backyard, or to walk or ride their bikes

CHRISTINA HUMPHREY

Christina Humphrey is a 7th grader at Redwood Day School, in Oakland, California. She started playing soccer at age 5 and has played Class I club soccer for four years. Her sister, now a senior in high school, also plays on a club team.

When you and your sister are at different tournaments, how do your parents get around to see everybody play?

Usually one parent will go with me and one will go with my sister, switching from weekend to weekend.

How do you feel about the life of a traveling player?

It's kind of confusing, because I don't really have time for anything but soccer. Like for the past two weekends, I had a bunch of homework and I had to do it in the car while going to soccer, because there were tournaments an hour and a half away, so it was kind of hard to find the time to do my homework.

Do you wish you had summers off?

Yeah. Because during the summer there's a lot of soccer. We have two weeks of soccer camp, and this past summer I had to go a two-week sleepaway soccer camp, and then we would have a bunch of weekend tournaments, like in Sacramento [90 minutes away], Mission Viejo [seven hours away] and Lodi [two hours away] and it would be a really long drive.

Do you wish it were different, that they could design a system where you could have more time to just hang out?

If I just hung out all the time it would probably just get boring, so I'm kind of happy. I guess it's different from how other kids live, but I kind of like the way it's happened, even if it's hard.

Do people at your level talk about getting college scholarships?

My coach always talks about college, and he gives us hand-outs about all these universities where these coaches are talking about what kinds of players they want to have for their team. They talk about high school, mainly.

*Some coaches don't want their players
to play on their high school team.*

My sister played on her high school team the past two years. Our club encourages you to play high school and club.

to friends' houses or to the local playground to play a pickup game or shoot some baskets. Plugging your child into an organized sport overseen by plenty of adults, with parents on the sidelines, seemed a wise and easy choice. And millions of American parents made that choice.

As soccer grew in the '80s and '90s, U.S. soccer successes mounted in the Olympics and the men's and women's World Cup competitions, and the number of collegiate programs multiplied. Professional soccer matches began to appear on the new 24-hour sports networks and cable TV outlets—including those by the first professional U.S. women's league (which disbanded in 2004)—and parents and kids began to see soccer not just as weekend fun but also as a ticket to a college scholarship or even a career path. Consequently, the excitement over soccer went from passionate to frenzied. To not sign your kids up for soccer seemed tantamount to denying them an opportunity for a college education. The pressure was on. Soccer mom and good parent became synonymous.

Get Organized

"The perspective today is that as soon as kids hit grade school age, they need to be involved in organized sports because everybody's doing it," says Lehigh University soccer coach Dean Koski, a father of four young boys, ages 7, 6, 4 and 3. "If you ask parents, they'll say, 'I want my kids to have the social opportunities, I want my kids to understand what it is to be part of a team,' and all those things. And I don't necessarily think those are the answers for kids. I don't think we can reverse the trend. All I think we can do is help parents find a level of moderation and balance about it.

"My wife and I are minorities in our neighborhood by not rushing our kids into organized sports. Everybody's playing soccer on Sundays and basketball through the winter, and these kids at 5 and 6 years old are going year-round with it. So before dinner and after dinner, our kids and a couple of the neighbor's kids are the only kids who are outside playing in the neighborhood. Everybody else is in their uniform and playing organized sports and eating fast food in cars.

"For me, as a college coach who stands in front of a bunch of parents who want their kids involved in soccer at the age of 5 because they want to have college opportunities, whether it be a scholarship or being able to play in college, I say to them, 'Look, I see the end product, and I can tell you right now that hands down, the best kids in our program, Division I, through my 14 years at Lehigh, have been kids who have played three sports, who have had balance, who maybe started late in soccer but they're really enjoying it and they can develop.'

"Most parents are pretty surprised to hear that, when they're thinking about having their kids specialize at 8 and 9. And I say you don't need to do that. Let 'em go out and have fun. Let 'em play. We've had three or four guys [from Lehigh] go on to play professionally, and all those guys have been pretty well-balanced in their backgrounds in terms of sports, which means playing two or three sports all through high school and never being fully immersed in just one. So I think there's a relationship there."

But sports are a mirror of the larger culture, and in our competitive society, parents are encouraging their children to specialize, to concentrate on one sport early, and to play at the top level. In today's youth sports, especially in soccer, that means playing for a club team.

CHAPTER 3

The Rise of Elite Clubs

It becomes this spiderweb, and you don't even know how you got caught in it. We started my daughter in soccer at age 5 because there weren't any kids her age in our neighborhood, and it was like, "Oh, isn't this cute? They're such cute little girls and little ball hogs and one's picking her nose, one's twirling her braid and this is so much fun." And then when she was 10, she and two friends went to see how it was for older girls doing a soccer tryout. They just did it for fun. And God forbid your kid has an ounce of talent and gets picked, then your life changes. And you don't even know when or where exactly how it happened; it just occurs. And before you know it, you've gone from little recreational soccer girls to select, and then club.

—ANNE VAN DINE, mother of Ginny Van Dine, who played for six years on an elite San Francisco Bay Area soccer team, until she quit after the fall season of her freshman year of high school and went on to play on her school's junior varsity soccer team

The second biggest change in the evolution of youth sports, after the increased opportunity for and participation of girls, is the rise of the elite clubs. Up until the early 1990s, the pinnacle of many young people's sports experience was playing for their high school team. Some athletes pursuing individual sports like ice skating or gymnastics might have had the Olympics as their goal from an early age, and may have moved to be with a special coach and worked with additional personal trainers. But the vast majority of kids played team sports in city recreational and parochial leagues or at the YMCA, Boys and Girls Clubs or the Police Activities League when they were in grade school and middle school. If they were particularly talented and motivated, they made their high school teams, and at that point ramped up their skill level as well as their time commitment to practice and training.

It was the high school stars who caught the eye of college recruiters. Some got scholarships; some made the college team but paid their own way. Some played only intramural collegiate sports and cherished memories of being on their high school team—the tradition, the local rivalries, following in the cleat and sneaker steps of community and possibly family members who had gone before them.

That was then.

Now private clubs offer the highest level, most competitive play. For a membership fee, between $500 and $5,500 a year, parents buy what they believe is the best opportunity for their child to get top-notch coaching and—if the child sticks with it through high school—get seen by college recruiters at the many weekend and holiday tournaments that are the clubs' lifeblood. For many parents, the long-term goal is that coveted college scholarship. Even when they're signing up a kid as young as 6.

And it's not just soccer, though the soccer club system came first. Now there are clubs for most other sports, many of which are part of the Amateur Athletic Union. There's AAU basketball, football, baseball, swimming, gymnastics, hockey and lacrosse. And what comes along with making the cut is a big jump in time commitment—two to three practices a week, in addition to two games per regular weekend and up to five or six games in a tournament—and cost: for dues, uniform and tournament fees, as well for the extensive traveling and overnight accommodations in what becomes virtually a year-round sport. The AAU reports that participation among girls nationally has gone up 55 percent in a decade, with 129,000 girls on AAU teams in 2005.

On top of club fees, many parents of club players are paying for personal trainers, commonly for kids 12 and up and occasionally for kids as young as 8. In my area, a pitching coach is $65 an hour, a goalie coach $100 an hour. Besides individual trainers, families can now turn to athletic training facilities, which are springing up around the country. Velocity Sports Performance, a national chain of state-of-the-art sports training centers based in Alpharetta, Georgia, has sites in 100 cities in the United States, including St. Louis, Kansas City, Philadelphia, Los Angeles, Alexandria, Virginia, and three in the Bay Area, in San Carlos, Concord and Dublin, in the heart of suburban club play. Founded in 1999, Velocity brings the latest sports training techniques from university and professional athletic programs to improve and maximize the athletic ability of athletes of all ages and skill levels. At Velocity you can "train like a pro," as its promotional materials say, even if you're an 8-year-old Little Leaguer. The price for kids 8 to 11 for three one-hour sessions a week for a month: $465. (The price goes down for three-, six- and 12-month packages.)

There are also sports summer camps to augment a player's training and conditioning in what might be called the off-season, except that the kids are still going to practices and playing their sport, even if they're not playing games for a seasonal record. Often there is an intimidation factor at play when players are informed of an "optional" camp or practice.

Gone are lazy summers when kids got to hang around the pool, the beach or the backyard, or do nothing and be bored, or hang out with friends. Gone is the spontaneous weekend away to the mountains to go skiing or jump in a lake. Gone is the ability to go on a family summer vacation when the family wants to go; now the coach tells the family the two-week window it has so as not to miss any games, practices or training. Threatened is the multi-sport athlete who wants to play different sports in different seasons, or a combination of club and high school sports. The club team owns you, and many coaches insist that you not play sports for your high school because they don't want you getting injured playing in an "inferior" league, they don't want you getting different advice from another coach in the same sport your club team plays, or simply because they want you to prove you are committed to the club team 100 percent—what parent Anne Van Dine refers to as "emotional blackmail."

And if you do miss a practice or a game or a tournament to go someplace with your family—a wedding, a bar mitzvah, a vacation outside the prescribed calendar dates—the consequence will be not starting in the next game, or having your playing time reduced. Some coaches are sensitive to the need for family time and do not punish players for taking it, but as one elite player told me, "That's not commonplace." And it's not just the coaches; the other parents will show their disapproval as well. "There's a silent shunning that goes on," says Van Dine.

I ask Caitlin Meyer, a 16-year-old super-talented Bay Area athlete who played club soccer in elementary and middle school and now plays AAU basketball and varsity basketball for her high school (see box on page 38) what happens if a parent raises an objection to the grueling schedule. She says, "The common response to parents saying, 'Look, my kid is burned out, she's getting hurt, she's getting sick, she's exhausted, they don't have time to do homework, they don't have time to be with friends,' is, 'Well, you want your kid to be a serious soccer player, and since you want them to be at that level, this is what it's going to take. And if your kid is too tired to do it, she should just play on a rec team.' It was like, 'You're making the commitment because if you don't, you're not going to achieve the top level of play or you're not going to get that college scholarship. It's not going to happen unless you're here. If you don't want to be here, you need to play for another team.' "

Fear of Being Left Behind

That's the ultimate threat: that your kid won't get the scholarship; that your kid might be left behind. When in fact most youth athletes will be left behind, even the ones who play club. Parents don't seem to want to face facts and do the math. Fewer than 1 percent of kids who do youth sports will get a college scholarship. As Jim Haner points out in *Soccerhead*, of the 8.7 million kids under 12 who are registered soccer players, only 7 percent will even make a high school team. And most of the kids who play on one of the nation's 3,500 travel teams will go no further. For those who make a high school team, there are 10,000 full-tuition soccer scholarships nationwide, about 60 percent for women's teams. A boy has a 1 in 78 chance of getting one.

"Where's the evidence that suggests we're going to get more scholarship dollars as a result of this investment?" asks Robert Cobb, dean of the College of Education and Human Development at the University of Maine and founder of the federally funded initiative Sports Done Right, which seeks to make interscholastic and youth sports in his state more positive, fun and inclusive. "There is no evidence. When you have fewer than 1 percent of the kids actually earning scholarships somewhere in sports, that leaves a big portion of them out of the winnings, that's for sure. And yet we create these elaborate tournament structures involving hundreds and hundreds of kids in an elite program in a region, with the parent expectation that they're all going to get scholarships, but the reality is that only one will get a scholarship. So you've created this whole structure in support of one kid getting a scholarship. Nobody in their right mind would want to be a party to that if they weren't the one kid. But that's what we do, and we hold out the promise and the hope that they will.

"I talk to coaches who will tell you that these elite teams are drawing kids off their JV teams, for example, who are not elite players, but they are numbers and they can pay. I've heard coaches bemoan the fact that kids are becoming really disillusioned, and it's just not right. Parents are being convinced by coaches who should know better. 'Oh, get him involved in this program, we want him.' They might as well just say, 'We want your $800 for the summer.' That might be more honest."

There's no question that the profit motive is a big factor in the new landscape of youth sports. Why do kids have to play year-round? Coaches may say and parents may believe that it's to keep the athletes' skills up and stay competitive. But one must also consider the fact that youth sports have changed from having mostly volunteer coaches in sports outside of high school and college to having, at the club level, professional coaches and trainers who rely on year-round play to make a living. If you're a soccer coach and the kids on your team want to play baseball in the spring, that's going to affect your income. So you may lobby them to stay with soccer to improve not only their skills but also your bottom line.

In December 2005, the Pittsburgh *Tribune-Review* reported that a school board member in Mount Lebanon, Pennsylvania, called for the firing of the winning coach of its girls' high school soccer team because he believed he gave preferential treatment to players who played on travel teams and attended the summer sports training camps at which he coached. The board member's concern over conflict of interest overrode his interest in retaining a winning coach.

"There are always going to be coaches out there trying to get money," says Monica Mertle, a varsity women's basketball player at St. Mary's College, in Moraga, California, a Division I school. "It's like that in every sport. My dad was my AAU coach in basketball, and the only thing he charged was what it cost to go to the tournaments. He wasn't making any money off it at all. So you can find places to play that are in it just to let you play basketball. Unfortunately, those places are getting harder and harder to find, because there's a lot of money to be made. A lot of parents basically end up buying their children scholarships with all the money they spend trying to develop them. And a lot of times they don't even end up getting scholarships."

Why are there so many tournaments, anyway? The coaches will

CAITLIN MEYER

Caitlin Meyer is an outstanding athlete, an A student, a student leader and an articulate, thoughtful young woman. She's president of her sophomore class at Bishop O'Dowd High School, in Oakland, where she plays on the varsity basketball team, which she made as a freshman. She also plays on an elite AAU basketball club team. Before high school, soccer was her primary sport; she played on an elite club team and was in the Olympic Development Program (ODP). Everything was in place for her to have a great soccer career in high school, but then things changed.

When did you start playing soccer?

I started in kindergarten, playing in a recreational league. Then I started to play Class III in Under 10s and played that for one year and then moved to Class I in Under 12s.

What was the time commitment like on the Class I team?

Oh, geez, it was pretty much my life for four years. Practice was twice a week, but as far as tournaments and games and summers, I was lucky if I ever had a free weekend. I could never have birthday parties because I was always away playing soccer. We never could plan vacations because I had soccer. And if you missed it, it was a really big deal and there were consequences—you didn't play.

In summers, all I had time for was soccer camps during the day, but after camp there was usually training. There were conditioning weeks where you'd have to go every day and just run. This started when I was in Under 13. That was pretty intense. I was in really good shape, but it was really hard. Then there were tournaments every single weekend. We'd go to San Diego [520 miles south] and all kinds of places. They were fun, but there were ones in Turlock [two hours away] and out there in the middle of nowhere, where we'd be staying at some micro hotel for the whole weekend. I basically lived soccer when I played Class I.

If you were in a big city like San Diego, would you have any time to experience the city?

There was a little bit of downtime, but the days were actually pretty long. We'd have two or three games per day. And we had to stick with the team, so we'd usually stay at the hotel and get dinner and then be back early enough to get to bed. So there really wasn't enough time to experience the cities at that age. We had games where you had to get up around 6 to get to our game at 7 and start playing our game at 8, so you couldn't stay out very late. So it was really strictly soccer.

At what age do kids start traveling?

I know for Class I, as soon as you start playing, you're all over the place. And that starts at Under 10, which means you could be as young as 8, but it's mostly 9-year-olds. Definitely the traveling starts early.

How did it feel to miss birthday parties and sleepaway summer camp that your classmates were getting to go to?

I got to go to soccer away camps with my teammates. But initially I couldn't understand why I couldn't go to my friends' birthday parties or why I couldn't have a birthday party. And I didn't really like it, but I got used to the fact that I was making this huge commitment to such a competitive team and that this is what I need to be doing so I have to live with it. I got accustomed to it, but it was definitely hard. It was hard for my parents, too, to have to plan things around my soccer.

*And you played on your school sports teams
in addition to your club soccer team?*

That was kind of a problem. That's why I actually had to stop playing on my Class I team. I was in 8th grade and in Under 15s, and soccer had become like a job, just because it involved so much of my time and so much work and it wasn't as enjoyable to me anymore, even though I was really good at it. But I just loved playing basketball on my school team, it was fun for me. So in 8th grade I ended up focusing on basketball and missing the first month of club soccer practice because my basketball team was playing for the championship and we kept winning playoff games. The soccer coach had known ahead of time that I wasn't going to be able to be there for a couple of weeks, but they were really mad and there was this big controversy and I ended up quitting my team and I basically haven't played soccer since. I was also in the Olympic Development Program at the time and got invited to go to the state tryouts to play on the Northern California state team, but I tore a tendon in my ankle there and had to stop. So that was really the last time I played.

*What did it do to your family life, from missing
family events to not eating dinner together?*

When I played for my Class I team, our lives revolved around me playing soccer. My parents really supported whatever I wanted to do. But I remember every Mother's Day we'd have to be somewhere at 7 o'clock, so we'd have to be up at 5, driving to a tournament, couldn't give Mom breakfast in bed, couldn't do anything like that. And as far as eating dinner went, I'd have a snack before practice and then come home and have to take a shower and then do homework, so we'd eat at like 9 o'clock. That still happens with basketball.

*Did you ever tell a coach you needed to miss a game
or practice because of a dance or something personal
that you wanted to do that wasn't a major thing but
something that was important to you as a developing kid?*

I didn't dare, because you're not supposed to miss soccer for anything. I guess you could for a wedding or something. They allow you to do stuff like that, but you can tell they're upset about it. I missed a day of a soccer tournament once, for my sister's wedding, and I had to go back to the tournament the day after, and I didn't get to start because I had missed the day before. Whenever you tell coaches you're going to miss something, they're upset about it. It doesn't matter what it is.

It was really hard when I was younger because I did miss out on a lot. I really tried to keep that balance, but it was hard lugging my huge soccer bag to school, leaving right after school, going straight to practice, not getting home till 7, doing my homework, then having to go to sleep, then tournaments every weekend. I couldn't hang out with my friends, I couldn't stay up late, there were just a lot of things I couldn't do.

I think that coaches and parents need to re-evaluate what they're doing and stop planning these tournaments where you have to leave the day after Christmas and you miss New Year's and you're gone for Thanksgiving. I think they need to look at families again and look at life when kids are growing up. It goes by way too fast to spend Thanksgivings away from the people you love. I think coaches need to realize that.

say it's so the athletes can compete against the best and be challenged, and, in the older age groups, be seen by college recruiters. But the teams and organizations that sponsor the tournaments are making money off the participation fees, and the communities where the tournaments are played—often in small towns in rural areas that have the space to construct large fields and sports facilities—have become dependent on this source of income. It has created a tourism industry for towns that would otherwise never have been a tourist attraction. The motels, restaurants, gas stations and shops depend on that revenue. The local chamber of commerce factors that revenue into their annual business forecasts. When the Little League Baseball Western Regional Tournament was played in San Bernardino, California, 64 miles east of Los Angeles, over 10 days in August 2005, drawing 50,000 people from 11 states, it brought $16 million into the community.

Tim Schneider, publisher of *Sports Travel* magazine, told the Salt Lake *Tribune* that the push to sell cities to youth sports tournaments and conferences is a lucrative and fast-growing trend. Ten years ago, only a few dozen cities in the country had sports commissions or someone selling their destination for sporting events. Now more than 350 cities have someone in that position, he said. "Once the events started, the hospitality sector got into it, and now there are more and more events."

Jeff Robbins, president and CEO of the Utah Sports Commission, estimates that major youth sports events in his state have contributed $40 million to $60 million a year since 2001, according to the *Tribune*.

"The Surf Cup is a great example," says Dennis Reichert, manager of his freshman daughter's Bay Oaks soccer club team in Oakland, referring to the big summer tournament in San Diego. "If you play in that tournament, you're required to stay at one of the tournament-approved hotels. It's so the tournament organizers can keep track of the economic impact, so they can go to the city and ask for certain services, and it lets them be armed with, 'Hey, the economic impact of this tournament is X millions of dollars with hundreds of teams coming in.'

"And for most clubs, running tournaments is a big fund-raiser. In Southern California, there are some clubs that run tournaments all year-round because if you have the infrastructure set up, it's a fairly easy way to make money."

So are kids playing more and more tournaments and giving up their weekends for the love of the sport and to hone their skills, or because their club team is now an integral part of a growing sector of the economy?

Linda Safir, an Oakland mother of three whose oldest daughter is a top-flight high school volleyball player and college prospect (see box on page 60), points out that some of the intensity of the year-round club programs derives from the club coaches' own professional goals. "A lot of these people are coaching high school, and their goal is to become a coach of a big-time college team. And if you have a winning team, you get visibility. So it may be an employment opportunity for that coach. It's also a venue for coaches to refine their techniques year-round. Some do it because they love volleyball, and some do it because they're looking for employment opportunities for themselves at a higher level. I don't think you make a lot of money coaching club, but you get a lot of visibility."

More, More, More

I ask Jim Thompson, former Stanford University professor and founder and leader of the Positive Coaching Alliance, which works with leagues and sports organizations to "honor the game" and combat the win-at-all-costs philosophy, why teams have to travel so much—and more every year. "Why do rich people need more money?" he responds. "It's a human tendency, greed. Whether it's financial greed or physical greed or emotional greed. We're the best team in the neighborhood, so now we need to be the best team in the region. It's the desire for more and more and more. Was it *ESPN* magazine that just had the top 6th-grade basketball player in the country on the cover? Why do we need to know who the top 6th grader in the country is? Maybe that kid will be another Michael Jordan. Can't we wait until he gets in high school or college to know that? It's that more, more, more."

"The message is being sent out there by these club organizations that your kids will be left behind if they don't participate at this level," says Carlos Arreaga, staff athletic trainer at Bishop O'Dowd High School, in Oakland, California. "And one of the things that's driving that is they're making money off of it. As much as they say they're doing this for the kids, is that truly what the philosophy of the clubs are? It's ultimately based on competition and who has the better club. I feel like there are some hypocritical messages being sent.

"It's really kind of sad because I think our kids, to some degree, are being used for financial gain and ultimately for adults. This is a trickle-down effect from professional to college sports. Years ago the talk was about college athletes and how they're being exploited for the universities' benefit. Now youth are being exploited to some degree for the adults' benefit. And that's not a healthy thing.

"In addition to working here at the high school as an athletic trainer, I've also worked as a personal trainer, and I'm also a strength and conditioning specialist and I'm certified to work with high school athletes doing personal training. I've done that for a few years and I've really thought a lot about this, and I've been very much in conflict about what's going on with youth sports. And I'm really pondering: Hey, is this really the right thing to be doing by running summer camps with kids and doing the training? Where is the balance? And what's the right thing to do? Because I don't want to contribute to that. So maybe I am, and I do feel conflicted about it."

But is it possible to make a high school team these days if you haven't played club?

"The kids who are really talented could," says Arreaga. "It's the borderline kids where it would really make a difference. Even at the college level, those kids who are skilled are probably going to make it regardless. For whatever reason they're genetically gifted, and those types of kids are going to be fine down the road. It's the kids who are average to below average who might need to put in extra time. But the perception among the kids is they have to play club or they won't make it."

"I think it's one of those myths parents buy into that if you don't keep up with the Joneses, you're not going to make the high school team," says Bob Tewksbury, former Cy Young Award–winning pitcher for the St. Louis Cardinals, who also pitched for the Minnesota Twins. Tewksbury is now a sports psychologist for the Boston Red Sox and host of a radio show in New Hampshire called *Sports from a Different Perspective*, as well as a youth sports coach and father of a son, 14, and a daughter, 12, both of whom play sports.

The significance of innate talent, Tewksbury says, is often overlooked by parents who believe they can produce a star athlete by following all the right training steps. He agrees with the American Academy of Pediatrics, which issued a policy statement in 2000 recommending that children not specialize in a sport until adolescence, when they are emotionally and physically more mature. The academy suggests holding off from specializing until age 12 or 13. Tewksbury would wait even a few years longer.

"In my experience as having played at the highest level of the pros for a long time, there's a thing called talent that I think people underestimate. And I think when parents elect to put children in early participation programs, for example at age 10, committing to being a full-time, year-round soccer player, they think that's going to equate to talent. Will their skill improve? Yes, it will. But you don't really know what your talent level is until you mature.

"The problem is the professionalization of youth sports. There are early-blooming kids and early-developing kids who are always going to have greater success because of their physical structure, and the later-maturing kids were traditionally held back because they weren't as good. Now we're labeling kids as good or not good at the age of 12, which is crazy! The research says specialization should start around age 15 or so. So if you have talent with the maturation process, now we can see how good you are. It's not determined when you're 10."

Tewksbury also objects to club coaches who would discourage or prevent kids from playing on their high school team. "And for what reason? For that 1 in 100 who gets that scholarship to play maybe on a Division I team? The odds of playing at a Division I level or getting a scholarship to play are incredibly against you. So the trade-off is what?

"I think it's a myth. It's a tidal wave of a belief system that's wrong. The elite club teams cultivate that. They say if you don't play for me, then you're not going to be able to play for that team. And parents believe that."

The devaluing of high school team participation is one of the biggest cultural shifts that have occurred thanks to the rise to club sports. Many club coaches discourage or prevent their players from going out for the high school team, even though the schools and the leagues in many cases guarantee there won't be a scheduling conflict. In my state, for example, the California Interscholastic League mandates that club soccer cannot run concurrently with the school soccer season. "The good news is the seasons don't conflict," one soccer mom of a club player told me. "The bad news is soccer lasts the whole damn year."

Yet even without conflicting seasons, some club athletes are still pressured not to play for their high school because they might get injured and become unavailable to play for the club team. Others simply believe that the level of play is not as competitive and that college recruiters will focus on the club teams, so why should they bother playing for the high school? What's in it for me? Fading is the value of representing something outside yourself, bigger than yourself: your community, your school. The high school club player is often driving toward a more personal goal: being seen by the recruiter, getting a scholarship.

Mike Riera is a nationally known parenting expert, the family and adolescent counselor for the *CBS Saturday Early Show* and a frequent guest on *Oprah* and NPR, author of *Staying Connected to Your Teenager* and co-author with Joe Di Prisco of *Field Guide to the American Teenager*, and head of the K-8 Redwood Day School, in Oakland, California. Riera, a multi-sport star athlete in high school who was captain of his basketball team at Wesleyan University, thinks it's a shame that kids are being discouraged from playing for their high schools. He told me, "You know, as corny as pep rallies are, it's a powerful experience in a kid's life when you're out there as a member of the team and introduced in front of the student body and everyone cheers for you and it's homecoming and everyone knows that's going on, versus on a club team, where it's just the parents and the players.

"My dad was a Hall of Fame high school basketball coach. And he was the P.E. teacher at the school. He saw the kids all day. And he would know when Johnny or Sherry's got a problem, because it would show up in practice, he would see them at school, he could call them into his office. He could really affect their lives. Whereas a club coach just sees them at practice. You don't *see* the rest of their life. I think club coaches miss the chance to really impact a kid's life by not being at school all the time."

Travel Treadmill

Riera is concerned about what travel teams do to families.

"Just the lifestyle it forces on parents, where one parent is always driving. And it rips families apart on the weekend. Mom or Dad is traveling, and the other is at home with the other kids or home attending to business, and it just pulls the family apart. Think of the number of social opportunities the player misses, and the number of missed opportunities for the whole family to do something together. I know people say there's a certain bonding that happens when you're on a trip and sharing a hotel room. And I'm not going to argue with that. But where are the siblings? They're not getting to spend the time with them. And it's like you have two different families at that point. So I don't know that you can measure the losses in this.

"When kids are toddlers, you often hear pediatricians telling parents, 'You've got to get the kid out of your bed. You've got to get her in her own bed, and you and your partner need to have a relationship, you need to have time with each other.' In some ways that's not too far from this. When parents are traveling all over the place, the child then keeps getting in the way of them spending time in their relationship. In our house, weekends are when we shut down and it's when we hang out and read the paper late and we make plans to do something and we do something entirely different that came up spontaneously. But if I was out of town and my wife was out of town always traveling with one of the kids, none of that would happen. So the best family time and best couple time would just go away. And that's really frightening that that can happen in families. I know families where the couple relationship hasn't gotten any stronger. It's going on fumes at this point, because they've got *this* kid doing this and *this* kid doing this, and there's never the consideration that for the kids' benefit, we need to pull back so that *we* can be connected, and that's going to be better for the whole family. But that's just not measurable enough somehow. It's not pragmatic and concrete enough."

"I'm a huge opponent of AAU baseball," says Bob Tewksbury. "I don't know who developed AAU sports, but they ought to be hung. I think it's an illusion. They tell parents, 'Johnny Smith played through our AAU program and now Johnny Smith is a major league baseball player.' Well, Johnny Smith could have stayed in the woods in New Hampshire and *still* become a major league baseball player because he had talent. And that is God-given. That's a gift, and you can't teach that. You can refine what you have, and people have different levels of talent. But I think that's a huge variable that has to be considered.

"People ask me all the time, 'You gonna coach an AAU team?' and I say no. I don't want to get into that chasing the Joneses.

"I grew up in a small town in New Hampshire with a blinking yellow light. I grew up in a trailer. My dad was an auto mechanic, my mom was a homemaker. I developed my talent not by playing on AAU teams. I developed my talent by throwing rocks at trees in the woods and throwing tennis balls at the schoolyard wall and by making up games with a bat and rocks out in the driveway. And I played on ball teams with all my friends, and I developed talent on my own through free play. That's how I developed my talent, because it kept it fun. The whole thing with specialization is not only the injury part but the burnout part. The numbers say that a huge percentage of kids stop playing sports before the age of 13. And I know there are a bunch of kids who stop playing because they're tired of it, they want a social life, they have other interests, they don't want the time commitment. And all they're trying to do is create a healthy balance in life.

"I just read an article in which a 9-year-old swimmer is quoted as saying, 'Dad, I've decided to retire.' At 9 years old!

"I pose the question on my radio program and to people when I talk to them: Are we talking about a small subgroup that's getting a lot of attention? Or is this really a national problem? In all the literature I've been able to pull up, and with all the organizations springing up like Sports Done Right, it seems as though this is a problem."

Tewksbury acknowledges that many of the players who come to the Red Sox played on AAU teams, but, he says, "Who knows if they got that far because of AAU or because they had talent? Would they

NANCY DUDLEY

Nancy Dudley, a writer and consultant in Chevy Chase, Maryland, an affluent suburb of Washington, D.C., is the mother of elite club hockey player Sean Heaslip, age 12, her only child, apart from a grown stepdaughter. Her husband, Mark Heaslip, a stockbroker, played hockey professionally for the New York Rangers and the Los Angeles Kings, and now plays on the Washington Capitals alumni team, and sometimes is a volunteer youth hockey coach. Sean is in the 6th grade at an all-boys Catholic college prep school called The Heights School in Potomac, Maryland. During the '05–'06 season he played for the Washington Little Capitals Pee Wee Majors, a AAA Tier I ice hockey team in the prestigious Atlantic Youth Hockey League (AYHL). He also played for his school soccer and lacrosse teams and attended a tennis camp in between summer hockey camps. For the '06–'07 season, he will play for Team Maryland, also a AAA Tier I team in the AYHL.

How has Sean's membership on an
elite travel team affected your life?

What I believe makes the difference is the attitude, the understanding and the value that the parents place on the participation in sports. That is the filter through which the whole experience occurs.

In our case, the schedule that we have, which is very intense, gives us a structure. It's a very busy structure. There's not a lot of downtime. But we create downtime within that structure. For example, on road trips, which are usually every weekend or every other weekend, you've got time in the car.

Now, you're not in the yard kicking a ball, but you're playing games, you're talking, you're together.

What makes the difference there is that I say, "That's family time," so I limit: Either there are no videogames or no electronics allowed in that car, or it's limited to reading or listening to a book on tape. So we can turn that time into non-electronic time that so many kids revert to when they're sitting around in downtime at home. Because let's face it, a lot of families have two working parents, and those electronics help you get your stuff done when your kids are busy doing that.

I'm married to a man who played professional hockey for the New York Rangers and the Los Angeles Kings and understands what it is to go to the top. But he does not visualize my son's participation in the sport of ice hockey as the path that he's going to have to the NHL. If he does end up excelling and gets a scholarship, all the better. If our son ends up going to play for Dartmouth College, wonderful. If he continues to play it as an adult and has it as a sport that he enjoys and keeps him physically fit, great. But the point of the whole sports exercise for us is to develop my son's character. It's a form of character development. It has to do with teamwork, it has to do with responsibility, it has to do with commitment.

And it forces my son to be organized in ways he would never dream of if he didn't have to be. For example, when I pick him up from school, he gets in the car, he's got a portable desk, he starts doing his homework right then and there because he's got hockey practice later on. And if he's going to do hockey practice, he's got to have his homework done. He places a value on his studies, all by himself. There's not a screaming match with that issue of homework. He goes to private school and he's got a demanding homework load.

When we drive away from school, his friends are playing at the basketball court and goofing off and having some time with each other. And I think about how Sean's driving away having not had that downtime. But on the other hand, he gets to have a whole other set of friends and a whole other peer group of people of very different backgrounds, which gives him more experience. There's everybody from super-super-rich people to the mailman to the single-mother maid. So that's nice, too. I saw that as an advantage.

At what point did he start playing on an elite team?

He's going into his third year on an elite team, but he was playing on travel teams and house teams before that. So he's been on a rigorous hockey schedule since the 3rd grade. And prior to that, he was at a hockey rink pretty much every weekend because my husband was coaching children at an outdoor rink near our home. So again, hockey was the structure by which we related to other people, by which we spent time outdoors. And the kids would have free skate, and that would be their downtime. There would be practices and there would be games, but the kids would choose to stay around the rink—they call them rink rats—and just goof off. Again, this outdoor rink is within a country club setting, so they take their skates off and go bowl or go eat, or go run around by the snow pile where the Zamboni dumps the ice. So within that world of hockey my son had lots of unstructured time, where he was independent and we didn't have to worry about him getting in trouble or getting kidnapped, because he was on country club property where we knew the parents and kids.

Does he miss out on much because of his demanding schedule?

Sean has been invited to many a fun outing, and Sean's not available, because Sean's getting in a car and driving to Philadelphia this weekend, or to Connecticut or whatever. So there are things that he doesn't get to do that would probably bring him into greater friendships with his classmates. But instead, he's in a car with either my husband and me or just my husband. Now I will say it sure has made for father-son unity, harmony, closeness and bondedness. And in this town, where you've got parents who've got to pull down six figures just to stay afloat, most breadwinners are working a huge number of hours and they don't have time with their kids. So that time that my husband and son are together is very valuable, and I think has served my son well.

And among the 2,000 families with whom we spent nine days in Quebec at an international Pee Wee hockey tournament, there is camaraderie, there is love, there is team spirit, a bondedness, a togetherness that comes from doing something, working hard and living side by side with one another and accomplishing things together. And with parents who don't have to do this. It is devotion, pure, unadulterated devotion to their kids that has them doing this. Because to play at the league level, you're talking five grand to play. And your kid could play up the street with the travel team for a couple of hundred dollars. So it is a sacrifice financially and time-wise. It's a sacrifice, but we think the rewards are worth it.

have made it had they been on a town team? That [AAU] is what they were encouraged to do by their parents.

"Maybe having played in the major leagues I have a different perspective. I understand how hard it is to play at that level. I saw kids who played 50 games a year in California, who had played tons more baseball than I had, who never made it. Why did I make it and they didn't? Was it because they played more games as a kid than I did? Maybe that hurt them. I don't know."

The level of opportunity varies from sport to sport. In soccer and volleyball, for example, club players have a clear advantage over non-club athletes as far as making the high school team is concerned, and in being seen by college recruiters. Travel-team baseball—called Extreme Baseball—is a relatively new phenomenon, having geared up mainly in the new millennium, so it's difficult to gauge its impact on athletic careers. (But it's having a big impact on the family: wiping out summer vacation plans.) High school basketball and football programs still seem open to raw talent the coaches can develop. That's how it used to be: Kids went to tryouts as freshmen and the most talented athletes or kids who showed the most promise got picked. Today the playing field is less level.

In fact, the rise of the elite clubs is changing the complexion of youth teams and the socioeconomic realities of high school athletics. Club teams are expensive, with the high cost of uniforms, fees and travel. A few kids may get scholarships or financial aid—and not all club teams offer these—but overall, the kids playing club sports are from middle, upper-middle and wealthy families. Poor and working-class kids are by and large left out, unless they get discovered playing street ball or playing in a recreation league and get sponsored to join a club.

Former Manchester United soccer player Gordon Hill, commenting on the state of American youth soccer in Jamie Trecker's column on the FOX Soccer Channel Web site, said, "I think we're missing

20 to 25 percent of possible kids in the pool—conservatively that's 2 to 3 million kids who don't play because their parents cannot afford it."

A soccer dad posted this response to Trecker's column on the issue of U.S. soccer becoming a sport of the well-off: "In the pay to play system, the buyers (parents/players) have three resources: talent, money and time. The sellers (clubs) have one resource—the game; with a hierarchy of quality. The higher the quality, the more buyers' resources they will attract. A club can sustain itself on volume (3,000 rec players at $50 a head), or it can make it on margin (300 elite players at $500 a head). They just have to compute the costs of good sold and set the prices."

If high school and college teams give preference to club players, then ipso facto they're favoring the privileged over the disadvantaged, widening the gap between rich and poor in an arena that used to serve as a great equalizer.

Joe Freeman, a writer for *The Oregonian* newspaper, summed up the situation succinctly in an October 2005 article: "Proponents say club sports improve the quality of high school play, offering rare opportunities to elite athletes and providing a year-round outlet for teenagers who wish to focus on a specific sport. But others say club sports—which can cost thousands of dollars a season—cater to the wealthy, decrease the number of high school athletes who play multiple sports and increase the demands on athletes when sports are meant to be fun."

We have to ask ourselves, is this the best thing for our kids? For our schools? For our families? And what is that year-round high-level play doing to all those young bodies?

Rise Up and Revolt: What You Can Do Now

- **Consider how joining an elite travel team will affect your whole family**. Will the parents and siblings be separated more weekends than not? Will it limit or eliminate your ability to take a family summer vacation? How will it affect your marriage if you and your spouse are going in different directions and sleeping in different locations each weekend? How much will you and your child have to give up? Is it worth it? Or will your child likely have a future opportunity—the high school team, a travel team when she's older—without sacrificing the early years of childhood and free play? Will it wipe out the chance for spontaneous weekend getaways or days at the beach or in the country? When my daughter's spring softball coach encouraged her to go to tryouts for the summer all-star team and she made it, we said no thanks when we realized it meant we would all have to give up summer weekends at the beach and the surfing and bodyboarding we love to do as a family. She was 10 years old. It didn't seem like something imperative for her to do right then. None of us ever regretted the decision.

If siblings are busy with their own games, and Mom and Dad are getting around to see and support everyone somehow, great. But if younger or nonathletic siblings are being dragged to games where they are bored on the sidelines or craving their parents' attention, which is predominantly focused on the playing field, resentments and disappointment can grow and last a lifetime. Michael Thompson, author of *The Pressured Child* and co-author of *Raising Cain,* told me, "There are many families where going to practices, attending tournaments, etc. become the main work of the family. They are spending time together, they are all interested in the same thing, and in a family where the parents are athletic and the kids equally so, it is arguably a reasonable thing to do. But in a family that has children with different athletic ability, or other interests, or just need recovery time at home, the devotion to athletics can be a huge burden."

- **Ask the coach not to penalize your child for attending family events.** The rule of thumb about playing time is to reward those who show up for practice and penalize those who don't. This is generally viewed as a fair system by players and coaches alike. But when there is no accommodation for spending time with your family—to attend a wedding, a bar mitzvah or a Mother's Day brunch, or go on a family vacation when the family wants to go, even if it's not during the coach-approved two-week break in the training and tournament schedule—that tells the child that sports and the team are more important than family. Playing at the rec level, this isn't an issue. Yes, it hurt my son's Little League team when they were headed for the championship and two of their best hitters had to miss a playoff game for their 8th-grade graduation. But they still won the local championship somehow. And when everybody was in the dugout for the regional championship a couple of weeks later, the team lost when those hitters just didn't have it that day. That's life. That's baseball. And the coach didn't hold it against them in either case. A club coach could adopt the same attitude and acknowledge that *life happens* and not insist his players miss their 8th-grade graduation dance for a tournament or risk being benched. There will be other dances, as there will be other tournaments. But their 8th-grade graduation dance happens only once, and if they miss it, they will never have the memory of that particular rite of passage, which their classmates will.

- **Keep academics a priority.** Often club volleyball tournaments in my state are scheduled to begin on Friday during the school year. That means that students, starting as early as 5th or 6th grade, miss not only Fridays but Thursdays as well, as their parents pull them out of school to travel to the out-of-town location. If you as a parent don't agree with putting sports before academics on a regular basis, and aiding and abetting the message that this sends to kids, think twice before you sign on that dotted line.

- **Consider not joining an elite travel team until your child is an adolescent.** Children are better prepared for intense play, practice and competition after they've gone through puberty. Travel soccer teams, for example, generally start at Under 10, which means 8- and 9-year-olds are spending weekends in motels, away from their friends and siblings, in intensely competitive play. State Cup competition starts at Under 11. Brian Doyle, director of coaching for Michigan's elite, nationally ranked Wolves-Hawks Soccer Club, told me, "A lot of guys believe we start the championships too early. Fourteen should be the first State Cup to play in. If you want to reduce stress, reduce the need to win. I personally believe the child doesn't really need to learn how to *win* the game until they're around 14. Before that, you're learning how to *play* the game."

- **Check your options.** Seriously question if an elite team is what your child needs or wants. Sometimes a child wants to join a Class I team just because his friends are going to. That may be a valid reason, but alternatively, you can evaluate the situation and decide that (a) it doesn't work for our family, or (b) he's a good enough player to make the high school team without playing club or (c) it's not a great choice for our family, so we'll put it off as long as possible and let him join in 7th grade so he'll have two years of competitive training under his belt going into the high school tryouts. One option is to do less competitive club play, such as Class III soccer, which is a step above recreation level but less demanding than Class I. They travel less and take summers off.

Another option is remaining at or dropping down to the recreation level. There's no shame in it! If you have a good coach and good players you enjoy playing with, you can have a great time without undue pressure. The status awarded elite teams may be overrated in terms of the athlete's actual experience. I know many rec players—from my kids' teams—who were extremely talented and went on to make their high school varsity teams without having given up their lives to year-round club teams in middle school. There's also the option of an alternative league. In my area, Babe Ruth offers a somewhat different experience from Little League. But there's also a Japanese baseball league that's less competitive than either of those. In basketball, there's an Asian league formed partially to allow kids to stay in touch with their community. Check the landscape in your area. You may find an array of alternatives to choose from and may be able to select one that fits your kid and your family better than the others.

THE HIGH COST OF CLUB:
FAMILY PROFILE

LINDA SAFIR

Linda Safir is a maxed-out mother of three in Oakland. Her son, Nick, a senior, has played varsity football and baseball at Berkeley's St. Mary's High School and will play both for Linfield College in Oregon, a Division III school. Her daughter Blaire, a sophomore at Bishop O'Dowd, is an outstanding volleyball player who made the varsity team as a sophomore, plays on one of the top Bay Area clubs, and is already getting letters from interested colleges. Youngest daughter Libby is in 1st grade, tried soccer this year but didn't enjoy sitting on the sidelines while the coach played faster, more experienced girls. Linda quit her job selling financial systems and consulting to hospitals when Libby was 3, but she's thinking about going back to work to help pay for Blaire's volleyball costs, which she laid out for me one Monday morning after a hectic spring tournament weekend.

When you got into club volleyball, did
you know what you were getting into?

No, I had no idea. And different clubs cost different amounts of money. Intially, in 6th grade, it was about $2,200 a year. But that was just the fee, and that didn't include a lot of your travel. Then Golden Bear, in 8th grade, was $2,500 to be a part of the club. Then there are fees for your outfit, which is about $250: They have at least three jerseys, for playing different days of a tournament; then you've got the sweats and the jacket, you've got the club backpack or bag. It really adds up. Her current club, City Beach, in Santa Clara [45 minutes away], charges one blanket fee for everything—for your daughter's accommodations, her uniforms, and airfare for the away tournaments (six or seven big ones a year; there's usually a tournament every two or three weeks from January until the end of June). The total fee for that is about $5,500.

But then there's *my* travel. Yeah, I could drive to L.A. [400 miles], but I drive a Suburban, so with the price of gas, it's cheaper to fly! Then there's the cost of my room. Sometimes I'll double up with another mom to cut the price in half, and the club gets good rates, but it's still $100 a night. If you're there three nights, that's $300. You go out to dinner with the parents or go out to dinner with the girls, and usually everybody puts $150 in the pot to pay for their daughters' meals. Then the chaperone manages the money, and if we need to put more money in, we do.

Then there's the eating at the tournament during the day. Maybe you're bringing coolers with food and drinks, but like yesterday I didn't have time to prepare the cooler, so it's $3 for a container of fruit, $3 for bottled water—this is where they get you. Over the course of yesterday, for various things—parking, coffee, lunch—I spent $100 for the two of us. And that doesn't count the price of gas, driving 90 miles to the venue in Sacramento. And that's not covered by the club because it's "local," even though it's an hour and a half away. So you have to get up at 6 to be there by 7:45. My husband, Tom, had to stay here with Libby. I got home last night at 7:30, and sometimes you don't get home till 10 p.m. And if it's a two-day tournament, even if it's only an hour away, if you have to be there at 7:30 in the morning, you maybe just rent a hotel room. So that's another cost.

Then there are the traveling tournaments, and the older you get the more traveling you do. This year we had Denver, Los Angeles, we were supposed to go to Atlanta. And that's a huge expense. And I have to decide, do only I go with her? It's in the summer, which means I have to make sure Libby's in a camp, or I have to bring her with me. Is Tom going to come? That means he needs to take vacation. Do we want to spend our vacation that way? Not really. But it would be really nice for him to be there, because I get tired of me being there and him being here. Then there's Nick. This is his last summer before he goes off to college. What about him while we're flying around to all these venues for Blaire?

So it's very expensive. We've calculated the total cost for our family at $10,000 to $12,000 a year, including my travel and her travel.

But this year, we have to factor in sending her to certain key college camps in the summer. She also made the NCVA High Performance Team, which gave her two options: She could go to Europe and play, which would be about $3,500. Or she could go to Orlando, Florida, and play on that team. So I thought, you're not going to Europe without me, and I'm not going to Europe to watch you play volleyball. If we go to Europe, it will be to see Europe!

So she's now deciding if she's going to play on the Orlando team. And it's still a huge expense to fly to Florida, plus the $575 fee for the five-day camp. She did that last year, when it was in Austin, Texas. That's the regional High Performance. She's waiting to hear from USA High Performance, which is part of USA Volleyball, the organization that picks people who will eventually be on the Olympic team. Two years ago she went to that in Colorado Springs at the Olympic Training Center. Then you automatically get invited to their Christmas camp, between Christmas and New Year's, which she went to when she was a freshman. That was more money, and more time away from the family. I haven't factored in how much it's going to be for these other camps. If she goes to Indiana, for the camp at

Notre Dame, it's $350 for four days, plus spending money, plus airfare—at summer rates. Then do we let her do a camp around here or send her to one somewhere else? At what point do we cut it off and say that's enough? Some girls go to summer camps every week of the summer that they're available. They go from camp to camp to camp. That's a huge amount of money.

Are all volleyball players wealthy?

I do find that it's an entitled group of people who play volleyball. And whenever we've had scholarship players, they don't last, because they don't have the family support for it. It's a cultural thing. Like this one girl who lived way down in a really bad part of Oakland, if we didn't go pick her up, she wouldn't be able to make it to practice. Her mother didn't understand the opportunity that was being afforded to her. You can't do it without family support. I've seen it happen with three different girls, where they just dropped out in the middle of the club season.

A 6th-grade friend of my daughter's said she went to a tournament and didn't get played all weekend. That must be hard on the parents who've gone all that way and paid all that money.

I've seen it happen, and it's a travesty. Yesterday a girl on Blaire's team hardly got played. And her parents are paying the same amount of money that we're paying. We had a tournament this year where Blaire only played one game. So you're just sitting there the whole day being a cheerleader, and it's humiliating. And I've known coaches who have done that for the whole season with people. And you do feel screwed. I think everybody should get some playing time.

How does Libby feel about sports?

She says, "I'm not doing a sport!" Because she gets schlepped around to Nick's football games, to his baseball games, to Blaire's volleyball games. Then there's the extra expense of my going to Target to buy her Polly Pockets or coloring stuff, something to keep her busy. I bought her a DVD player so she can watch a movie. It just keeps adding up! It's really crazy.

Do you spend money on trainers?

Well, now that Nick is going to be playing college football, that means he's got to bulk up. So now he'll be going down to Mavericks, a training facility in Emeryville [20 minutes away], and working out with Anthony at $30 an hour. Blaire goes down and works out with Anthony twice a week. So that adds another $60 a week to Blaire's kitty, another $240 a month.

And then if you get an injury, you have to go see Stan Nakahara, the resident local guru trainer, who for a mere $130 will work on your injury and make you feel better. Blaire had a problem with an ankle one month and I spent more than $200 on Stan. So there are all these hidden costs.

Some of the girls come from families that are loaded with money, so not only do they do all the conditioning and all the stuff that we do, but then they have a private coach on a daily basis. There's one girl who has a nutritionist who calls her from Los Angeles every single day to go over what she ate to make sure she's eating all the right things.

Then Blaire has a tutor for biology, because kids also need to get good grades to get into a good school. She does that with two other girls, so we split that three ways, but that's $90 a month.

So she has something every night. She's got conditioning Monday night from 8 to 9, which means you leave at 7:30 and get home at 9:30. Tuesday night we drive down to Santa Clara, so we have to leave at 6 and I get home at 10:30. Wednesday she goes to biology tutoring from 8 to 9:30 in

Castro Valley [20 minutes away]. Then Tuesday night, back down to Santa Clara. And Blaire's doing homework the entire time in the car. And I've got Libby in the car on the way down, then I pull over and meet Tom, who works in Sunnyvale [just north of Santa Clara], and Tom takes Libby home in his car. Then Friday Blaire goes back to Mavericks for conditioning. Then on Saturday, if she has a tournament, we're up at 6 and we're out of here. So she doesn't get a lot of sleep. And if the team is staying in a hotel, there could be three or four girls to a room, and you're sharing a double bed with someone you don't really know that well, so you're not sleeping particularly well. It's very, very taxing. She comes home on Sunday nights and she's just exhausted.

Playing club volleyball has been a very positive thing for Blaire, but it is a huge financial burden and commitment.

CHAPTER 4

The Risks to Young Bodies

I have seen overuse injuries in the Pony League my son played in. Some of those kids are so worn down from throwing so many pitches. Their shoulders are aching. One kid at one point could only throw underhand, but he was still out there on the field playing. Isn't that insane? I'd never do that to my child, even if they loved the game that much. You've got to protect those kids, because they're not going to be able to pitch in college, if they make it that far. They will have worn their arms out or pulled something in their shoulder.

—LESLIE OLNEY, mother of an athletic daughter and son in Southern California

Parents are as much the culprits as coaches in wanting their kids to play year-round. We know some parents who won't let their kids take a single break, so that they're playing every single weekend, four or five games a week, just to make sure they're in the ballgame. So it's not just the coaches. It's a societal trend of being hypercompetitive in everything, whether it's pre-applying for preschool when your child is 2, or hiring professional writers to do your essays for college. America has just become a supercompetitive society in all aspects.

—JANN KING, mother of two star athlete sons in Oakland, California

One of the big consequences of the rise of elite clubs and the trend toward specialization is that many young athletes are now playing virtually year-round, putting more stress on their growing bodies than anyone ever imagined. Once they're playing only one sport, they're using the same muscle groups exclusively, which causes repetitive stress or overuse injuries.

Dr. Ronald Kamm, M.D., director of Sport Psychiatry Associates, in Oakhurst, New Jersey, told me, "We enacted child labor laws 80 years ago to protect children from all this work. And now basically we're making play into work. And they're working as hard as they used to in the sweat shops, some of them. I'm concerned about it, it's out of hand, and kids do need downtime and seasons off and multiple sports. There is the occasional prodigy who just loves the sport and is focused on it, maybe a Tara Lipinski or a Tiger Woods. But most kids do better with many sports. It protects them and they don't get overuse injuries as much and it keeps them from burning out."

Injury occurs when a tissue or structure, such as a tendon or bone, gets worn down by repetitious motion. With rest, the tissue can heal and engage in more work without further injury. But without rest, the body's inflammatory response kicks in, which ultimately causes damage.

"When it comes to preventing the overuse injuries, the simple thing to do is, instead of playing one sport year-round, they should be playing two or three sports," Dr. Robbie DaSilva, of Midlands Orthopaedics, in Columbia, South Carolina, told Joey Holleman of *The State* newspaper. "Then they don't strain the same joint year-round."

"Children are especially susceptible because their bones are still growing," Holleman wrote in an August 2005 article titled "Take Me Ouch to the Ballgame." "The growth plates at the ends of the bones are spongy, rather than the hard bones of adults. In general, bones stop growing in females around age 13 and males around 15. Until those ages, young athletes' bones need a break from repetition."

"The No. 1 risk factor is year-round playing of a sport," Dr. James Andrews, a nationally prominent orthopedic surgeon based in Birmingham, Alabama, told the Cincinnati *Enquirer*. "It starts with minor injuries, and by the time they are in high school, it turns up as a serious injury." He estimates he's treating four times as many overuse injuries as he did in 2000, including chipped bones, torn elbow ligaments, cracked kneecaps and lower back damage.

"We used to see these injuries in the 15- to 18-year-old range," Dr. Anthony Stans, pediatric orthopedic surgeon at the Mayo Clinic, in Rochester, New York, told the Minneapolis *Star Tribune*. "Now we're seeing it in kids as young as 8 or 9."

Playing year-round baseball, or playing in multiple baseball leagues during a season, is particularly risky. Dr. Andrews, who is senior orthopedic consultant for the NFL's Washington Redskins and medical director of baseball's Tampa Bay Devil Rays, says that 10 years ago he did the so-called Tommy John surgery to repair the ulnar collateral ligament in a pitcher's elbow (named after the first professional baseball player to have it done, in 1974) only on adults. In 2004 he did 51 of the surgeries on children, at a cost of about $8,000 each to the athletes' parents. "I shouldn't see any of those," he told *People* magazine in 2005. "It's completely preventable."

Dr. Timothy Kremchek, the Cincinnati Reds' medical director and chief orthopedic surgeon, and team orthopedic surgeon for professional soccer's Cincinnati Kings, did 10 Tommy John surgeries in 10 days on baseball pitchers ages 9 to 19 during the summer of 2004, and also took the knife to a high school gymnast with a torn triceps and chipped elbow bone and a young volleyball player with a bad shoulder. "I love sports, and I love to see kids enjoying their sport," he told the Cincinnati *Enquirer*. "But I'm telling you, we need to re-evaluate where we are as a society on this."

Stephen Boyer started playing baseball when he was 8 and played in two leagues at the same time, sometimes having a game every day, occasionally experiencing pain and playing through it. By the time he was a high school sophomore, the Utah teen needed Tommy John surgery for his second overuse injury. His first was an injury to the growth plate in his arm.

"There are pitchers all over Salt Lake doing the same thing he did and they're 8, 9, and 11 years old," Stephen's mother, Jan, told the Salt Lake *Tribune*, reflecting on whether she should have made sure he had some time off. "I wonder if it would have made much of a difference. I don't know how many tournaments I would have kept him from playing in, but I probably would have made him take three months off each year instead of letting him play year-round."

Bob Tewksbury, who works for the Boston Red Sox, says that overuse injuries have become so rampant that major league scouts are no longer turning to the South and West—regions where athletes have more opportunity to play and train because of the mild weather—to find pitchers. They're realizing that guys who have been taxing their arms year-round, for years on end, may have only so many throws left before they'll end up on the disabled list. Scouts are now turning to the East for talent, figuring the players' arms there might last longer.

"There's an incredible increase in [the Tommy John] injury, and that injury is strictly an overuse injury at a young age," Tewksbury told me. "So these guys are playing more and more baseball at a younger age and they're getting hurt. So what the special teams are looking at is: How much wear and tear has this guy got? Where does this guy go to school? I know they look at how many college innings pitched and say, 'You know, this guy pitched 200 innings in college and he's gonna break down.' And some teams will go back and ask, 'What did he do as a youth? Where did he play, how much did he play? Did he play on a specialized team? And does he have a greater chance of being hurt?' So they're shying away from those types of players, for the most part."

So let's get this straight: Parents are putting their kids at risk having them play year-round so they can one day play professionally, and the pros are starting to be wary of players who may have worn out their arms trying to get to the majors.

"The problem comes in, especially with younger players, with their participation in the elite travel-ball programs not affiliated with Little League, where they have no oversight in how much a pitcher can be used," Little League International spokesman Lance Van Auken told *People* magazine in June 2005.

"The average kid we operated on had only the week of Thanksgiving and the week of Christmas off," Dr. Andrews said in the same article.

Mark Verstegan is a Tempe, Arizona, physical trainer who has helped Nomar Garciaparra, Curt Schilling and Brett Favre, to name just three pro ballplayers, recover from injuries. Verstegan told Phoenix *New Times* writer Robert Nelson that baseball is one of the world's most physically lopsided sports, because whether you bat right or left or throw right or left, when you're playing, half your body is doing one thing, and the other half is in a subordinate role, making it about the worst sport to focus on exclusively throughout the year. "Having a kid only playing baseball is like taking a tree and forcing it to grow in only one direction," Verstegan told Nelson. "You're going against nature. And you're guaranteed to end up out of balance." He says the best baseball players he has seen were involved with other sports when they were young.

Katie Graeve played soccer from age 5 and became captain of the women's varsity soccer team at Eagan High School, in St. Paul, Minnesota, but spent half of her high school soccer career on the sidelines with her leg in a brace. The center midfielder tore the anterior cruciate ligament (ACL) in her right knee before the beginning of the season in her junior year, and tore the ACL in her left knee two games into her senior season. She has endured two surgeries and eight months of painful physical therapy.

"I played basketball back in the day," she told the St. Paul *Pioneer Press*. "I wonder if I would have kept another sport, and not played soccer all year-round, if that would have helped."

I ask Caitlin Meyer, the AAU and Bishop O'Dowd High School varsity basketball player, if she sees a lot of overuse injuries.

"I know I have shin splits from playing basketball," she says. "We never stop playing. We get a month off twice a year. I have shin splints that will never go away. Every day I'm in pain. When I wake up, when I walk, when I run, I'm always in pain. All summer we're training and conditioning, going to tournaments. Then we have a month off, and in September we start right back up again. We start having practice only two to three times a week, but in November we practice every day and have games on the weekend usually.

"People who don't have a specific injury like my shin splints, their bodies become so tired that they're sick all the time or getting hurt in the same place, like getting knee injuries in their left knee all the time. I know one girl who's always getting back injuries. She'll do something funny and tweak something in her back and have to sit out for a couple of weeks, and she'll go back and play and be fine and then the same back injury will occur.

"There are a lot of overuse injuries. I know I go down to the training room at school to get therapy for my shins, and there are constantly the same kids working on the same things. There are always athletes hurt, always."

"When you look at the physical stress that's being placed on the body, the bottom line is kids are doing too much," athletic trainer at Bishop O'Dowd High School Carlos Arreaga told me. "Kids' bodies are not developing at a faster rate than they were many years ago. There are developmental stages that the kids have to go through. I work with a lot of kids dealing with injuries and also doing strength and conditioning training, and I'll often hear coaches say, 'So-and-so has got to get stronger, they've got to bulk up.' That may be true, but, as I tell the coaches, their bodies are going to develop when they develop, when they mature. And that might not happen until they're 18, 19 or 20. So to think that if you take a kid and have him lift weights every day that all of a sudden he's going to be this bulky, strong individual, that's not reality. Everyone's going to do it at a different level."

The Costs of Specialization

Even though sports medicine specialists, college coaches and orthopedic surgeons keep hammering the point that playing multiple sports is better than specialization for young athletes, some parents and coaches at the youth level continue to insist that the three-sport high school athlete is going the way of the typewriter, and that to compete in today's world, focus on one sport is a must. And a surprising number of parents think that means specializing at the youngest levels.

They should talk to Monica Mertle, who didn't do any sports until 5th grade and still ended up getting a college scholarship to a Division I school, St. Mary's, in Moraga, California. She told me that as a young girl, "I did all stereotypically girlie things: acting, dance, ballet, singing. I didn't even like sports before 5th grade." At that point she joined for social reasons when everyone was going out for the basketball team at her K–8 Catholic school in Santa Rosa, California, "and I ended up falling in love with it." She also joined the volleyball team and played on both until high school, when she specialized in basketball. After playing "in some low-key YMCA leagues" in 6th grade, she moved on to AAU basketball in 7th. "And that's when it got really serious. That's when it became all year."

Monica questions the reasoning of pushing kids to specialize at a young age in order to get a scholarship down the line. "The parents have such an important role in this," she says. "I mean, when you're 5, you're going to do what your parents say. At that age, their kid should be playing on the swings and maybe have a good time with their sport, and practice on the weekends or whatever. Grade school is a good time to do what you want and try out different sports. By the time high school came around, I was completely comfortable making the decision that I just wanted to play basketball.

"If you get too serious when a child is 5, 6, 7 years old, it's easy to understand how it becomes a chore. Because kids that age want to go to the playground and run around and play in the dirt. They don't want to do all these drills. A parent really has to be in tune with whether their child is having fun. Because the minute it stops being fun, they don't want to do it anymore."

Parenting author Mike Riera sees the benefit of exploring multiple sports in terms of children's personal growth. "Why the pressure for a kid to know what their sport is when they're 10 years old? If we're really trying to develop kids who are multifaceted and kids who have multiple intelligences, then they need to play a variety of sports. They need to play the one where they're the natural, and they need to play one where they're not so good. And they have to know what it's like to be picked last. So the kid who's great in soccer may be a lousy basketball player because they don't have that kind of coordination. They need to know what that's like, instead of being protected, going for the soccer all the time."

Kids who specialize, play year-round and/or play the same sport on multiple teams are especially susceptible to overuse injuries because their young bodies are still growing. *Time* magazine writer Christine Gorman, in a June 2005 article on why more kids are getting hurt, explains, "The constant repetition is particularly brutal on joints and growth plates—the areas of developing bone tissue that are the weakest parts of a child's skeleton because they haven't completely ossified." Gorman notes that doctors find injuries tend to cluster at different ages: heel problems in children 9 to 12, elbow problems for those 10 to 12 and knee injuries for athletes 12 to 14. And girls are more likely than boys to tear their ACL, "a tough ribbon of tissue that holds the knee together."

"Twenty years ago, it was rare for someone under age 15 to have ACL surgery," Dr. Daniel Green, a pediatric orthopedic surgeon at New York City's Hospital for Special Surgery, told Gorman. "Now it's commonplace."

Injuries on the Rise

There's a booming business in youth sports injuries. Children's Hospital Boston opened a Division of Sports Medicine in 1974, the first clinic of its kind in the United States, and served about 250 athletes that year, according to Dr. Lyle Micheli, one of its founders and the current director. Micheli told the Salt Lake *Tribune* he now sees more than 300 children a week. In a 2005 interview with the *New York Times*, Dr. Micheli said that 25 years ago, only 10 percent of his patients came to him for injuries caused by overuse, but today it's 70 percent.

According to the U.S. Consumer Product Safety Commission, 3.5 million kids younger than 15 received medical treatment for sports injuries in 2003, more than four times the number since 1995, when it was 775,000. And many youth sports injuries—some studies say 30 percent or more—are caused by overuse. The high cost of sports medicine treatments (like ACL and Tommy John surgeries) and expensive—increasingly common—diagnostic tests (like MRIs) are driving up the cost of medical care in general, so there's a price being paid by the whole society, not just sports parents.

The five most common overuse injuries are shin splints, bone fracture, knee damage, heel injury and Little Leaguer's elbow. Among the other afflictions kids frequently suffer: Sever's disease, which affects the growth plates of the heel and occurs frequently in soccer players ("Ten or 15 years ago we never saw Sever's disease in young girls," Dr. Lyle Micheli told *People* in June 2005); Osgood-Schlatter disease (OSD), which causes knee pain in soccer and basketball players; gymnast's wrist; and Little Leaguer's shoulder.

Parents need to keep in mind what overuse injuries can mean for children: missed school, bench time when their team plays, hours of painful physical therapy and, in very serious cases, surgery and rehab. And injuries kids get today can cause lifelong ailments, including

THE FIVE MOST COMMON OVERUSE INJURIES IN YOUNG ATHLETES— AND THEIR COSTS

Tom Groeschen, staff writer for the Cincinnati *Enquirer,* compiled this list for a September 2005 article on youth sports injuries.

1. **Shin splint:** Painful damage to muscles, tendons or bones in the front of the lower leg. It's caused by extended running, running on hard surfaces or poor shoes. Shin splints can afflict young soccer, cross-country, basketball and volleyball players. Cost to treat: $2,000 or more, including X-rays (about $80 to $150), MRI scans ($900 to $1,500) and leg braces or crutches ($50 to $250). Treatment does not involve surgery.

2. **Bone fracture:** A break or crack in the arm, leg, wrist, collarbone, ankle or other bone, caused by stress. It commonly results from pounding on the basketball court or football, soccer, field hockey or lacrosse field. Think of the bone as a green tree limb, very pliable until it starts to split with constant use. Cost to treat: $1,500 to $2,000 without surgery; up to $5,000 if surgery is needed.

3. **Knee damage:** Typified by abnormal tugging of the muscle on the undersurface of the kneecap, leading to quadriceps fatigue and pain. It's common in almost all sports, especially those that involve running and weight training, and it might be the No. 1 chronic pain complaint of young female athletes. Cost to treat: $5,000 to $7,000 with bracing, surgery and rehab.

4. **Heel injury:** Usually, inflammation at the point where the Achilles tendon attaches to the heel bone. It's very common

in youngsters who play a lot of running games such as soccer, football and basketball. Cost to treat: $500 to $700, including arch supports. Surgery is usually not needed.

5. **Little Leaguer's elbow:** A catch-all phrase for any overuse injury to elbow bone or cartilage in kids, especially young pitchers who repeatedly work their arms hard. Cost to treat: $5,000 to $7,000. Surgery is common.

chronic pain, osteoarthritis, tennis elbow, Achilles tendonitis and shin splints, and may require surgery when they're adults.

The saddest fact is that most overuse injuries are preventable. Dr. John P. DiFiori, associate professor and chief of the Division of Sports Medicine at UCLA's Department of Family Medicine, who has studied overuse injuries in young athletes for several years, told the Salt Lake *Tribune* that young athletes have a better chance of avoiding overuse injuries if they avoid heavy training loads and early sport-specific training and take adequate rest periods.

"An emphasis on one sport under the age of 10 should be avoided," said DiFiori. "Parents are so focused on winning even when their children are 8, 9 and 10 years old because they think it will give them an extra edge to get a college scholarship."

The hardest pill to swallow, for kids and some parents, is the need for rest—rest between seasons, rest during the week and rest after an injury.

Dr. Timothy Kremchek, the Cincinnati Reds' orthopedic surgeon, told the Cincinnati *Enquirer*, "Just today, I had a 9-year-old girl in my office and she could barely walk. Her foot and ankle hurt her so badly. She plays soccer on three teams, and I said, 'We'll put you in a boot for three weeks.' The first thing the father says is: 'We've got the championships in a week. Can she play in a week?'

"I said, 'You've got to be kidding me.' I think once the dad realized what he had said, he took a step back. But that's the mentality you're dealing with."

Dr. Robbie DaSilva, of Columbia, South Carolina, knows what to say to parents who think taking six months off to rehabilitate after a serious injury will kill their child's potential college scholarship or professional sports career. First, he reminds them that very few young athletes ever reach those levels. Then, "I tell them if that child was meant to be the next [pro pitching great] Greg Maddux, he's still going to be the next Greg Maddux even if he takes the fall season off."

All of the doctors and athletic trainers Joey Holleman talked to for his article in *The State* agreed that "basic parenting skills might be as important as medical expertise in preventing the more common overuse injuries." Dr. John Batson, a pediatric specialist at Moore Orthopaedic Clinic, in Columbia, told him, "If your child's out there on the field limping, that's not a good sign."

Recreational leagues and colleges have put rules in place precisely because athletes and parents can't be trusted not to put winning over kids' health. Sometimes institutions have to save us from ourselves. In college, athletes may not practice more than 20 hours a week under coach supervision. But teen gymnasts often train 40 hours a week when they're in high school. Little League had tried to protect kids' arms by restricting the number of innings a player could pitch, setting it at 6. But as parents of pitchers (like me) know all too well, an "inning from hell" can go on for what seems like hours when the kid on the mound is getting shelled. In 2006, Little League Baseball tested a new pitch-count rule, with about 500 of the 6,400 U.S. Little Leagues voluntarily participating. The new pitch counts vary according to age group: Kids 10 and under are limited to 75 pitches a day, and teens 17 to 18 to 105 pitches. Rest rules are also age-based: Those 7 to 16, for example, must take a four-day break from the mound after throwing 61 pitches. These limits must be approved by Little League's board before being mandated, possibly in time for the 2007 Little League World Series.

Young pitchers who play on an elite travel team in addition to their Little League team are putting double the stress on their arms. And for those who play only at the elite level, there is often no one counting pitches. "Tournament teams and traveling teams operate by the coach's philosophy and integrity," Oakland baseball mom Jann King told me. "You either like it or you find another team that fits your philosophy."

Dr. Micheli recommends that if a child is spending more than 18 to 20 hours a week in a given sport, he or she should be monitored by a sports doctor. "Nine-year-old gymnasts easily go over that," he told the Salt Lake *Tribune*.

Dr. Jack Vander Schilden, an orthopedic surgeon in Little Rock, Arkansas, is horrified by the number of games young athletes on club teams play in a tournament weekend. "Six games, three on two days in a row!" he exclaimed to *People*. "The pros couldn't tolerate that!"

And remember, the pro baseball and football players take four to five months off every year.

Weighty Issues

Overuse injuries can affect young athletes in all sports, but some unhealthy trends are sport-specific. One common to youth football and wrestling is crash-dieting and using more drastic methods to achieve sudden weight loss before a mandatory preseason or pre-match weigh-in.

Some coaches look the other way and some parents lend a hand as football players from 2nd graders to high schoolers starve, sweat and purge to quickly shed pounds to gain a competitive advantage. If they succeed, they get placed on a team with younger, lighter kids, then after the weigh-in, bulk up to dominate.

A child of 8 died in August 2004 while trying to make a 135-pound limit for a football team in Liberty, Kansas. Over the course of two hours, young Ryen Vanden Broeder jogged, spent time sweating out water weight in a sauna and then worked out on a treadmill before he collapsed. Heatstroke was the official cause of death. He weighed 139 and had to make 135 for a team of 3rd graders.

"It can be very dangerous to lose weight quickly," Bill Dietz, director of nutrition and physical activity for the national Centers for Disease Control and Prevention, told the Lexington *Herald-Leader* in November 2004. Dietz has studied the deaths of young wrestlers. He said many kids resort to crash exercise regimens "because it's far easier to drop a few pounds of water weight than body fat," but they risk dehydration, which can lead to heatstroke, especially in the hottest time of the year, when football weigh-ins take place. He explained that without water, the body generates more heat than it can radiate, perhaps causing cardiac and brain dysfunction. He also said some people incorrectly believe that physical activity is the best way to lose weight. "People lose weight by changes in diet—physical activity is to maintain weight."

Some kids take diuretics they find in the family medicine cabinet, some wear plastic garbage bags to sweat weight off, and some kids force themselves to vomit.

"It's part of the little league football culture here," high school coach Doug Bills, president of the Utah Football Coaches Association, told the Salt Lake *Tribune*, which did a month-long investigation into the practice in November 2005. "As a coaches association we don't encourage kids to lose weight at all. We are always telling kids that [success] at the little league level does not mean success at the high school level. There's no correlation at all."

In 1997 the NCAA and National Federation of State High School Associations implemented rules for wrestling weight loss that measure body fat and won't let wrestlers compete if they drop below a certain level, usually 5 percent. (See Coach Greg Strobel box opposite.) But younger kids' weight-cutting practices still go unchecked. A 13-year-old cited in the Salt Lake *Tribune* story lost eight pounds, or 7.4 percent body fat, in three weeks to weigh in at under 100 to be able to play with 12-year-olds, yet in the season he weighed 115. The same boy got down to 104 pounds for a wrestling tournament the previous June, and his father told the *Tribune* he didn't see anything wrong with it. "It's not like he dieted all summer," the father said. "Three days before the weigh-in, he started eating just salads and losing water. He happens to have the metabolism to be able to do

CUTTING WEIGHT: WHAT'S HEALTHY, WHAT'S NOT

COACH GREG STROBEL

Greg Strobel is the men's wrestling coach at Lehigh University, which in 2006 won its fifth straight team title in the Eastern Interscholastic Wrestling Association Championships, an impressive feat in a very competitive conference. He has been to six Olympics since 1984 as a coach and administrator, including serving as assistant coach in 1996 and head coach in 2000. And he was a national champion when he was on the Oregon State wrestling team. I contacted Strobel after MTV broadcast an episode of its *True Life* documentary series titled "I'm on a Diet" featuring Cory Cooperman, one of his star team members. Cooperman was EIWA champion in his weight class, 141, in 2006—his third EIWA title. An MTV episode summary claimed Cory was living on toast and water so he could lose 10 pounds a week. I asked Coach Strobel to explain the whole weight-loss issue in his sport.

*Is crash-dieting to make weight condoned
by the parents, coaches and leagues?*

It's not condoned. There are some kids who cut weight the wrong way. Or they try to make weight the wrong way and cut too much weight in a given week, and they make weight, and then they binge and put it back on again, and then do it again the next week, and it's a vicious cycle.

The MTV thing was interesting because they had three people. One person did it exactly wrong, one person did it exactly right, and Cooperman was kind of in between. He did it mostly right but not always right, according to what I believe is right. The girl who did it exactly right was the biggest one there, and she lost the most weight—effectively—and it stayed off. The girl who did it wrong was a beauty pagent person who crash-dieted and she ended up gaining weight.

What did Cory do that was wrong?

Just the kinds of foods he ate. I believe in fresh fruits and vegetables. He said, "All I ate today was a PowerBar." Well, that wouldn't be real food.

MTV said that Cory is now on a diet of toast and water. Doesn't an athlete need protein? How could he perform on that?

You can't. You have to eat all the four food groups, you have to have protein, you have to have carbohydrates, you have to have fats, you have to have all of that stuff or you can't perform. You could go toast and water for one day, but you can't do that for a season—or for a week, or even for more than a few days. I had a couple of my guys a few years ago try the carb-free diet. That lasted about a week. Because you can't go work hard and wrestle hard and burn up thousands of calories a day and just eat protein, because carbs are where you get your energy. And they just crashed miserably. And I asked, "What's wrong with you guys?" And they said, "Oh, we're trying this diet." And I said, "Well, it doesn't work."

I believe we do it the right way here at Lehigh. I've been an advocate of good weight management—I don't even call it weight cutting—and what that means is getting down to a lean weight. We go by percentages. So if someone's in a weight class of 141, I'd like him to always be at no more than 3 percent overweight (3 percent of 141 is about four or five pounds). And then as he gets closer to weigh-in day, I'd like him to get within 2 percent. And that's done just with portion control when they're eating. Then, right before weigh-ins, kids will not drink water for—what I preach is less than 12 hours.

Because water's heavy—a gallon of water weighs eight pounds. And then they work out a little bit. I just went on a bike ride and lost three pounds. So I could just work out for 45 minutes to an hour, I can lose three to four pounds, maybe even five, because I'm 195 pounds. Then I drink three pounds of water and I'm back to where I was before. That's a reasonable thing to do before weigh-in. So you ask the question why wouldn't a guy be at 141 all the time? Because they want to be as big as they can be and still make their weight class. So a 141-pounder will really be about 145, 146, maybe even 147.

It's a fine line. Say I worked out a little bit like I did today, let's say I lost four pounds, and then I made weight, and then I'd have to wrestle one hour later. Now if I worked out too hard to make weight, I wouldn't have the energy to go wrestle a match. And it's critical that you rehydrate, because you can't function in a dehydrated state. Studies show that even a 2 percent dehydration affects your performance. That's why I want my guys walking around at no more than 3 percent over their body weight. Once in a while I'll have a kid who doesn't do it right: they binge eat on the weekends; then they spend Monday, Tuesday, Wednesday starving themselves because they binged on Saturday. And that's what we try to keep kids from doing. The NCCA has come out with some really good rules that keep wrestlers from cutting too much weight.

I do see kids in little league wrestling, kids who are prepuberty trying to cut weight. And that just doesn't make sense to me. Why in the world would you not just wrestle where you are? I'm coaching college and Olympic-level athletes. Why would you do this to a kid who's out playing a game?

Do you see weight cutting affecting performance?

Oh, yes, all the time. Not among my guys. I might have a couple of guys who of their own volition do it wrong, but as a general rule, our team is not a weight cutting team, and we're generally smaller than most of the people we wrestle. And once in a while we'll come up against a team that will cut more weight than we do, and we know it and we pick up the pace and we wear them out. Because they're not used to going when they're that tired.

So you can walk in a room and you can tell? You can see it in their pallor?

Oh, yeah, you can see it in their face.

So the NCAA is doing what it can, and after that, it's up to the individual coaches?

The NCAA and the high schools have good weight management rules. Then it's a matter of educating and changing a culture of how it used to be. What I mean by that is, the parents of the kids, they wrestled, and that's the way they did it. And the grandparents wrestled, and that's the way they did it. And then the coach, that's the way his coach did it. And so it's a culture of here's the way we did it, and you can do it that way, too. And what needs to change is: Here's a better way of doing it. And then it takes a generation or two for that to actually catch on. You can legislate rules that change, but the real true change has to be a cultural change.

it. . . . If a kid doesn't have any weight to lose, it's different. Then it's unhealthy. He didn't need an IV like some have."

And how healthy is it for a 95-pound 12-year-old who belongs at that age and weight class level to have to go up against a 115-pound, 13-year-old hulk?

Cynthia Ferrari, a psychotherapist, in Castro Valley, California, who specializes in treating patients with eating disorders, says she finds them cropping up across the board in sports. It's not just a problem in women's gymnastics and ice skating. She's seen it turn up in women's track and field and even basketball and soccer, sports where one wouldn't think slimness mattered. "The coaches let the players know what they consider an ideal body, and they make little comments and it puts pressure on the athletes," she told me. "The athletes themselves also figure out how to lose body fat, etc., through eating disorders even when their coaches aren't necessarily encouraging or promoting the behavior. What's really scary is that the athletes are sometimes encouraged *after* they've reported to their coaches what they're doing, because the coaches are either uninformed about eating disorders or don't recognize that it's not 'just a phase' that will stop after they discontinue their sport."

Ferrari says the weight-loss practices of male wrestlers can become a lifelong problem. "Overall, only 5 percent of men have eating disorders. But the bingeing and weight cutting wrestlers do in high school can become a behavior pattern that stays with them after they stop competing."

Bulking up rather than slimming down is the flip side of the weight issue. In youth football, the trend is that bigger is better, especially in high school. So kids are doing what they can—from pigging out to ingesting steroids and supplements—to increase their body mass. Once again, youth sports is using professional sports as a model, and youth football teams are fielding a bunch of Refrigerator Perrys with the hope that intimidating size will translate to success on the field at the prep level, a scholarship to college and even careers in the pros. (William Perry was 6 feet 2 inches and weighed as much as 370 during his nine-year NFL career.) Unfortunately, it could in fact translate to serious health consequences from being overweight, including chronic diseases such as diabetes, to death on the field due to stress and dehydration.

Thomas Herrion is a recent tragic example at the pro level. After struggling to break into the NFL for a few years, he was aiming for a spot on the San Francisco 49ers' roster when he collapsed in a preseason game in Denver in August 2005 and died. His weight: 310 pounds, considered average today for an NFL lineman.

"My fear as a health professional is that bigger is not healthier," senior athletic trainer and research coordinator for the University of Wisconsin Health Sports Medicine Center Tim McGuine told Dennis Semrau, a reporter for *The Capital Times*, a newspaper in Madison, Wisconsin, that looked into the issue in August 2005.

Semrau noted that on a local high school football team, the Lancers, 11 of the players weighed 240 pounds or more, including two tackles at 310 and 295. Their three rival schools each have at least six players over 240 on their squads.

"I've talked to coaches and parents who want their kids to get big even without regards to the type of body mass they're adding," McGuine told him. "For example, I see numerous 'big' kids but estimate they have 20 percent to 30 percent body fat. I try to argue that we're not doing these kids any favors with their long-term health and I would rather see kids weigh less but have more lean [muscle] mass."

Juicing

Many kids will turn to high-protein supplements—or worse, steroids—to increase their size and strength, which put a lot of stress on the kidneys and liver. And at the start of the season or in summer football training camps when it's hot and humid, overweight kids can get dehydrated, may pass out, and in some cases have died.

According to the Centers for Disease Control and Prevention, as many as 1.1 million young people 12 to 17 years old have used performance enhancing drugs (PEDs) or sports supplements, and steroid use—or "juicing"—among high school students more than doubled between 1991 and 2003. Statistics from the National Institute on Drug Abuse reveal that 3.4 percent of U.S. high school seniors admitted using steroids in 2005. And who knows how many kids surveyed didn't admit their usage?

"Depending on which national studies you read, estimates of usage among kids in 8th through 12th grade ranges between 4 and 11 percent," says Mark Fainaru-Wada, San Francisco *Chronicle* reporter and co-author with Lance Williams (see box on page 88) of *Game of Shadows: Barry Bonds, BALCO, and the Steroids Scandal That Rocked Professional Sports.*

Fainaru-Wada wrote a story for the *Chronicle* about Rob Garibaldi, a young baseball player in Petaluma, California, who was encouraged at 16 to use legal weight-gaining supplements by his high school coach, who was also a supplement salesman, and by 18 he was using steroids he procured in Mexico. His parents and psychiatrist say it was use of those drugs, and the resulting depression, rage and delusional behavior he suffered from, that led him to commit suicide at 24, in 2002, by shooting himself with a .357 Magnum he had stolen the day before. Garibaldi's father, Ray, told Fainaru-Wada he had confronted Rob a month earlier, demanding to know what drugs he was on. Rob erupted and started choking him, screaming, "I'm on steroids, what do you think? Who do you think I am? I'm a baseball player, baseball players take steroids. How do you think Bonds hits all his home runs? How do you think all these guys do all this stuff ? You think they do it from just working out normal?"

Weight training and conditioning are part of high school sports

STEROID USE AND TEENS

LANCE WILLIAMS

My colleague Lance Williams is an investigative reporter for the San Francisco *Chronicle* and co-author with Mark Fainaru-Wada of *Game of Shadows: Barry Bonds, BALCO, and the Steroids Scandal That Rocked Professional Sports*. Their reporting of the story of Bay Area Laboratory Co-Operative, the supplement company that was surreptitiously supplying anabolic steroids to athletes, and the publication of their book in 2006, contributed to Major League Baseball's finally adopting a steroid policy.

I've heard you say the reason you two pursued the BALCO story so doggedly was because of the trickle-down theory that what pro and Olympic-level athletes do influences young kids in those sports.

We think that's the reason for concern about steroids at the elite level. It's not so much a concern about the elite athletes' health, although that's important, too. But young athletes model the stars. High school kids all think they could be pros. Or the good ones do. And if they get the idea, as they have, that steroids provide that route to make you a star, they're going to use them. And, really, I think the drag on it is the expense for the high school kids, not that they have any awareness that it's a bad idea. I think the belief is widespread that this is the way to do it.

What is the expense?

You'd probably have to have $75 or $100 to get some crappy old weightlifters' steroids. And you have to have your kit—syringes and the whole bit. But the really good stuff, the undetectable stuff or growth hormone, that can cost many thousands of dollars. To fill a syringe with growth hormone can cost $900. That's not one you're going to see the kids using.

How do kids get started using steroids?
Do their coaches know about it?

In our reporting, we've met young athletes and their kin, and they've told us there's a whole code that the coaches use in talking to the boys to tell them to use steroids. One phrase is: "You need to get bigger." Another is: "You need to get serious in the weight room." We talked to the mom of a Division I college baseball player, and he was told, "You need to take a trip to Mexico," a reference to where athletes can buy steroids cheaper. So by using phrases like that, the coaches can later say, "I never told him to use steroids."

It's hard for some teenage boys to gain weight. My son was pretty serious about weight training. He's a long, tall, lean guy. He's about 6 feet 2 inches and he lifted weights throughout his junior year in high school trying to gain some weight, and he also did some flaxseed oil and powdered supplements. And he only went from 162 to 165, despite fairly intense weight training and playing two other sports and eating all the time. It's just not that easy for some kids to gain weight. And when the coach says you need to get bigger, the way to get bigger is to use anabolic steroids, because that will help you put weight on—muscle on—right now.

Are steroids more dangerous for teens than adults?

The psychological effect of the drugs is, some people think, more intense on teenagers than it is on adults. There's this depression factor that can come in when you cycle off. You have to take them in a cycle. If you did steroids all the time, a man would lose the ability to produce testosterone naturally, and you'd have to take them the rest of your life. So they have to cycle off them. But when they come off them, then there's no testosterone, and typically the mood really crashes. That's worse with kids, according to some studies.

That's the real reason for the concern that we had that was reflected in the reporting for our book: the effect on the prep programs, which are already, in my opinion, kind of messed up, to the extent that they have professionalized sports, where the program isn't about participation but about getting Division I scholarships. They do turn out some elite athletes, maybe one every couple of years, but in the meantime, the whole program gets distorted.

How were the high school kids influenced by steroid use by the pros when it was underground, before your reporting exposed it, before the congressional hearings, before your book came out and before Major League Baseball formally adopted a steroid policy?

At least since the late-'90s, and for some people since the mid-'90s, it's been an open secret. You'd hear about it from your coach or other kids. The nexus is weight training, which didn't used to be part of baseball at all. That's where you meet the gym rats and hear about the steroids stuff. So that's where it comes from.

How can coaches recommend something to kids that not only is damaging to kids' health but also seems like cheating?

There's a whole mentality in the sports world now, at the elite level, that you're just doing it to compete with the other guys who are already doing it. And there's something to that in a way. If you want to get a pro contract, and they're trying to pick between two guys, and the other guy has 15 extra pounds of muscle that he just picked up because he's using steroids, that would be a tremendous temptation to do it.

Now that the ubiquity and health risks of steroid use have been exposed, do you think people are starting to turn away from it?

Well, there's a lot more awareness of it being bad. A lot of people didn't even know these things existed at all. I was kind of like that. I knew almost nothing of this topic until I had to work on it as a story. And I thought I was a pretty good baseball fan. Now that there are more testing and penalties, they're going to screen out casual users or new users or dumb ones. But a really dedicated drug cheat can find his way past most tests for a long time and eventually maybe gets tripped up. But it's easier to beat the tests than it is to catch the guys cheating.

The way tests are done, you have to program in what specific substance you're testing for. So the whole thing with BALCO was, well, we'll take this known steroid and change a molecule around so it won't look the same when it comes out on the mass spectrometer and they won't believe or realize it's a steroid. I think if the technology of the testing changes, that could change everything. But until then, the cheats will be ahead of the testers. But to the extent that there's attention and penalties and rigorous testing, you are going to discourage it.

It's like the old theories of vice control at the police department. You're not going to get rid of prostitution, but if you don't do something, there are going to be hookers on every corner, so you have to control it and you have to stay after it. I think that's where steroid policing is now. They have no hope of eradicating it, but they can control it and try to lasso it and minimize it.

programs, and anabolic steroids allow for significantly quicker recovery time from workouts and injuries, so more stress can be put on muscles in a smaller amount of time. A steroid abuser generally can work on the same group of muscles every day without needing any time for them to recover. So the athlete will get much larger than a nonuser during the same period of time.

Symptoms of steroid use include dramatic gains in size and strength, cysts, oily hair and skin and changes in behavior including paranoid jealousy, delusions, increased irritability and aggression, often referred to as 'roid rage. Steroids can also cause male-pattern baldness and shrunken testicles.

According to the American College of Sports Medicine, steroid use by adolescents has been linked to early heart disease, an increase in tendon injuries, liver tumors, testicular atrophy, severe acne and premature closure of growth plates.

Long-term health risks of steroids—which can be easily obtained on the Internet and injected or taken in pill form—include heart disease, stroke, kidney malfunction, liver disease, HIV risk, disfigurement, depression and premature death. When high school steroid use hits the evening news, it's often because an athlete who was juicing has committed suicide.

When a junior varsity baseball coach told Texas teen Taylor Hooton, an outgoing, popular athlete, that he needed to get bigger if he wanted to make the varsity baseball team at Plano West High School, he began using anabolic steroids and went from 175 pounds to 205 on his 6 foot 1½ inch frame. He stopped taking them in May 2003 and slipped into a depression and, a month after his 17th birthday in July that year, committed suicide by hanging. "It's a pretty strong case that he was withdrawing from steroids and his suicide was directly related to that," Dr. Larry W. Gibbons, president and medical director of the Cooper Aerobics Center, a leading preventive medicine clinic in Dallas, told the *New York Times*. Taylor's father, Don Hooton, a director of worldwide marketing for Hewlett-Packard, founded the Taylor Hooton Foundation to fight steroid abuse and travels around the country speaking to high schools to build awareness of the dangers and prevalence of steroid use. "Don't tell me it's not a problem," Hooton told the *Times*. "My kid just died."

High schools are concerned about teen steroid use, but few have established testing practices. The tests are very expensive—costs can run as high as $250 each—and there is debate about how widespread steroid abuse is, how urgent the need for testing is, what appropriate punishment would be and who should mete it out, should a test come out positive. New Jersey was the first state to step in and mandate random testing of high school athletes participating in state championship events in the 2006–2007 academic year, a policy that would affect about 500 athletes. Anyone testing positive could be banned from competition for a year. When acting governor Richard J. Codey signed the executive order in December 2005, he estimated at that 8 percent of New Jersey's 220,000 high school athletes—more than 17,000—were abusing steroids.

Codey told the Associated Press, "We've all seen the statistics and read the articles about the impact steroids have on kids. This is a growing health threat, one we can't leave up to individual parents, coaches or schools to handle."

Other states began to take action around the same time. The executive committee of the Virginia High School League enacted emergency legislation in September 2005, making students caught abusing steroids ineligible for two years. New Mexico started random testing in four school districts in early 2006, hoping to expand the program statewide. In Central Florida, the Marion County School District enacted a random testing policy in 2006. In the spring of 2006, a bill based on the Olympic Committee's anti-doping model was before the Wisconsin Senate's education committee. Stevens Point school board member Mike O'Meara, who lobbied for the bill, told the Wisconsin

State Journal, "When schools of less than 1,000 children have [football teams with] offensive lines averaging 250 pounds . . . that's not happening by genetics."

In October 2005, California Governor Arnold Schwarzenegger outlawed performance-enhancing dietary supplements in high school athletics because, he said, they "could pose a health threat or create an unfair advantage." The year before, he had vetoed a similar bill when he was under contract to a publishing firm, American Media, Inc. (which also owns the *National Enquirer*, the *Globe* and the *Star* tabloids), whose muscle magazines relied heavily on advertising from the supplements industry. (When it was then revealed that he was executive editor for both *Muscle & Fitness* and the firm's *Flex* magazine, earning him at least $1 million a year while he was serving as governor, there was an uproar over conflict of interest, and in July 2005 he quit that role.) The law Schwarzenegger signed prohibits use of dietary aids banned in college and Olympic sports and requires that high school coaches be trained in the dangers of these supplements by 2008. The California Interscholastic Federation mandated that, starting in the 2005–2006 academic year, student athletes must sign a pledge not to use any of the specified performance-enhancing substances before they are allowed to participate in interscholastic high school sports.

Heatstroke on the Gridiron

Even players who have not resorted to PEDs are at risk at football camps occurring under the hot summer sun. Before specialization and year-round play became the norm in youth sports, kids played baseball in summer and football in the fall, with only a passing camp held close to football season's start. Full-contact play in summer football camps was forbidden in Oregon until 2005, when member schools of the Oregon School Activities Athletic Association successfully lobbied to have the ban dropped so they could keep their competitive edge. This "athletic arms race," as Brian Meehan, writing in *The Oregonian*, put it, has put players at risk for heatstroke.

In fall 2005, the OSAA instituted a regulation that requires coaches to use a computer model to calculate heat and humidity for the practice location; if it's too hot, the coach is obliged to limit the practice. But there's no such provision to protect players enrolled at football summer camps; the OSAA has no control over summer programs. And there's no limit to the number of camps a player can attend.

The trend is fueled by the quest for athletic scholarships, Meehan pointed out in his August 2005 article, when in fact there are a lot more academic scholarships to be had. Tim Welter, executive director of the OSAA, told him, "There is 30 times the money available for college academic scholarships than for athletic scholarships."

Americans love to fight regulation, but we're talking about our children's health here. As parents, we inoculate our kids against disease, we pay thousands to the orthodontist so they can have straight teeth, we insist they put a coat on when they go out in the cold. From the minute they emerge from the womb we are concerned about protecting their health. So why, when they get to be on a competitive sports team, do we suddenly throw health concerns out the window, fighting and bending the rules designed to protect them?

There is only one reason: Because winning has become that important. The time has come to get our priorities straight. No trophy, no scholarship is worth endangering our child's health. We seem to have lost sight of the fact that these athletes are children, not facsimiles of professional players. We can't abdicate our role as protector because we've been seduced by the siren call of the scholarship. And remember, they didn't start out with a win-at-all-costs mentality—the kids getting Tommy John surgeries, the kids crash dieting, the kids taking steroids. They're kids. They got involved in sports because they love to play.

Rise Up and Revolt: What You Can Do Now

- **Encourage multiple sports.** Listen to the orthopedic surgeons. Playing different sports can prevent repetitive stress injuries. Support your child in playing multiple sports—seasonally, not year-round—as long she can, even in high school. College coaches say multi-sport athletes are often their best players. It's good to learn and grow in different sports, and it's better for your body to not use the same muscle groups all the time.

- **Resist the push to specialize at an early age.** The American Academy of Pediatrics recommends that kids wait till puberty to specialize in one sport. There is no evidence that specializing early increases the likelihood of being an exceptional athlete in a sport. The best, tallest basketball player in 4th grade can be completely overtaken in 8th or 9th when he stops growing and his classmates go through puberty, catch up to him, then grow taller and display an increased athleticism. If you decide when your kid is 5 that he must specialize in soccer to get a scholarship when he's 18, you may be preventing him from finding out when he's 11 that he's a great pitcher or has a passion for hoops.

- **Lobby your interscholastic league to mandate a break in training.** The trend in year-round play has spilled over into the high schools, so that football players, for example, are going to camp all summer and training all year. The Utah High School Activities Association has imposed a rule that teams must have 12 weeks of dead time, when there can be no practices or coaching of any kind, paid or volunteer. The rule is universal, assuring that teams and coaches get a break without their having to worry about falling behind while their opponents continue to train. Twelve weeks off a year is precisely what Birmingham orthopedic surgeon Dr. James Andrews recommends for anyone in an overhead-throwing type of sport to avoid overuse injuries. And just think: If it works for Utah, it could work in your area.

CHAPTER 5

Child's Play

There's just no time to sit down and listen to music or hang out. I cherish any free time I have, any time I can just sit down and listen to my favorite songs or watch a show and not have to worry about anything.

—CAITLIN MEYER, 16, varsity high school and AAU basketball player, president of her sophomore class

The biggest crime is there's too much organized sport and not enough kids going out into the yard and kicking the ball around. Things are out of balance in that regard. Kids don't think about it. They'd be much more inclined to pick up their PlayStation than to grab a ball, call up some friends and say, "Hey, let's go to the schoolyard," and play basketball, football or soccer. If it's not an organized game, they don't do it.

—JEFF GREEN, assistant coach of the California State Girls Under 16 soccer team

Amid all the gains of playing sports—the physical benefits of healthy exercise, skill development, agility, balance and coordination; the social benefits of building relationships, learning how to work as part of a team, leadership, time management, decision-making, focus, discipline and goal-setting; and the psychological benefits of increased confidence, self-esteem, dealing with disappointment and frustration and learning how to be both a good loser and a gracious winner—I am concerned about what children have lost or given up as youth sports has evolved into its dominant role in contemporary family life. The landscape of childhood has changed, and so many things I took for granted as part of childhood have fallen by the wayside, from Sundays off to lazy, open-ended summer vacations.

But perhaps the most dramatic change has been the decline and near disappearance of unstructured play. For many kids, childhood is a rat race in which they go from school to practice to home, where they wolf down dinner (if they haven't already stopped for fast food), do homework and crash and then get up and do the same thing the next day, unless they're traveling to a tournament to play multiple games, squeezing in homework and what passes for family time on the way to the motel.

It was a stunning sign of the times when the Lego Corporation announced in June 2006 that it would close its Connecticut toy factory and move the operation to Mexico as part of a worldwide effort to trim staff and production costs. Lego had appeared recession-proof since it entered the market in 1932. Its colorful plastic building blocks seemed eternal, an integral part of childhood. The company showed a loss for the first time ever in 1998. CEO Jørgen Vig Knudstorp told NPR in a June 21, 2006, interview explaining the reason for the company's decision, "What's going on is that traditional toys are disappearing because children have overscheduled lives now and there's little time for free play. And then of course there is the impact of new media and digital toys such as games and things you can do with the Internet and so on."

When little kids don't have time to play with blocks, you know we're in trouble.

Not only have toy habits changed, but by and large today's kids are not playing in their own neighborhoods, or even in their own backyards. If they're not scheduled for a game, a practice, a lesson or a playdate by an adult, they aren't out. And if they're in, to relax they will more than likely choose to play a videogame, watch a TV show, surf the Internet, talk on the phone or instant-message a friend on their cell phone.

A 2005 Kaiser Family Foundation study found that during the school year, children ages 8 to 18 spend, on average, 6.3 hours per day with media—mostly television, personal computers, videogames and music devices. Seventh to 12th graders spend another 53 minutes per day on the phone.

Going outside to play is no longer the common first choice of children. For many, the only time they're outdoors is when they're on a field of play, aiming to score points. They're not wandering aimlessly on a path in the woods. They're not riding their bikes to the park.

Brian Doyle, director of coaching for the Michigan Wolves-Hawks, an elite soccer club in the Detroit suburb of Livonia, had to devise a program to make sure his players were coordinated. "We put our children through coordination exercises with a private trainer at the indoor facility where we train, because children in my time, we jumped fences, we climbed trees. These are the things that make a child a coordinated human being—riding a bike and falling off that bike, running through fields and playing games. Well, children don't do that anymore. If children go one block around the road, their parents are nervous. They have to literally have them in their sights today, when they're 10 and 12 years old.

"When I was growing up, we were allowed to ride our bikes to the park. I rode my bike almost every day to Binney Park in Old Greenwich, Connecticut, to play baseball or soccer or football. Today, every child's life is choreographed. They're dropped off at school, they're picked up from school, they're taking violin on Monday, soccer on Tuesday, whatever. I think children today are not allowed to be children as we were when I was growing up. That's just a change in the landscape of America."

Children's outdoor activities have been declining since the mid-'90s, with a particular acceleration in the new millennium, according to the 2004 results of the annual National Sporting Goods Association survey of physical activity. Little League participation is down

21 percent since its peak in 1997, but baseball playing in general—pickup games, playing catch, playing pickle—has declined almost twice as fast, according to the NSGA survey.

Bicycle riding has decreased 31 percent since 1995, according to the NSGA survey and American Sports Data, Inc., a research firm. *Bicycle Industry and Retailer News,* a trade magazine, reports that in 1995, 68 percent of children ages 7 to 11 rode a bike at least six times a year. In 2004, that number had dropped to 47 percent. And sales of children's bikes fell from 12.4 million in 2000 to 9.8 million in 2004, representing a 21 percent decline.

When I was a kid, your bike was a ticket to independence. In today's parlance, it was empowering. I'd take off, choose my own route to adventure, have independent time away from my family and along the way imagine all manner of worlds I was traversing. My bike was a motorcycle, a sports car, a horse or a chariot, and my terrain was a track, a moonscape, a motocross course, far removed from the city sidewalk visible to those around me. When my sister and I took off together, we were a pack of wild wolves, a leather-jacketed gang of teenagers, a pair of explorers investigating the unknown. It was sport, transportation and freedom, all rolled into one. It was cheap, accessible technology that inspired imagination and hours spent outdoors; literally freewheeling fun.

We lived in the Southern California city of Pasadena, a lovely and diverse community 10 miles east of Los Angeles, nestled below the San Gabriel Mountains. Our home was near the Arroyo Seco, a giant gash that cuts through the stately homes on the town's western edge and, if you follow it north a couple of miles (and we would), ends at the Rose Bowl. The arroyo is a sand-colored, rocky canyon with a trickle of a steam at its center during the brief winter and dry as toast the other 10 months of the year. We played in that canyon as if it were our private back lot for a Western movie. With its granite boulders and manzanita bushes, the terrain looked just like what we saw in TV and Hollywood Westerns that were filmed just a few miles down the freeway. One day we were cowboys, the next we'd be archaeologists digging up ancient Egypt. We could be anything we wanted, and we could get there on our own and stay virtually as long as we liked. Our parents knew the hot sun would drive us home before too long.

Today, outdoor play is more likely to be organized, competitive and supervised by adults. A study by the University of Michigan Institute for Social Research found that from 1981 through 1997, children's time spent playing organized sports increased by 25 percent, while time in unstructured play fell by about the same amount. The study also found that kids have 12 fewer hours of free time per week, eat fewer family dinners, have fewer family conversations per week and take fewer family vacations.

The United Nations' International Labour Organization reports that U.S. workers now work more hours than any other industrialized nation and take fewer vacations. And the vacations they do take are briefer than they used to be. In fact, the shrinking family vacation has become such a trend, it's begun to affect the tourist industry. Wisconsin secretary of tourism Jim Holperin cites youth sports schedules as one of the reasons, according to a July 2005 article in *The Capital Times*. Parents forced to work around summer tournaments and year-round training are forgoing the two-week family vacation and reducing getaways to a few days away not far from home. So not only are kids having less downtime and family time during the school year, they aren't getting as much of a break in the summer, either. And the family is missing opportunities to relate in a fun, relaxed atmosphere away from the stresses and demands of the home environment.

Out of Their League

With so much of children's active time spent in organized sports, kids have less experience making up their own games or picking teams by themselves. Usually if they're playing a game, adults have made up the rules and are there calling the fouls and telling the kids if the ball is in or out.

Parenting author Mike Riera thinks kids miss a lot by not generating their own pickup games on a playground.

"When you have kids who are on a team, that's a ready-made activity," he says. "All they have to do is get there. Then the coach takes care of everything, the parents get them to the place. There's a certain infantilization that's going on. What's missing for me is playground sports. When you show up at the park, you sort of have to read the culture of the park. How do I get into the game? Or you have to decide with some friends: Are we going to play baseball, are we going to play cards, are we going to play football? You have to have that social engineering that goes on. You have to deal with how you pick sides. All that stuff is so important to growth. Before the game's even started they've gotten this great education. And I worry that kids are so used to getting plopped down, that it creates a weird kind of entitlement that all they have to do is get there, then everyone else takes care of them and that's the way it should be—and they should have nice uniforms. I miss the days when you'd just go to the playground, kids just choose sides and you figure out how to make it fair, how to make it a good game and you go from there. This is all too ready-made."

Dean Koski, the Lehigh University men's soccer coach, calls it "the scourge of the soccer mom generation." Since contemporary children have always been told by adults how to play, they don't know how to play on their own.

"I didn't get married till I was 39," he says, "so I spent a good part my 20s and 30s being an uncle and watching my nephews grow up. And every time they'd come over and visit me, I couldn't get them out in the backyard playing on their own. They wanted me to come out. It bothered me that they wouldn't go out and just have a catch and run, even though they were close in age and could have decided what they wanted to do. Then it dawned on me that ever since they were 5, they'd always had an adult organizing them. And then I started to make the correlation to my own teams:

"From time to time I'll give the players an opportunity to go organize themselves. I'll tell them, 'Go make three teams of seven and make sure they're fair, and I'll be back in a few minutes,' and these are 18-to-22-year-old very bright men, who wrestled with that activity because they'd never really had to do that. It's not an incrimination, it's a commentary on how our kids are being developed as they're going through organized sport at a very young age.

"Obviously organized sport is my vocation and my avocation, so I'm a proponent of it, but I worry that we're taking away from kids opportunities to pick their own teams, solve their own conflicts, be creative—to do all the things our generation did as kids without an adult being present.

"I'm looking at this generation of kids and seeing that they don't have good leadership skills, they don't have good conflict resolution skills, they don't do well when I tell them to go organize themselves because they've been structured from the time they were 5. And 99 percent of the kids we recruit will say, 'I've been playing soccer since I was 5 years old.' Again, that's not a bad thing, but it shows the extent of it and how dominant it can be in their lives.

"My wife and I talk about how as parents, we could either pre-pare the path for our kids or prepare our kids for the path. And hands down, the kids who come into our program whose parents have prepared their kids for the path are going to be more success-ful. But the children of parents who have prepared the path for their kids every step of the way, through school, through sports, through everything, have more trouble adjusting because they've always had Mom or Dad be there. The parents have good intentions, but the end product is that they're not helping their kids develop the skill sets for independence."

"There are kids who've never played pickup anything," says Cathy O'Keefe, instructor of leisure studies and therapeutic recreation at the University of South Alabama since 1975. "I don't know if it's a result of our excessive obsession with safety and that's what parents want—to make sure their children are always supervised by an adult and never on their own—or if it's a fear of liability that fuels the oversupervision of children, where everything has to be organized. It's probably a combination of the two. And then the kids don't get a sense of what they're able to do, and so they lose confidence in their ability to do anything and just keep looking to adults."

O'Keefe has no doubts about the value of play. She uses it in her work with adults with developmental disabilities, with acute and chronically ill children, and with nursing home residents. Though she works with the disabled, she says everyone has basic developmental milestones that have to be reached. "We talk a lot about intellectual developmental milestones, and lots of educators have a good bead on that. The motor learning people have a good bead on the physical milestones; they know when kids need to walk and they know what skills build on what skills. It's the affective developmental milestones that we often overlook."

She told me of the work of Stanford professor Albert Bandura, a psychologist known as the father of cognitive theory, who has said that when you're little, you need to know what you're feeling, where the feeling is coming from and how to appropriately moderate the intensity of your response. "And those three key affective developmental milestones are met wonderfully through play," O'Keefe says. "Because play gives children the ability to explore a range of emotions, play gives children the ability to do cause and effect, which means if I build the sand castle, then I have the effect of happiness; in other words I can cause it myself. And then there's the appropriate moderation of response: How happy should I be? How upset should I be? Play allows kids to play-act all that stuff out. Kids play-act house and they do their little skits. They're acting out the way that people respond. And they get to practice how they respond. For kids who don't get that, either everything's a big deal or they underrespond."

O'Keefe says a psychologist friend told her, "You don't realize how many kids we see in trouble with conduct disorders and they don't even know what they feel. You'll say to them, 'How do you feel?' And they'll say, 'I don't know.'" The psychologist used to think they just didn't want to tell her; then, after she got into sociopsychology, she realized they don't really know, because they're out of touch with their feelings. "So, naturally," O'Keefe told me, "if you don't know what you feel, and you can't know where those feelings that you are having are coming from, can you imagine how out of control your life must seem?"

Unstructured play stimulates kids' imaginations, which they need to develop and exercise. "Children who don't develop their imagination," says O'Keefe, who has five children of her own, "lose their sense of awe and wonder at the things they can't conceptualize until they actually play enough *to* conceptualize. And so later on it's very hard for them to visualize something imaginative."

Sport psychiatrist Dr. Ronald Kamm explains, "What kids are missing by having the adults organize their sports is the creativity that comes from organizing their own play—the backyard, sandlot games kids used to have, where a couple of kids would emerge as leaders and they'd select the other kids and they'd decide how far apart the bases should be and no hitting to right field 'cause we only have six guys; there'd be a lot of improvisation and creativity. Now kids are just automatons and directed by the coaches to do everything. They don't exercise much choice. It's not play, it's really *a* play: It's like being in the school play and having the director direct you, as opposed to having free play, like in recess, and constructing your own sport and your own game."

So how are today's kids going to explore their feelings and learn conflict resolution if they play only in the context of organized sports? How are they going to develop their imaginations if they never have downtime? And if they never experience nature beyond a manicured sports field, how can they come to appreciate it?

Nature-Free Childhood

Richard Louv, San Diego *Union-Tribune* columnist and author, is particularly worried that children are losing their connection to nature because they are so rarely in it. His provocative 2005 book, *Last Child in the Woods: Saving Our Children from Nature-Deficit Disorder*, offers a sobering perspective on how little time children now spend in nature in particular and engaged in free play in general. He notes that city parks used to be places where urban kids could kick around and experience nature to some extent, but that in cities across America, open park greens have been converted to sports fields for youth leagues. And even gorgeous new developments with beautifully designed open space areas have rigid restrictions and covenants that preclude the kind of messy, inventive, creative play engaged in by previous generations.

"We're the get-off-the-grass generation," Louv told me, noting that the trend is so evident that the makers of Tide soap sponsored a study to find out why fewer grass stains were showing up on the knees of kids' pants; they obviously had a vested interest. "Someone came up to me at a book signing and told me that her community association had just outlawed chalk drawings on the sidewalk. We moved to Scripps Ranch [north of San Diego], which was kind of close to the way I grew up, because there are a lot of eucalyptus forests in the canyon, and there's a lake within 10 blocks. So I figured that would be good for my boys. We didn't read the fine print, and not too long after we moved in, I realized that the community association is going around the canyons tearing down forts and tree houses, and I had encouraged my boys to go down and build a fort." He refers to these and other restrictions as the criminalization of outdoor play.

"I consider this a kind of cultural fascism that we don't really see directly, and yet it's creeping up on us. And almost all the developments built in the past 30 years have those kinds of restrictions. They're enforced in varying degrees, but the mere presence of them is discouraging, I think, because it sends a message, and kids hear that message."

Even recess is an endangered species. A first-of-its-kind study, by the U.S. Department of Education, of food and exercise in American schools, whose results were released in May 2006, found that 7 to 13 percent of elementary schools nationwide had no scheduled recess. The decline began in the late '90s, and the No Child Left Behind Act, passed in 2001, was really the death knell for recess and P.E., as the need to prepare students to pass standardized tests became public schools' overriding concern. Nonacademic parts of the curriculum, including recess, P.E., art and music, were pushed aside to make more room for math, science and language arts. Nearly 40 percent of school districts have cut or eliminated recess nationally.

Yet a national survey conducted by the PTA in 2006 found that 9 out of 10 teachers believe recess and free time spent with peers is an important part of the school day and crucial to a child's social and emotional development; 3 out of 4 parents and teachers believe recess should be mandatory; two-thirds think kids need unstructured play during the day; three-fourths say taking a break in the day helps children concentrate; and more than half of PTA leaders think their daily recess is at risk.

"If you look at Atlanta, there's a new school district building schools without playgrounds at all," says Louv. "A big school district in Broward County, Florida, started putting up signs on the playground in 2005 that say, 'No Running.' This is why I talk about a culture of fascism, which is really insane."

Yet educators are somehow baffled that kids are squirming in their seats instead of paying attention in class, and the nation puzzles over high child obesity rates. According to the American Obesity Association, teen obesity has increased 200 percent in the past 20 years. And a Centers for Disease Control and Prevention statistic reveals that of children who are overweight today, 70 percent will become overweight or obese adults.

"We have this weird habit of preaching at kids about child obesity and saying you've got to get your kids to exercise and get your kids away from the television, but we don't tell them what to do with the kids once the TV's off," says Louv. "The *New York Times* recently had a huge slick-paper insert that was put out by Kaiser Permanente and San Francisco State University and I think some insurance company, and the headline was 'Child Obesity,' and in the whole thing, which must have been 8,000 words, there wasn't one mention of kids going outside into nature. There were vague suggestions about parents taking their kids outside, but in a list of recommendations of what to do, the only clear one was get your kids in organized sports. Well, the irony is that the greatest increase in child obesity occurred during the same two decades as the greatest increase in history of organized sports for kids. Obviously they were eating a lot of French fries along the way. There were other factors, but clearly organized sports is not doing it when it comes to childhood obesity."

But, Louv points out, the same parents who try to protect their kids from injury outdoors may fail to see that highly competitive year-round sports come with their own health risks.

"Physicians are seeing many fewer broken arms and legs," says Louv, "which every kid had when I was growing up from falling out of trees. They're seeing hardly any of those; what they are seeing is more repetitive stress injuries.

"The insanity there is that we enroll kids in organized sports and structured activities because we're afraid to let them outdoors on their own. We're afraid of the bogeyman, we're afraid they're going to get hurt. Increasingly, parents are afraid of nature itself. So we enroll in these things, or we let them sit in front of a videogame all day, and instead of a broken leg or an arm that heals relatively quickly, they end up with injuries that last for the rest of their lives. And that gets into the area of comparative risk. We really need to think, as a society, in terms of comparative risk rather than just think they're going to go outside and it's going to be dangerous. The most poisonous spider we know of in North America lives in our closets and likes to hide in our teenagers' jeans on the floor: It's the brown recluse. It doesn't much like living outside, it prefers living inside with us. But parents are terrified their kids are going to go outside and get bitten by a spider."

Since the 1980s, parenting has become a fearful enterprise. There's fear of child abduction, fear of injury—and the parents are confronted by institutional fears, chief among them: fear of liability.

"I think this is coming from something deep in the culture that has to do with the litigious worries, but is something else: this absolute mania for control and neatness," says Louv. "And I think it comes from a generalized fear of The Other—of crime, of race, now of terrorists. And I don't think it's something we've looked at closely enough.

"I try my best not to blame parents too much. And I'll be the first to admit that my kids did not have the kind of freedom that I did—I had a complete free-range childhood—and it wasn't because I wanted then signed up for every program, but because of fear. I was afraid of the bogeyman, too. But I have made a big effort to encourage boredom—the right kind of boredom—and my wife and I made a big effort to take them fishing and hiking and all of that. I'm not pretending the free-range childhood of the 1950s is going to return. We have to be a lot more intentional, though. And that takes a different mind-set."

In his book, Louv offers a random biographical sample of great

REALITY CHECK—NOT MANY KIDS ABDUCTED BY STRANGERS

One of the reasons parents are reluctant to let their children play outdoors unsupervised is fear of abduction. This fear grew from a number of highly publicized cases of abduction, beginning in the 1980s. Yet kidnapping of children by strangers is in fact quite rare. According to the U.S. Department of Justice National Incidence Studies of Missing, Abducted, Runaway or Thrown Away Children [NISMART-2], 797,000 reports of missing children are made to police annually. Here is the breakdown of why they were reported missing:

Child ran away	48 percent
Benign misunderstandings	43 percent
Lost, injured or stranded	8.5 percent
Total	99.5 percent

The number of kids actually kidnapped per year is between 90 and 300. There are 70 million children 18 or under in the United States. Thus, the chances of your child being abducted are somewhere between 1 in 350,000 to 1 in 700,000. By comparison, the chances that a child will be killed in an automobile accident are 90 in 400,000.

According to an article in the February 1998 issue of *Redbook* magazine, a recent study of parents' worries by pediatricians at the Mayo Clinic, in Rochester, Minnesota, revealed that nearly three-quarters of parents said they feared their children might be abducted. One-third of parents said this was a frequent worry—a degree of fear greater than that held for any other concern, including car accidents, sports injuries or drug addiction.

thinkers, innovators and activists, including science fiction writer Arthur C. Clarke, inventor Thomas Edison, naturalist Jane Goodall, poet T. S. Eliot, author Mark Twain and first lady Eleanor Roosevelt, who all have cited time spent wandering, dreaming and contemplating alone in nature when they were young as a great influence. Of Roosevelt, who would disappear into the woods and fields for hours to read books and write stories, he says, "For Eleanor, literature, nature, and dreams were forever linked. We can only imagine how this little girl would have developed without her time in nature, but surely her fragile power needed protection as it grew, and time and space to hear an inner voice."

Parenting expert Mike Riera sees downtime, free play and daydreaming as a crucial part of childhood that can affect who we become as adults.

"My wife's an architect, and she tells me all of the hours she spent under the window outside, behind the bush, where she constructed little cities. And I tell her about the hours I would be playing basketball. I could go three hours completely entertained, not practicing any drills but just being both teams and being the announcer interviewing myself and just that whole creating a world. And I don't know if our kids get much of that. That was a common experience when I was growing up. We all had ways of doing that.

"I think there's a little fear of kids being bored. What's wrong with staring out the window for a while and not being so efficient? I think efficiency has taken over a lot, and that's what we see in sports: How efficient can you get to be the great player? And I think that anything that's great or worthwhile has had some leap of imagination along the way that was not predicted. We're not that rational of beings. We're not that linear in the way we do things. But we want the security, and the security is this club team system, and, boom, you follow this and you go all along the way, and at each place you'll get feedback on what you need to do to improve, and you can get the full scholarship to college, which is really what most people are aiming for." Even though only 1 percent or less get one. "And how many people get damaged along the way?"

Creativity versus Productivity

If kids rarely play outside on their own, rarely experience nature, never get downtime—time to be alone, to do nothing, to be bored, to daydream—how will they develop creativity?

Louv says, "I think this gets to the whole issue of what we really value in this society. I don't think we value creativity. I think we value productivity. And we don't recognize that in the long term, lack of attention to creativity reduces productivity. We don't look that far."

To try to understand the changes in youth sports and childhood, I went to see my old professor Harry Edwards. This wasn't exactly *Tuesdays with Morrie*, but my Monday with Harry turned out to be fascinating. Edwards was a sociology professor at UC Berkeley for 31 years. I took his popular, eye-opening Sociology of Sport class when I was an undergraduate at Cal, and seeing him now, all these years later, I felt he was as charismatic and captivating as I remembered. I drove down to the southern end of San Francisco Bay, to San Francisco 49ers headquarters in Santa Clara, to interview him; he's been a consultant to the football team for 20 years and does player personnel. He explains that it's his job to "separate out the merely disturbed from the truly demented among prospects and candidates so we don't get in too far over our heads in terms of what we can manage. Guys come in about four different gradations: You have no maintenance or low maintenance, moderate maintenance, high maintenance and 24-hour surveillance."

Edwards was a college athlete himself, starting at Fresno City College, where the record he set in the discus throw in 1960 was not broken until 1999. From there he went on to play basketball and track and field at San José State College (now University). Over his varied and colorful career he also worked in the NBA with the Golden State Warriors for 10 years, in Major League Baseball for five years under Peter Ueberroth in the Office of the Commissioner, and was director of parks and recreation for the City of Oakland under Mayor Jerry Brown, 2000–2003.

Edwards gained notoriety for allegedly having inspired the dramatic protest at the 1968 Mexico City Olympics: As "The Star-Spangled Banner" played and the U.S. flag was raised, on the medal stand African American San José State College teammates Tommie Smith, who won the gold, and John Carlos, who earned the bronze, in the 200-meter run, each bowed his head and raised a black-gloved fist in the Black Power salute to protest racism in the United States. (They were immediately thrown off the team by the United States Olympic Committee.) Edwards, then a young sociology professor, had urged a boycott of the games (which never materialized) by all black American athletes as a protest against racial discrimination, and his group, the Olympic Project for Human Rights, counted Smith and Carlos as members. The two runners decided to go to the games and planned to make the gesture if they won medals.

After leading me through hallways at 49ers headquarters lined with framed jerseys of players like Y. A. Tittle, Joe Montana and Ronnie Lott, Edwards opened the door to a terrace where we could talk. Sitting at a patio table outside the building on a mild and sunny January day, with the 49ers practice field glistening green before us and the Santa Clara Youth Soccer Park, featuring three pristine fields, on the other side of us, I was perfectly situated to grasp the connection between youth sports and the dream of playing in the pros.

"The whole context of youth has changed in the past 30 years," Edwards began. "There was a time, believe it or not, when youth was a time of frivolity and play and even to some degree experimentation and role playing: Who am I? Who do I really want to be? and so on.

Over the past three decades, since the onset of highly saturated media presentation and intrusion, principally television, youth has come to be seen more and more as a highly productive period culminating in 18-year-olds coming out of high school signing $10 million basketball contracts and $90 million shoe deals. You have high school girl singing groups like Beyoncé and Destiny's Child at 17, 18, 19, coming out of high school signing multimillion-dollar record deals. You have rappers, 18, 19 years old, driving $150,000 Lamborghinis with $100,000 worth of diamonds around their necks, living in $15 million homes, all projected by the media into the living rooms. You have 14-year-olds signing soccer contracts for $10 million. Tennis players—14, 15 and 16 years old, making $10 million a year. Golfers 16 years old signing contracts. Tiger Woods, 18, 19, coming out and now he may be one of the richest sports figures in the country.

"All of this has projected youth as a *productive* period, as opposed to that age of frivolity, role playing, experimentation and, more than anything else, being a child. That is gone. Along with that has come all the accoutrements of production and productivity; the adult access and vices: the sex, the drugs, the alcohol, the materialism. So now you get parents at the lower end of the socioeconomic structure where athletes in the so-called major sports have traditionally come from—the basketball players, the football players, the baseball players—they are pushing their kids into these blue-star camps, one camp after another, and this is after having played basketball or football all year in school. Now in the summer they're in the camps.

"If they're from the middle class, they look at the NBA and the NFL, and they say, 'Hey, my kid is not gonna go out and compete with LeBron James. But maybe my kid can get on that soccer team, or maybe my kid can get on that golf tour, or maybe my kid can get into tennis, so let me get them involved in these camps where they have the possibility of moving up the ladder and becoming productive. Maybe even becoming a superstar.'

"The core of the issue is not what's happening with any particular class, but what's happened in terms of the very definition of youth in this media-saturated age, where the emphasis is on production. These kids can produce beyond the wildest dreams of their parents, their class, their community. And that is what a lot of this push is about.

"You eliminate that evolution from 30 years ago, when childhood was in an age when you had three networks and you got the NBA on tape delay and maybe you'd get *a* football game on Sunday in your area, and maybe *Wide World of Sports*, which was as likely to be about downhill skiing in Norway or bull riding in Wyoming as about playing golf or tennis—you eliminate that and all of this goes away; you're still talking about kids. And sports figures are golfer Arnold Palmer or Bob Gibson, the pitcher for the Cardinals, or Kurt Flood, another great Cardinals player, or basketball players Bill Russell or Bob Cousy; these were *grown men* in their mid- to late 20s and so forth, not somebody who has been pushed since they were 8 years old and somebody found out they could run a little faster than everybody else or hit a tennis ball a little bit harder or maybe swing a golf club a little bit more accurately."

Alvin Rosenfeld, whose landmark book *The Over-Scheduled Child* was published in 2001, told the *Washington Post* in 2005 that things have only gotten worse for kids in years since his book came out. "It goes back to parental anxiety, an almost nonacceptance of the child's inherent nature and [an attempt] to convert them into some accomplishment machine."

And when a child achieves, parents can see the tangible evidence: the trophy, the scholarship, the spot on the roster, the endorsement deal. What they might be losing along the way is harder to see.

"The problem is that what is lost in a family life to a driven athletic schedule is ineffable: time to cook together, time to hang out, time to read a book, lying on your bed," Michael Thompson, author of *The Pressured Child: Helping Your Child to Find Success in School and in Life* and co-author with Dan Kindlon of the *New York Times* bestseller *Raising Cain: Protecting the Emotional Life of Boys*, told me. "Call me old-fashioned but I think that downtime in the context of family is often what people remember about their childhoods."

Thompson, an author and psychologist who specializes in children and families, wrote a poignant essay for the op-ed page of the Boston *Globe* in 2004 talking about how he rediscovered "a fantastic lost world of family traditions" when he visited a children's summer camp in Vermont, 40 years after he'd attended one himself. It was a world, he wrote, "where people sit and eat three meals together every day, serving their food from platters and talking with one another throughout the meal. A world where 10-year-olds set the table for dinner and clear it, without complaint. A world where 13-year-old boys don't play video games every night, or watch TV, or sit in front of computers. Instead, they lie in bed and read—comic books, novels, sometimes even grown-up novels. In this world 11-year-old girls walk together holding hands as easily as they laugh and talk. No frenzied instant messaging here. Instead, they sing. Every morning, as they make their beds and sweep out their rooms, they sing together. One girl starts a song and the others join in, spontaneously."

Thompson wrote that he "was struck hard by how rarely children engage in these activities anywhere else: not in schools, not in neighborhoods, not in families. Summer camps are one of the last places that kids can learn the so-called family values that hard-pressed families no longer have the time to teach." And he noted wistfully, "The only place a child from a high-pressure family can enjoy some peace and quiet, and perhaps a good night's sleep (with a lullaby), is away from home.

"Why does it matter?" Thompson asked rhetorically. "Because children need it. Children don't develop because they are pushed, prodded, and pressured to develop for sports teams or 'good' colleges. Development is their biological and psychological imperative.

It is the job of adults to create environments where children have the time, freedom, and safety to grow up at their own pace."

I think most parents would agree that Harvard is a "good" college. Yet they might be surprised to find out that the undergraduate dean, Harry Lewis, sends out a letter to freshmen telling them not to pick up the pace to compete at one of the nation's top learning institutions, but to slow down, get plenty of rest and relaxation and cultivate the art of doing nothing. Carl Honoré quotes from Lewis' letter, titled "Slow Down," in his book *In Praise of Slowness: How a Worldwide Movement Is Challenging the Cult of Speed*. "Empty time is not a vacuum to be filled," writes Lewis. "It is the thing that enables the other things on your mind to be creatively rearranged, like the empty square in the 4 × 4 puzzle that makes it possible to move the other fifteen pieces around."

Lewis concludes, "In advising you to think about slowing down and limiting your structured activities, I do not mean to discourage you from high achievement, indeed from the pursuit of extraordinary excellence. But you are more likely to sustain the intense effort needed to accomplish first-rate work in one area if you allow yourself some leisure time, some recreation, some time for solitude."

Alone Time

"Poet Marianne Moore wrote, 'The cure for loneliness is solitude,' " says parenting expert Joe Di Prisco, who co-authored *Field Guide to the American Teenager* and *Right from Wrong: Instilling a Sense of Integrity in Your Child* with Mike Riera. "I always want to put in a good word for loneliness in kids.

"Team sports are great if they're organized the right way and if their purpose is clearly articulated: that it's about sportsmanship, playing hard, competition, respect for your opponents, respect for the game, and, to quote Bob Ladouceur, the winning football coach at

[Concord, California, high school] De La Salle, it's about love—love for your teammates. So those are great things.

"Here's something you don't learn from team sports: how to be alone. And what are we talking about here? The development of a child, at any age. And if your child is so programmed into finding meaning exclusively or predominantly through team sports, then there's not a lot of opportunity to be alone, to entertain oneself, to take chances that being dedicated to a team doesn't allow you to do."

If downtime and alone time are as important as the psychologists, parenting mavens, educators and sports medicine doctors say it is, why do we so easily give in when the youth sports machine starts to gobble up more and more of our kids'—and our—lives?

Sometimes coaches have to be the voice of reason when parents are blinded by the gleam of imagined trophies just over the horizon. When high school football teams in Oregon began having full-contact camps throughout the summer, rather than passing camps only in August, right before the start of football season, one coach spoke out in *The Oregonian*: Tom Smythe, whose high school coaching career spans four decades in the state.

"For crying out loud, football at the high school level is supposed to be fun," he said, urging the Oregon School Activities Association to address the issue. "How is it fun when a kid has to give up a summer job, summer baseball, summer basketball or his family? How about giving the kids some family time? Maybe let them have some freedom to go with their girlfriends to the beach. Or maybe just to lounge around and do nothing. Isn't that what summers are for?

"My teams at Lakeridge and McNary have never lifted a finger in the summer and between them, we've won three state championships and 80 percent of my football games. Well, what does that tell you?"

It tells me that kids who take time off to recharge can still be successful. And that reducing their stress might be a key factor in kids' doing well.

Why Kids Need Downtime

Peggy Wynne, MFT

Is it hard to convince parents that kids need downtime?

Yes. Especially the baby boomers, who come from this place that more is better. And this idea that downtime is not good, that if you're not productive, then something's wrong, and you're not going to achieve. If you're not either studying your Spanish flash cards or out there practicing soccer from age 3 on, you're never going to get into Stanford. So the kids never learn to self-soothe or self-satisfy. That's a big issue when they get older, in terms of impulse management.

What are the consequences of that?

What happens is, if kids don't learn to entertain themselves, play by themselves, be creative in their own head, they're always looking for someone else to stimulate them. And what I find is when they get to be adolescents, they look for those quick fixes—drugs and alcohol—because that's a great way to get some kind of reaction to something, rather than learning how to make yourself happy doing something else. You're always looking for something to make you happy rather than learning how to make yourself happy. And that's a really big issue in terms of kids. That's a skill you want to teach our kids: how to self-entertain. And that goes for relationships as well: If you're always looking for someone to make you feel good, that never works very well.

Then there's the issue of kids' only experience of play being organized sports refereed by an adult, so they aren't learning how to make up their own games and solve their own disputes.

I think that speaks to the notion that you're not teaching your child to think, you're kind of doing it for them.

And that's one of the big consequences when they get to be adolescents: If, by the time they're teenagers, they don't know how to make decisions based on what's good for them and what works for them, they're basing their decisions on all the wrong things: Are they going to fit in with the right crowd, are they going to make their friend happy, are they going to look cool if they do this? Part of the work of being a parent is getting your kids to make those decisions for themselves. And always being monitored by someone else and never being able to make calls for yourself is a huge problem.

A lot of parents think their kids won't get into trouble if they're always playing sports.

That's a fallacy. I can't tell you how many kids I know who are good students and are on varsity first string who are getting drunk and driving around, doing drugs and having sex without condoms. They're all doing it. Having your kid in sports does not stop that at all. It keeps them busier and it might tire them out a little. But they'll still face the peer pressure of it.

I think it takes a really strong family to be able to say no to some of those pressures and not just do what everybody else is doing, but to have your own family values about what's important and raise your kids to go off and be successful and go to four-year colleges and do well. But a big piece of it is that everybody has to learn how to self-manage, and when you grow up in an environment where everything is managed for you, then it's much harder to learn that. I think that playing sports is a really valuable tool—learning how to be on a team and work with other people is a really valuable tool. But I think it's isolated as the only skill that children have to learn. I think it's one of many.

Rise Up and Revolt: What You Can Do Now

- **Promote free play.** Kick your kids out into the yard so
  they can make up their own games, build forts, sail bottle-
  cap boats in puddles and streams or shoot baskets on their
  own. Let them ride their bikes around the neighborhood
  and to the park, if you live in safe area. Be realistic about
  your fear of danger and the likelihood of harm or abduction. Teach your kids to be independent and responsible
  and trustworthy. Stay in cell phone contact if that will help
  you be less anxious. Take them to the park or the beach or
  the woods with no agenda and let them run around and
  make up their own games while they're there, with you as
  their base of operations to return to for food and hugs.
  Play *with* them. Get down and get dirty. Let them lead you
  with their imagination rather than you leading them with
  your instruction. "Children love it when parents enter into
  play with them," says Cathy O'Keefe, the University of
  South Alabama instructor of therapeutic recreation. "We
  all need play that doesn't have an end product in mind,
  even as adults. So when we play with our children, we're
  actually doing ourselves a favor. We're giving ourselves a
  chance to re-enter the world of the frivolity of play. That's
  what makes play different from sport or recreation. Play is
  its own end, an end in itself. It's not a means to an end, like
  sports might be a means to a trophy or a means to being
  selected for something else. Play is just play."
- **Take summer vacations as a family.** This is a time for
  relaxation, renewal and bonding. A week or two together
  without the pressures of work and school and sports and
  the family dynamics you're locked into in your own home
  can provide opportunities for fun and connection that are

less available during the rest of the year. Don't give this up to a team itinerary! Give your family what it needs. The team can do without you for a while. You and your children will have more to give after you recharge your batteries.

- **Set aside a family night or day for fun** each week or as often as you can. Play board games, watch a movie together on TV, rent a DVD, go to the movies, take a hike, go on a picnic. Decide by consensus what fun activity to do.

- **Help save recess!** The cutting of recess has become so prevalent that in March 2006 the National PTA (which boasts nearly 6 million members) and Cartoon Network launched Rescue Recess, a national campaign to champion the importance of recess for kids and fight for its survival. They developed the campaign (to which Cartoon Network has pledged $1.3 million) with input from an advisory board drawn from the Centers for Disease Control and Prevention, NAPSE, the President's Council on Fitness and Sports, New Leaders for New Schools and Health MPowers. Find out more at www.rescuingrecess.com, and you and your kids can join the letter-writing campaign to your local and state school officials.

- **Fight the forces that are cutting P.E.** Again, with obesity rates rising, this is no time to have kids get *less* exercise. Schools pressured to improve scores on standardized tests have erred in taking time for physical training and exercise away from kids. They need it, and studies show exercise can actually benefit kids' ability to learn in the classroom. According to a Department of Education report issued in May 2006, only 17 to 22 percent of schools provide daily P.E across the elementary grades, and the average number of days per week of P.E. is 2.4 in 1st through 5th grades.

According to the *Shape of the Nation Report* released in 2006 by the National Association for Sport and Physical Education (NASPE) and the American Heart Association, only 36 states require P.E. for elementary school students; 33 for middle school; and 42 for high school. Twelve states allow P.E. credits to be earned through online courses. One of the benefits of P.E. is that it provides a way for kids to try out new sports in a relaxed, less competitive setting, which can lead to their pursuing one or more of those sports outside of school. And kids whose families can't afford the cost of youth leagues or club teams deserve the opportunity to learn and play sports in school.

- **Bring back intramural teams.** If we're concerned about obesity and diabetes and that 70 percent drop out of sports by age 13, how about lobbying school boards and administrators to reinstitute intramural competition in high school, which got dropped some years ago in most places? More sports options are better than fewer. For kids who played at the rec level and are not skilled enough to make the high school team or don't want to make the time commitment that would involve, how about providing a vehicle for fun and exercise and continued love of sports? If there's a budgetary reason to say no, organize parent volunteers to oversee the program.

CHANGES IN HOW CHILDREN SPEND THEIR TIME

According to a survey of children between the ages of 3 and 12, conducted by the University of Michigan's Institute for Social Research Center, between 1981 and 1997:

- Free time declined by 12 percent.
- Playtime dropped by three hours per week.
- Unstructured outdoor activities decreased by 50 percent.
- Structured sports doubled from two hours, 20 minutes per week to five hours, 17 minutes.
- Studying increased by almost 50 percent.

CHAPTER 6

Growing Up Stressed Out

Of all the kids that I've worked with, no one has ever complained that they weren't doing enough. I've never had a kid who said, "I wish I'd been signed up for one more sport this season." I think that's significant.

—PEGGY WYNNE, marriage and family therapist in San Francisco and Pleasanton, California

Children are not born obsessed with speed and productivity—we make them that way. . . . One of the first phrases my son learned to say was, "Come on! Hurry up!"

—CARL HONORÉ, from his book *In Praise of Slowness*

It's not news that we lead busy lives. In the majority of contemporary families, both parents work outside the home, maintaining their own demanding schedules and stress levels, and layered upon that are their children's schedules and all their extracurricular activities, from Scout meetings to music lessons to sports practices and games. Many athletic kids are playing on more than one team per season, or on elite traveling teams that operate 10, 11 or even 12 months a year, with loads of drive time built into the weekday schedule and motel stays booked on the weekends. Ask a parent "How are you?" and the common response is "Busy."

Days and periods of rest used to be built into even the most high-powered lives. People didn't used to work or schedule youth sports games on Sundays. Evenings were for family dinners, a moderate amount of homework and relaxing from a hard day's work. Weekends were for fun and relaxation, with maybe one youth game on Friday night or Saturday. Now many parents are checking work e-mail daily, nightly, hourly, so they're never really disconnected from their job concerns, and kids have loads more homework, on top of practices and games throughout the seven-day week. Families are taking fewer vacations, and the ones they take are shorter in duration. So many of the release valves we used to rely upon are no longer in the picture.

Reflecting on this change is not merely an exercise in nostalgia. It's a reminder that Americans didn't always live the way most of us are living now. This new version of childhood is only 15 or 20 years old. It was ushered in by the baby boomers when they became parents and decided their kids should be denied no opportunity, and that they would be involved in their children's lives in a way their own parents rarely were. People seem to have accepted the idea that we live in a 24/7 world, as the expression goes, and high-pressured youth sports commitments are part of that. But what kind of a toll is this taking on children and families?

Cathy O'Keefe, the University of South Alabama instructor of leisure studies and therapeutic recreation, says, "I tell my students all the time, your generation is going to have a conflict that I don't think any of us have had. There have never been more than 24 hours in a day, but there's far too much now to do within that 24 hours and far too much pressure about what you do in that 24 hours. And I think we're reaching a critical point where a critical mass of young people are going to be unable to handle it, and may be uninterested in handling it."

As adults' lives have speeded up in response to the increased pressures of a tight global economy, where downsizing, union-busting and merger mania have made working adults feel insecure and vulnerable, kids' lives have kept pace. The kinds of pressure parents internalize— to succeed, to never fall behind, to keep up with the Joneses—have trickled down to the children, who are urged to work hard, to stay ahead of the curve, to excel and win prizes, be they the shiny gold kind you can put on a trophy shelf or the college scholarship that will help the family bottom line and bring prestige to the parents who have sacrificed so much of their time and money to help kids get there. And there's no time to waste. Coaches of grade school children are already talking to them about college scholarships. Middle school kids are urged to join elite teams so they'll get a spot on the high school squad. Prep students are skipping the high school team altogether so they can get more exposure to college recruiters at the club tournaments. Kids are now always looking ahead so as not to fall behind.

Carl Honoré, author of *In Praise of Slowness,* who calls the predominant contemporary parenting style the roadrunner approach to raising children, writes, "In our turbo-charged world, the hurry virus has spread from adulthood into the younger years. . . . Young people today are certainly busier, more scheduled, more rushed than any generation ever was. Recently, a teacher I know approached the parents of a child in her care. She felt the boy was spending too long at school and was enrolled in too many extracurricular activities. Give him a break, she suggested. The father was furious. 'He has to learn to do a ten-hour day just like me,' he snapped. The child was four."

We are clearly modeling our type-A behavior and our anxiety about failure to our kids. They feel the pressure to excel, whether it's communicated overtly or indirectly. What puzzles me is that when I was growing up, I felt that in every one of my classes and on any given playing field, there were kids who were above average, average and below average, and everyone knew who they were, including the parents. But in the current era, it seems that virtually all parents want their kids to be No. 1, and believe they can help them be that simply by providing the right opportunities and training. "It is no longer enough to keep up with the Joneses' children," says Honoré, "now, our own little darlings have to outpace them in every discipline."

"The trouble is it gets globalized, so that everybody has to do it that way," Bay Area therapist Peggy Wynne told me. "The parents are abdicating their responsibility to nurture their kids in a healthy way. It's nice to give your kid opportunities to do things and be in sports and a variety of activities, and that's healthy and good for them. Yet what I see kids and parents struggle with is: Where are the boundaries? I urge parents, especially with kids in elementary and middle school, to pick one sport a season to participate in. But the parents who have the kids in multiple sports that overlap are the parents who are afraid to say no because they're afraid to let their kid not be as exceptional as he might be. We have this cultural expectation that we have to nurture our child's every teeny little gift, and if we don't nurture it to the best of our ability they'll never become exceptional. I really think that's a detriment to kids, because kids can't just be OK anymore. They have to be exceptional. And that's hard."

Wynne says that a lot of the stress issues she deals with in family therapy involve parents' overscheduling their kids and the pressures that go with that. "I think from a psychotherapy standpoint, the majority of the issues have a lot more to do with the parents than the kids," she says. "The parents end up overscheduling their kids because of that competitive nature that adults have with each other about having to prove that their kids are the smartest and brightest.

"It's not just sports," she adds. "It's like that thing of trying to get your kid into a preschool before they're born. And middle school parents are worried about what college their child is going to attend. So it's this societal and cultural pressure that I see as one of the big factors in why kids are overscheduled and why it's creating the stress in families that it does.

"A lot of the cultural pressure comes from the top down," says Wynne. "High school sports today is what college sports used to be like—the attention, the focus, the practices—it's all just dropped down a level. It used to be that kids could play high school sports for fun. It's not like that anymore. It's much more competitive. Kids used to use sports as a tool to be well-rounded, as something to try and something to do and a way to make friends—that just doesn't exist anymore. And that's the real tragedy. Sports for kids 5 to 18 used to be a way to socialize, a way to have fun, to learn a few new skills, but it was not the intent of making pro athletes or getting a scholarship to college. But now, people are thinking about that in the 8th grade.

"I see a lot of high school kids who are so stressed out, trying to get into the right college and getting good SAT scores, and they're all taking special classes to make sure they can do everything. And it's really a drain to be a 17-year-old kid and have the weight of all this, which emotionally they're really not prepared for. They're supposed to be goofing around being kids."

"My take on overscheduling is that kids in general are very robust and like and enjoy a wide range of activites," says Marin County psychotherapist Madeline Levine, author of *The Price of Privilege: How Parental Pressure and Material Advantage Are Creating a Generation of Disconnected and Unhappy Kids*. Levine raised three boys, all of whom played on elite travel teams and two of whom played on varsity teams in high school. "The data that we have says that the majority of kids actually say that they participate in extracurricular activities for fun, as opposed to because my parents said so or because I'm supposed to get into college or stuff like that.

"So the fact is that being involved in after-school activities is good for most kids. What is not good for most kids is parental criticism of their performance. In particular, girls are susceptible to both emotional and academic problems when their parents are critical about extracurricular performance. The great predictor of depression is perfectionism. So always pushing your kid and saying, 'That wasn't good enough,' is a great setup for depression.

"I think an important question is: What is the difference between what kids need and what the current culture is? Are they the same? I think the answer is no.

"So just because the culture is involved in something doesn't mean it's good. And I think the burden of it falls heavily on mothers. I think we feel guilty if we're not doing what we see as everything we can. So I think there needs to be some education about what children need. In fact, what children need are intact moms. The most predictive factor in a child's health is his mother's mental health. So if we're stressed and gulping our dinner and racing around, the fact is, we're not doing a good job, even though we think we are. And if you have to buck the culture, you're probably not as alone as you think you are."

Hard to Say No

As a parent, it's hard to say no when a child shows an interest in a new sport or activity. How will he or she discover an aptitude or a passion without trying it on for size? The stress often comes in when there are too many activities in a week, and when a child has to choose between appealing options.

In my family, Kyle, my firstborn, tried out new sports as they came along—first rec league soccer (not in kindergarten, but a couple of years later), then Little League baseball, then CYO basketball on his school team, starting in 3rd grade. His conflicts emerged later, when he had to juggle soccer and fall ball (baseball) in autumn, and spring soccer and Little League in the spring. He ultimately saw that one sport per season was the sanest approach.

He also made quite a mature decision—all on his own—to drop basketball in 8th grade. His school team had been building toward a championship season since it started in 3rd grade. Our school had never won the CYO championship in its history, but the coaches felt this team had the right stuff, and that these boys were the ones to do it. They had come very close in 7th grade, and all signs pointed toward ultimate victory in the 8th. But just before the start of the season, as Kyle faced increased academic stress plus entrance exams and applications for college prep schools, and he looked ahead to all those practices, all that pressure to win and all that time he'd be spending on the bench, since he wasn't one of the top players, he realized he just didn't love basketball enough to go through all that, and he quit the team. They did go on to win the championship, and Kyle was in the stands cheering his classmates on, but he did not regret his decision.

Things were even more complex with my daughter, Hayley. She started off in gymnastics in preschool but by 2nd grade wanted to check out the team sport all her friends were playing: soccer. We explained that she couldn't do both because they happened at the same time on Saturday mornings, and as working parents we could not take her to weekday afternoon classes. She elected to give up gymnastics. In 3rd grade, her school basketball team started, and she took up city league softball, whose season partially overlapped with basketball.

Then, in 4th grade, the school volleyball team started, and she decided to play spring soccer while also playing softball, so we were really in for it. The volleyball team starts practicing before soccer season is over. The basketball team starts practicing before volleyball is over. And in the spring, she sometimes had conflicting basketball, soccer and softball games. She'd have to decide each weekend which coach she'd have to apologize to, which team she'd have to let down, and shoulder the stress of that process—all at 10 years old. Some days, the timing was such that she could make both scheduled games on a Saturday, so long as she changed uniforms in the car as we rushed between the two fields at opposite ends of town or in different cities.

The next year, in 5th grade, she was elected to student council, joined the 4-H Club and started taking acting classes at the local repertory theater. Were we insane to let her add more after-school activities to her—and our—already crowded sports schedule? Well, it's tough when you have a child who's enthusiastic about learning new things and demonstrates leadership skills and athletic talent. She realized it had been too stressful to play two spring sports concurrently, so she dropped softball in favor of spring soccer. That was a hard decision, because she had great coaches, a nice team, and she was becoming a good pitcher, batter and fielder. But I respected her for seeing she needed to make a choice. She planned to drop volleyball the next winter, but after she happened to go to a preseason practice with a friend and had such a good time, she came home and asked if she could stay on the team. We said yes, and it turned out to be a fun season and a great bonding experience with her classmates. If we had imposed our will, she would have missed out on that.

Sometimes she's been wiser about monitoring her stress level than we have. That year, when her fall semester after-school acting class ended, she told us she didn't want to sign up for the spring class. Rather than really hearing her, we encouraged her to stick with it because we knew she liked acting (she'd attended drama camps for several summers) and she was getting a higher level of professional training. She did the class, didn't have a very good time, and at the end of it, said, "I want to take a break from acting" and canceled plans to attend the theater camp she'd previously enjoyed so much. That taught us quite a lesson.

"Part of growing up is having to make choices," says San Francisco psychotherapist Dana Iscoff. "That is also something we as parents have to give our kids. It's not just giving them opportunities, it's also giving them the capacity to make choices. Sometimes you can't do both things, so how do you make that decision? And how do you deal with the loss? But that's part of what life is about: You can't do it all."

Iscoff says that for little kids, offering limited choices is good, because children may be inclined to say yes to everything that's offered, or be overwhelmed by having to choose among several atractive options. So parents could offer a choice between two sports—"Do you want to play soccer or Pop Warner football?"—or suggest a combination of one sport and one extracurricular activity: "Do you want to do soccer and dance? How about basketball and art class?" She says parents should resist the temptation to overschedule children with too many activities. The child might not complain going into a season of different activities every day, but may end up showing signs of stress, from crankiness to a dip in academic performance.

When kids reach middle-school age, Iscoff says, they can have more of a role in deciding what they want to do.

"A patient of mine just told me about a situation where his kid, who's in 7th grade, wanted to play in an important game for his school team while he was also playing for an elite team," she recalls. "The father had set a rule that if there was ever a conflict, he had to play with the elite team. So when this conflict came up, his father wanted to hold him to it. But the kid took issue with that and said that he felt like his school team was his peer group and that's who we wanted to play with. It was for a big playoff and he was the star pitcher, and it wasn't a very good team but it was the first time they had ever made the playoffs. So the father ended up saying, 'OK. If this is what you're deciding, then you need to tell the coach of the elite team and you have to handle it.' So the kid ended up handling it. He talked to the elite coach, who was really understanding, and played on the school team and they won! The kid learned a lot about decision-making, about what's important. His loyalty to his school peers overrode his loyalty to the elite team. His school peers were really depending on him and he came through for them. And the next night he played in the big game with his elite team."

Iscoff admires the dad for being flexible. "This was a case where this father let his kid make this decision, even though his first response was 'No, we had an agreement and this is what you have to do.' He let up on that and let the kid make his own decision and it ended up being a really good learning experience for the kid.

"It's a fine line for us parents determining where we step in and where we back off; when we let them work out stuff on their own and when we say, 'You know, you're overdoing it.' Like so many aspects of parenting, we have to kind of keep our eyes on our children and listen to the kinds of decisions that they're making and help them. Maybe say, 'OK, you try this, and if it doesn't work, then we'll have to revisit it.' Ultimately it's a better experience for the child to have a parent who supports them at that age when they can make their own decisions, but who also can intervene when it's just too much."

When Too Much Is Too Much

Sometimes parents' expectations can slip out of synch with what kids really want.

"I had one dad who absolutely refused to discuss any changes to the soccer schedule," therapist Wynne recalls. "He was just unwilling. I think the kid was in 6th or 7th grade, and was in two competitive sports on traveling teams and OPD. And it was really, really tough on him. The kid was not happy, and he was suffering emotionally and suffering socially."

Wynne says she suggested the boy quit one of the sports, and the father absolutely refused. What happened then? "The family left treatment."

Sometimes a child's parents are in conflict over what is a desirable level of involvement in sports, leaving the child caught in the middle. Diane Ehrensaft, a psychologist at The Wright Institute in Berkeley, California, and author of *Spoiling Childhood: How Well-Meaning Parents Are Giving Children Too Much—But Not What They Need,* recalls a case in point:

"This is a post-divorce situation of a father who is zealous about his child's team sports, and is the coach, and the mother who is an artist, and the child is very artistic. The mother is adamant that this child should not have to be entrapped in his father's mania about sports. It turns out that the child is extremely talented both in art and in sports. He plays on soccer teams, he plays baseball, and he was invited to be on a traveling all-stars team this summer, and he goes to a 12-month school, so he normally doesn't have summers off. Basically the mother backed off and said, 'OK, if this is what he really wants, the team has to understand he's in school, but I'll go along with it.'

"And the outcome was, at the end of the summer, this child was sobbing in my office about what a horrible experience it was for him. And how he was miserable every day and he was in over his head, out of his league, and felt pressured to do things he wasn't ready to do and felt everyone was angry at him because he didn't play hard or well enough. And this is a kid who was very hard on himself to begin with."

And how old is this boy? "He is 9," says Ehrensaft.

Doesn't the father see how unhappy he is?

"The father doesn't see; the boy hides it from his father. But his mother sees. The mother finally yanked him out and said, 'I'm not doing this to this kid.' And of course that creates tension between the parents—and this is a child caught in the middle between two value systems.

"There's is a belief system around commitment that I've heard from many parents—and it's one of the biggest tensions post-divorce, usually a father-mother split in heterosexual families around sports mania—that our children are not committed enough, and the commitment to sports is one where once you make it, you've got to keep it—and that this is a value that we're teaching.

"It's in this context where playing becomes hard labor. And it's not just around sports, it's around everything. And whatever activity kids take up, it's not about having fun, it's about doing it well and excelling. And there absolutely is a devaluing of nothing-time, where you do nothing or are not doing anything productive. That's our culture. We live in a society that works longer hours and takes fewer vacations than any other industrialized country but Japan. That's where the mania around sports is embedded.

"I'm concerned that we're robbing children of the opportunity to play. We're squelching the creativity. And we're creating anxiety disorders. Is this what we want for our children?"

I ask Ehrensaft what she means by anxiety disorders, and how and when they surface.

"Here's how it typically shows up: with sit-down strikes. The kids collapse in early adolescence. And this is the time that you want them to start thinking about sports more seriously. They say, 'Forget this. I've had it. I'll never touch a baseball again.' And they're old enough then to walk, to say, 'I refuse.' So rather than starting out with it being fun and really enjoying the pleasure of it and then moving to 'Do you want to do this more seriously?' you often completely foreclose that possibility by starting too soon with too much and too much pressure and seriousness about it."

Beware of Burnout

According to an oft-quoted study by Michigan State University, 70 percent of kids who play youth sports quit by the time they're 13. For some, it's because they've had bad experiences or they develop other interests, but for others it's due to parental pressure or because they are simply burned out.

Some kids train hard from kindergarten on, rack up the trophies and take all the right steps to make the college team, only to find out when they get there that they've lost their love of the game.

Lehigh University soccer coach Dean Koski reflects, "I worry that I'm dealing with 18-to-22-year-old, very talented, very bright kids who are playing at the highest level of soccer in the country, and they aren't passionate about playing—not all of them—but you can just see it in their eyes, you can see it in how they practice, because they've been doing it since they were 5 and that's all they've been doing. Understandably, they've lost some of that passion to show up at practice and have fun and get after it and go to games and get after it, because they've just been doing it over and over and over again. I worry about that.

"My first year of recruiting at Lehigh 14 years ago, I'd recruited a guy who I thought was going to be a great fit for Lehigh. He was my top kid, and on the third day of preseason, he said, 'I don't want to do this anymore.' I said, 'What do you mean?' And I remember to this day that he said, 'Because I've been playing since I was 5 and I thought this was going to be fun, but it's not fun anymore. I'm sorry.' And this happens annually. This year there's a kid whose twin brother plays for me, and he called me a week before preseason and told me, 'Coach, I just can't do it anymore. I just don't have the passion to play. I thought I could do it, but I think I'd be cheating you and the team because it's no longer there inside me.'

"At least one a year is going to say, 'I don't want to do it,' or if they're not saying it, they're hiding it pretty well, and are playing for other people, i.e., their parents, their coach or their girlfriend or even sometimes for me."

What's really hard on kids is when they want to quit but fear that they can't because it would disappoint or anger their parents.

Judging from her experience on a Class I soccer team in elementary and middle school, Caitlin Meyer says it seemed as if many kids were playing club because their parents wanted them to. "I played with a lot of kids who were really good players but didn't want to put up with the stress and the time commitment that it became for them, but their parents wanted that for them, so their parents made them be there. That was another unfortunate side effect: parents wanting their kids to be superstars and get college scholarships and play professionally, which rarely happens. I don't know if every single parent realizes that playing on this club team isn't guaranteeing a college scholarship or playing professionally. It's just bunch of kids. I think parents often got carried away."

I ask Caitlin what percentage of athletes she played with would have liked to quit but stayed on the team because their parents wanted them to stay.

"On my team of 15 girls, there were probably at least five or six who really didn't want to be there. As kids get older and become more independent, they can say, 'I really don't like this anymore,' and so as we got older, those kids dropped out and went to different teams that are not as intense. Some kids quit the sport altogether because they're so frustrated with what it has become. I know some kids who went through that whole experience, being really good and playing at that level, and then felt it was all about the coaches. Or it was all about saying you played for that elite team, and it wasn't really worth it anymore."

The pressure to meet parental expectations of success on the field are magnified when your dad or mom is your coach. To avoid any sense of favoritism, the parent-coach may be excessively hard on his or her child. Conversely, the coach might be unable to conquer an innate bias toward his or her own child and give that player more playing time or a better position on the team, which can foster resentment among the child's teammates and their parents. Either way you slice it, it's the kid who suffers. The vast majority of volunteer parent-coaches I've observed have been outstanding role models and evenhanded with all their players. But it can definitely be stressful to be the coach's child.

Soccer mom Anne Van Dine saw a girl on her daughter's Class I soccer team torn up and embarrassed by her father's unrelenting coaching style. In one game, when she was in 8th grade, the girl actually slowed down in the middle of a play to shout at her father,

Signs of Stress or Burnout in Your Child

- Complains of physical symptoms, such as headaches and stomachaches
- Starts asking to skip practice, seems uninterested in other favorite activities
- Finds it hard to keep up with schoolwork, and grades begin to fall
- Can't relax when there is downtime
- Younger child acts out; older child appears anxious or depressed

"Would you just shut up?" and then kept running. One of the referees asked him to leave during another game that year.

"Her dad was the Under 10 and Under 12 coach for our club team," says Van Dine. "All the girls ended up hating him, including his daughter, and he was asked to leave and not return as a coach. He would scream at his daughter, like, 'You're not being aggressive! You don't have enough touches on the ball! It's *yours*! It's *yours*! What are you doing? What are you thinking?' And going nuts, like a dog on a bone. Just in a frenzy.

"That was the worst parent I've seen," says Van Dine. "In fact, that girl, who is now a freshman, has dropped out of sports completely."

Sometimes kids express their feelings of burnout by switching sports when they get to high school.

A mother of two athletic teen boys in Marin County, California, told me she's seen a number of kids who've played Class I soccer up through 8th grade and been groomed to be superstars who as incoming freshmen decide to play a different sport in high school. Sometimes it's football or cross-country, whose seasons conflict with soccer. "I've seen some parents who are pretty devastated because their kids don't want to play soccer, and they're starting out with a brand-new sport," she says.

Another way kids express burnout even if they stick with their sport into high school is by complaining of injuries. High school athletic trainer Carlos Arreaga says he sees that all the time in kids who have been playing at the elite level for a long time. "It might not be something real significant, meaning a serious injury, but they complain about this pain that they have in their body and they'll continue to complain about it over and over again. I've learned over the years that there's some sort of connection here with what's going on in their sport. And ultimately the injury might not the root of the problem. It might be that they're just not having fun in their sport, they're burned out and this is one of the symptoms of it, and perhaps it's their way to get out of it. Kids will use that at times, because here in the training room, at all levels—high school, college—it's a safe haven for them to be able to express that and to have a place to go."

Pressure Drop

The pressures on kids are tremendous—to succeed, to not let their coach or their teammates down, to get their homework done and keep their grades up while playing sports, to make the cut on a higher level team, to constantly improve and excel. Sometimes a kid may want to quit a sport or drop back to a less competitive league but feels the pressure of the parents' great financial sacrifice.

When University of Maine dean of the School of Education and Social Science Robert Cobb was developing the principles and standards of Sports Done Right, his initiative to make interscholastic and youth sports a more positive, inclusive and sportsmanlike experience, he held a major summit at the university, inviting hundreds of kids from across the state to come and talk about their sports experiences. He told me that kids on elite travel teams are well aware of the thousands and thousands of dollars their parents have spent on team membership dues, tournament fees, transportation and accommodations. "The kids recognize the investment the parents are making and the sacrifice they're making on their behalf, and that becomes a not-so-subtle pressure to stay with it and specialize in it. We've had kids say they felt like they couldn't make the choice to drop away because their parents had spent so much of their money in getting them this far."

Traveling to tournaments is stressful in it itself, even though the young athletes enjoy playing the games once they're on the field. It may be a parent-child bonding experience for some, but many parents I spoke with did not confirm that.

"It's not like 'Kumbaya,' 'The Circle of Life.' There's a tenseness," says Van Dine. "It's more time in motion: making sure we can find the place, especially if the Yahoo directions are wrong; making sure they have their white jersey and their blue jersey and their gold socks and their blue socks. It's more logistics. I do know there are girls on the team who barely chat with their parents. Like when we had a tournament in Lodi [two hours away] over the Halloween weekend, we had to drive up Friday night after school, and the girls have to get up at 7 to be on the field by 8 o'clock and the game starts at 9, then they play the game, then they have maybe an hour and a half before the second game."

One mother of three told me she would drive her older daughter, an 8th grader on a Class I soccer team, to her out-of-town tournaments while her husband stayed home to go to their two younger daughters' games. But their time in the car was not warm and fuzzy. On the way, the girl would be anxious about the upcoming game and not want to talk. At the motel and on the field she'd be with her teammates. And on the way back, she would snap at her mother's comments on the match, because the mom hadn't played soccer and didn't fully understand the intricacies of the game. If the girl's team had lost and the mom made supportive remarks, like, "Well, I thought you played well, they were just a tough opponent," her daughter would lash out at her because she was feeling bad after the loss and didn't find her mother's comments perceptive or helpful. That family quit the travel team after two years and the girl went on to play basketball for her high school team.

"Kids respond to stress just like adults do, with higher levels of cortisol and adrenaline," Susan Toole, a Dayton, Ohio, area psychologist told the Dayton *Daily News* for a story about overscheduled kids' stress. "And they tend to get sick, just like adults."

Tim Anderson, a pediatrician in Burnsville, Minnesota, finds kids are coming in with headaches and stomachaches. "A lot of them suffer from stress and anxiety and they don't know why," he told the Minneapolis *Star Tribune*. "And then we look at their schedules. They have expectations that they have to be on the hockey team, the math team, the debate team.

"The physical [overuse] injuries they receive from playing too much are tragic. But most of those will heal," he said. "The bigger concern is what overscheduling is doing to their minds and families."

"What you have to do, and this is my stance in general about kids, you have to look at that kid in front of you and see how the kid is doing," advises psychotherapist Levine. "So if the kid is doing well and enjoying his sport and keeping his friends and doing well in school, fine. If the kid is having somatic symptoms—headaches and stomachaches, migraines, saying, 'I don't feel good, I have a belly ache, I can't go today'—or is teary, which is a sign of depression—'Do I have to go again?'—to me, that's my definition of overscheduling, whether that kid's involved in five activities a week or one activity a week. That kid's resources are being overwhelmed and tend to show up in symptoms. So if your kid's not symptomatic, let him run, let him enjoy it."

One major cause of stress is pure exhaustion, and a contributing factor is playing or training seven days a week at all hours of the day. Often kids don't come home from practice till late at night. And some have practice or games very early in the morning.

"I think the biggest challenge for us is sleep," says Nancy Dudley, whose son, Sean Heaslip, is on a AAA Tier I ice hockey team in the Atlantic Youth Hockey League. "My son is 12 years old and he comes home from soccer practice at 10:30. He has a light dinner before he goes to hockey practice, and he's starving again when he comes home. So he eats a second dinner and goes to bed at 10 minutes to 11. Most of his classmates are asleep at 9 o'clock."

Louie Reed, a sharp, enthusiastic 7th grader at Redwood Day School, in Oakland, is an elite club hockey player on the Under 14 team of the San Jose Junior Sharks. His team practices at the same facility where the professional Sharks practice, which is 45 miles down a crowded commute corridor from where he lives.

POSSIBLE SIGNS OF OVERLOAD
IN YOUR FAMILY*

- You have fewer than five family dinners at home together per week
- You have no downtime as a family to do unstructured, spontaneous activities together
- You're having to miss one event to attend another
- You're forgoing vacations together, visits to extended family and social events for your children's activities
- You, as a parent, have no time for hobbies or activities of your own
- Your children are often tired, cranky or hypercritical of their performance
- Your children have trouble sleeping or have lost their appetite
- Your children have no downtime

Source: William J. Doherty, professor of family social sciences and director of the Marriage and Family Therapy Program at the University of Minnesota

"I drive down there three or more times a week for practice," he says. "On Tuesdays practice is at 6 p.m., so it usually takes an hour to an hour and 15 minutes, because it's right in the middle of rush hour. And on Saturdays and Sundays it's usually at 7 a.m., or can be as late as noon."

He also plays on his school basketball team and says, "This year I'm probably going to play volleyball also. But hockey's definitely my main sport."

I asked him if he has any downtime.

"Yeah, I have some during the week, and my hockey practices on the weekends are always in the morning. Like last weekend I had a 6:15 a.m. practice, so I went down to San Jose and came back and went to my friend's birthday party that started at 2 p.m. Sometimes it interferes with stuff like that. Like, I have to leave Thursday to go to a tournament in Arizona, so I'll miss the dance. I miss some stuff, but it's not like I'm not doing anything fun; I'm doing my favorite sport. It's definitely worth it."

The travel schedules for hockey players can be especially brutal, because there are a limited number of rinks where kids can train and play, and in competitive leagues on the East Coast, players routinely zigzag across many states and up to Canada for competition. Rick Sullivan, who's been a youth hockey referee for five years in Vermont, is shocked that the state tournament is scheduled during the week in the school year.

"It's two and a half hours away from Brattleboro, up in Burlington," he says, "and it's the kind of tournament where if you win you play again, and they play on weeknights. So the Brattleboro parents have to go up, then if they win, drive back down and go to work, and the kids go to school—these are 10- and 12-year-olds—and then they have to drive back the next day. But the power is up there, so all the games are there. Why not have some down here? The answer is always 'If you don't like it, then don't participate.' But I'm amazed the parents put up with it."

Sports parents put up with a lot of disruptions to family life. Some can lead to stress, and some can lead to disconnectedness. As we're about to see, one of the biggest changes in today's families is the willingness to give up the most basic of family rituals: eating dinner together.

Rise Up and Revolt: What You Can Do Now

- **Make sure your kids have downtime.** To get it, it may mean dropping one sport or activity while keeping another. At our house, we instituted one "unplugged" night per week, during which no one could watch TV, play videogames or be on the computer. That left room for solitary pursuits like reading or doing art and interactive ones like playing board games or taking an after-dinner walk. We kept it up for a whole school year and then loosened the requirement over the summer, when there was more downtime all around. By the next school year we were living more balanced lives and it wasn't as necessary, though occasionally someone will suggest, "Hey, let's have an unplugged night!" My kids are good at self-monitoring for overload. They're very social and they love playdates, but I've seen them turn down invitations to gain some precious downtime on a weekend when they've had a scheduled activity every other day of the week. And when they ask, "What are we doing today?" and I say, "Nothing," they tend to exclaim, "Yes!"
- **Check in with your child regularly for signs of burnout.** Is your child still having fun? Is she sticking with a sport or a team to please you, or out of fear of the coach, or does she truly love what she's doing? If she wants to quit, let her quit. If she wants to try out for or switch to another sport,

let her go. And let her know that whatever she decides, you will love and support her either way, no matter how much time and money you've invested in this sport so far.

- **Stick to one sport per season.** It reduces stress on the child and the family. It eliminates a whole raft of logistical complications. It can be hard to say no to a kid who wants to do two sports she enjoys simultaneously, but sometimes one has to make choices beneficial to everyone involved. Help your child grow by helping her through a tough decision. If she finds she really misses the sport she gave up, she can go back to it next season. She's young. She has time. Let go of the fear that she'll be left behind. Missing a season won't leave her out of the running forever.

- **Challenge the number of tournaments travel teams go to.** It keeps escalating. Limit travel to what's genuinely needed and what's reasonable. If last year you went to six tournaments and this year the coach wants to do eight, say no if you think six was plenty. Consider your child's needs foremost. Does he really need to do this to stay competitive? Or is it to satisfy the coach's need or the other parents' need? Is it a reasoned proposal or one offered out of a possibly unrealistic fear that a neighboring team will surpass yours? If your players are disciplined and talented, do they really need more competition and less free time to be winners? Think of the added stress to your child's mind and body. Think of the benefits of staying home: the financial savings, the chance for your kid to connect with non-team friends and siblings, the opportunity for you to connect with your spouse and other loved ones. Parents on elite teams often get to vote on how many tournaments they go to. Don't be afraid to speak up at the meeting and say no if that's how you feel. Don't be intimidated by the coach or drowned out by the most gung-ho parents; if you are given a vote, exercise your right to use it.

- **Propose eliminating tournaments on holiday weekends.** I know this is precisely contrary to the current practice, but how many Thanksgiving dinners have to be sacrificed before the dominant sports culture acknowledges that this is a national, *family* holiday that kids should get to spend with their families? And Christmas vacation: Shouldn't kids who work hard in school all year long get to enjoy the downtime of two weeks off without leaving the morning of December 26 to travel to a tournament that ends on New Year's Eve? Or how about a three-day tournament that week instead of a five-day one? How about seeing a difference between the biggies (like Christmas and Thanksgiving) and other, less family-centered holdiays? Some have told me the holiday tournaments are designed so parents can get the time off or have the time to drive instead of fly to the tournament. But again we must ask ourselves: Are we sticking to these demanding schedules because it's what's best for our developing children or because it suits us adults somehow? Lehigh University men's soccer coach Dean Koski says, "I've spent far too much time away from my family during summers and holidays because this is when major tournaments are being held. If I want to stay ahead of the curve, or even up to the curve, I have to be at these tournaments. I've often said if all the college coaches got together and stopped going to these tournaments during the holidays, the parents would stop having them during the holidays. They would reschedule them at times that made sense."
- **Challenge the need for seasons to overlap.** The most stressful sports times in my family are the few weeks sprin-

kled throughout the year when my daughter's seasons overlap. Volleyball starts before soccer is over. Basketball starts before volleyball is over. Spring soccer starts before basketball is over. But what I've realized is that it's often not the games that overlap. The double duty is caused by the coach starting preseason practices early, by a month or more, to get ready for the season. Or he schedules the team to participate in a preseason tournament when the kids haven't practiced at all, and they get trounced! What is the value of that? It may be impossible to address the problem of a city league (like our soccer team's) season overlapping with our CYO league (like our volleyball team's). But when basketball overlaps volleyball, that's a case of two teams in the same school-sponsored league. We, as parents at the school, could voice some objection to the athletic director, the coaches or the league. Decisions about when to start are generally made by parent-coaches sitting around a table. Claim a voice at that table. Note: Coaches seem to accept it when players on club teams say they can't start working out with the school team till their club playoffs are done. How about if players on the other school teams use the same rationale?

PLAYER PROFILE

KAITLYN MOORE

Kaitlyn Moore is a poised, articulate 7th grader at Redwood Day School, in Oakland, California. She plays for an elite suburban club soccer team and is a former member of the San Francisco Ballet Company.

How did you do club soccer and ballet at the same time?

I quit ballet this year, after three years, because it was hard to get homework done and stuff. And actually to get more into soccer. And sometimes my knees would start hurting at games.

Was it a tough decision to choose to give one up?

From my other ballet class, in San Leandro [her hometown, 30 minutes east of San Francisco], I never really loved ballet because I had a really strict teacher. So I never really liked ballet when I went to San Francisco. So I was kind of relieved to quit.

What's your stress level like now?

In terms of homework, it went down a lot because I don't have ballet four times a week now on top of soccer. When I'd finish my ballet class in San Francisco, I'd take BART [the subway] to Orinda [a 45-minute ride], and so it would be hard to get homework in, because I'd have soccer or ballet every single day of the week. So I'd get home at 6 or 7, and I'd have to do all my homework, and then we'd have a late dinner and I'd have to take a shower. I'd get to bed late, and then it would be really hard for me to get up early because of all the stress.

That's a lot of effort to go to for something you didn't like that much. Does that mean your parents wanted you to do it?

Yeah. My mom. And sometimes I'd be in performances, like *The Nutcracker,* and they'd like that. Sometimes I'd have to miss soccer practices for ballet, but usually ballet would be before my soccer practices, so I would just go anyway and try to make it. Because (the coaches) are OK with it if you at least try to show up to the practice, even if there were just 30 minutes left.

How about sports—does that come from you?

I like sports. I like doing soccer. And my mom and dad really like me doing it. It's really healthy exercise.

Do you play on Bay Oaks (the local elite club team)?

I used to be on Bay Oaks, then I left and went to Lamorinda. I've been doing it out there [about 20 minutes from her school in Oakland] for three years. My mom wanted me to have a bigger challenge, I guess.

If you're going to tournaments on the weekends, how do you get to spend any time with your friends who aren't on the soccer team?

I usually try to do stuff on Fridays or on Sundays when I come back home. But I do miss a lot of things, like I missed a birthday party because I had to go to a tournament.

Do you ever get to go to sleepovers?

Yeah, but then if I have a game at 8 the next morning, and I have to be there an hour early, I have to get up at like 6 to get there by 7 to play the game at 8. We have lots of games at 8, and it's really tiring. And sometimes I'd really like to watch TV, but with practices and all, I only get to watch like one show a day. It's really tiring.

Do you ever wish that things were different so you could have more free time and summers off?

Yeah. My season just ended, but sometimes I then go into indoor soccer (during the break between club seasons). But it would be so much better if I could spend more time with my friends.

CHAPTER 7

Guess Who's Not Coming to Dinner

We have not eaten dinner together for years. My kids come home from practice at 7:30 at night. And most of the time when they come home from soccer they're not hungry, because they're all revved up. So family meals have gone by the wayside.

—TESS AMATO, mother of three star athletes who played club and varsity soccer in high school

The irony is, statistically we have more kids playing organized sports than ever before, yet we have a higher obesity rate in kids as well. I think one of the reasons kids are obese is that they're not eating good meals. They go play organized sport and then they come home and that's it; they've had their activity. They don't extend it. They're eating fast food in cars, they're not eating good meals, they're eating on the fly all the time, they're eating out in restaurants a lot because they're traveling. I think the whole lifestyle has really been skewed in such a way that we ought to pause a little bit.

—DEAN KOSKI, Lehigh University men's soccer coach

OK, so youth sports have messed with our weekends and our summer vacations. But when they say we can't have dinner together, them's fightin' words. I'm ready to draw a line in the tablecloth.

Eating together is the cornerstone of family life, the ritual that nourishes us in more ways than one. It's the time kids learn manners, learn to listen to their siblings, absorb adult vocabulary and ideas as their parents express opinions about the day's events in terms that reflect their values as members of this family and part of the community. It's when family members find out what's going on in one another's lives, hear of their triumphs and disappointments of the day and how they're feeling, what their aspirations are, their likes and dislikes. It's a time to relax and enjoy one another and eat good, healthy food, and perhaps try new tastes and explore unfamiliar cuisines from different cultures to expand the palate and add to our repertoire of favorite dishes. It's an opportunity to come together and connect, to share, to laugh. And it's too important to give up just because we're busy.

There is a mountain of statistical evidence that eating dinner together is not just a nice thing to do, it's also a predictor of kids' success in many areas—physical, academic and psychological. And, conversely, not having frequent dinners together is a predictor of negative behaviors, chief among them substance use and abuse.

Research by the National Center on Addiction and Substance Abuse (CASA) at Columbia University has found consistently in studies conducted since 1996 that the more often a child eats dinner with his or her family, the less likely that child is to smoke, drink or use illegal drugs.

Perhaps the most striking fact the studies reveal is the difference a few days make: Children who eat family dinners five times a week are more likely to be emotionally well-adjusted and do well academically and socially, while children who eat dinner together with the family two times a week or less are more prone to getting in trouble at school, being depressed and getting involved with illegal drugs.

A 2000 CASA teen study found that children who never eat dinner with their families are 61 percent more likely than the average teen to smoke, drink or use illegal drugs, while children who eat family dinners seven nights a week are 20 percent less likely to engage in these activities.

CASA's 2003 teen study showed that kids who eat dinner with their families often are less stressed and less often bored, which is significant, because teens who are frequently bored and have a high level of stress are at three times the risk of smoking, drinking, getting drunk and using illegal drugs.

A 1997 study by psychologists Blake S. Bowden and Jennifer Zeisz of De Paul University in Chicago found that teens who ate dinner with the family were more well-adjusted emotionally, and that adjustment was correlated more to shared meals than any other factor, including gender, age or family type. The researchers found that mealtimes served as a "marker" for other positive family attributes and helped teens cope with the stresses of adolescence.

Maintaining the family dinner hour is tough for parents who seem to have no control over coaches and leagues that schedule practices or games at dinnertime. Jim Thompson, founder of the Positive Coaching Alliance, told me about a woman "who signed her kid up for Pop Warner football and found out that they had five practices a week during the summer, scheduled at 5:30. 'If every practice is at 5:30, then when do we get dinner?' she asked. 'We don't get dinner together for an entire summer!' And the guy who ran the league said, 'Hmm. Sounds like a new parent.' "

Some parents reschedule the dinner hour rather than give it up completely. If a kid's practice is early, they eat early before practice. If the kid gets home late, the family eats late. Families with kids on elite travel teams face even more daunting challenges. They not only have busy weeknights, but are also traveling to tournaments on the weekends. The kid and maybe one parent end up eating many meals in fast-food or chain restaurants rather than having home-cooked food around the dinner table with their whole family. "I can't tell you how many meals we've eaten at Applebee's," one traveling soccer mom told me. And the food they order at places like that are higher in fat and sugar content than what they would likely prepare at home.

Kids who frequently eat dinner at home tend to have healthier diets overall. A nationwide study of 9- to 14-year-olds reported in the

Archives of Family Medicine in March 2000 found that boys and girls who ate dinner with their family "every day" or "almost every day" were more likely to eat more servings of fruits and vegetables, less fried food and soda, have higher intake of some nutrients (calcium, fiber, folate, iron, vitamins C, E, B6 and B12) and have a lower intake of saturated fat than kids who "never" or "only sometimes" ate with their families.

And a University of Minnesota study published in the *Journal of the American Dietetic Association* found that children who ate family meals ate more fruits and vegetables and fewer snack foods than children who ate separately from their families.

First Generation in History to Give Up the Family Meal

Alice Waters has been one of the most influential figures in American cuisine over the past 35 years. As owner of Chez Panisse, which is consistently listed as one of the nation's best restaurants, and through other ventures, Waters has championed the value of organic, locally grown and produced food, eaten seasonally. In a 2005 speech she gave to the USDA Nutrition Connections Conference in Arlington, Virginia, Waters laid out her concerns about our society's trend toward abandoning eating together as a family.

"Time was," she began, "just about everyone on earth had to spend the better part of their lives hunting and gathering and growing food; and just about everyone had to spend a good part of every day cooking and sharing food with some kind of extended family. Food is no longer integrated into everyday experience, as part of our culture. Sure, there are a few times when we celebrate, like Christmas and Thanksgiving, but the celebration of food prepared and shared with family is not a daily ritual any more. The shared enjoyment of the sensual pleasure of eating is just not an everyday part of life for us.

Here we tend to think of food more and more as our own private fuel, and less as an occasion for getting together. For most of us, eating dinner is not primarily about the pleasure of the table, but in fact people's desire for pleasure can actually be the biggest motivator for healthy eating.

"Only in today's world—a world that's increasingly noisy, fast, and out-of-control—only in today's hectic world could the preservation of simple pleasure become an urgent issue. And it is an urgent issue, because so many of us no longer have that moment in the day to sit down and communicate around the dinner table. In fact, we may be raising the first generation in history that doesn't have to take part in the family meal. This deprives our children of what I believe is the most important educational experience of all. The dinner table. The place where we learn by experience the art of sharing. The place where we learn consideration, generosity, and patience. The place where we learn to control our natural greed. The place where we learn to cultivate our gift for empathy.

"I learned these values almost unconsciously at my family table as a child. But many children grow up today without any kind of family meal. Some studies say that as many as 85 percent of all children don't sit down and eat with their families at dinnertime.

"Instead of family meals, the meals of children are likely to be cooked by strangers and to consist of highly processed foods that are produced far away. And while they are eating, they are absorbing messages—fast-food messages—that come with this food. These are a set of values that are indoctrinating our children, telling them that speed is a virtue above all others; that food is cheap and abundant; that abundance is permanent; that resources are infinite; and that it's OK to waste."

Concerned about the children in her own community, Waters started a program in 1996 at Martin Luther King Jr. Middle School in Berkeley, through her Chez Panisse Foundation, so kids could regain their connection to the food they eat and learn the joys of cooking and eating together. Called The Edible Schoolyard, it is part of

FIVE NIGHTS ARE BETTER THAN TWO*

- Compared to teens that have family dinners twice a week or less, teens who have dinner with their families five or more nights in a week are:

  32 percent more likely never to have tried cigarettes (86 percent vs. 65 percent).

  45 percent more likely never to have tried alcohol (68 percent vs. 47 percent).

  24 percent more likely never to have smoked pot (88 percent vs. 71 percent).

- Teens who have family dinners twice a week or less are three times more likely than teens who have dinner with their families five or more times a week to say all of their friends use marijuana (9 percent vs. 3 percent).

- Teens who have dinner with their families five or more times a week are almost twice as likely to receive A's in school compared to teens who have dinner with their families two or fewer times a week (20 percent versus 12 percent). Teens who receive A's and B's are at half the risk of substance abuse as those who receive grades of C or lower.

*Source: National Center on Addiction and Substance Abuse (CASA) at Columbia University 2003 survey of 12- to 17-year-olds

the regular curriculum of the 900-student public school, not an elective for some, but a course for everyone. The program has two components: the garden and the kitchen. Students rotate through each in 10-week blocks, meeting once a week for an hour and a half. For example, in the garden, which is just over an acre, they'll dig and plant, water, prune and weed, and harvest the vegetables, grains, flowers and seeds. In the kitchen, a class of about 30 kids, divided into groups of 10 at three work tables, learns preparation and cooking techniques, follows recipes and, in the last half hour of each hour-and-a-half lesson, lay down a tablecloth, set the table, decorate it with flowers and share a meal together and then clean up.

While this is an unusual curriculum for a public school, what's truly remarkable is how rare an experience it is for these kids to share a home-cooked meal around the dinner table. King is a good microcosm of American society because it's big and it's very diverse economically, racially and culturally. There are 20 different languages spoken within the student body.

"We see between 60 and 90 middle school children every day in our classes," says Edible Schoolyard administrator Chelsea Chapman, "and it's consistent across the board: When you ask kids who they had dinner with the night before, they say, 'Oh, the PlayStation' or 'The Xbox 360.' It's very rarely with a family member. And we see that among the more well-off kids, the low-income kids; it's really consistent. The one population that we don't get that response from is our ELL (English Language Learners) students, who are more recent immigrants to the U.S. and continue to have the tradition of the family eating together."

A Place to Talk

The kids at King not only find out how to grow food and cook it, they're also taught how to conduct themselves at the table. Learning to wait until everyone else is served is a novelty for a lot of the kids in the class, says Chapman, as is the art of conversation. One adult is stationed at each table to facilitate a real group discussion, making sure it doesn't dissolve into a bunch of little side chats. At each table there's a set of 50 cards with open-ended questions to be used as conversation starters if the need arises. Sample questions include: "If you could change one law in our country, what law might you change?" "What would you like grown-ups to know about what it's like to be a kid?" "What's one thing you're really proud of about yourself?" "What's one thing you really like about your mom?" But often lively discussions take off without ever having to resort to resort to the cards.

"The dinner table is where you have the civic conversations," says Chapman. "It certainly was when I was growing up. That's one of the places you talk about all the big-picture stuff, not to mention having that daily check-in with your family members.'

Esther Cook, who has been the teacher chef at The Edible Schoolyard for nine years, agrees. She came from a big family, where "dinner was easily an hour every night with lots of conversation with five kids and two parents. And that experience, that feeling and those memories are something I think about at least once a day, every day. It stays with you. It's huge. And if parents are giving up their time with their kids, then kids are getting their information and their ideas and feedback and everything else from their peers, and they're losing a lot. It's frightening that they're not getting input from adults."

Dinner was the glue that held my family together when I was growing up. We were no paragon of *Leave It to Beaver* perfection, but despite our problems and sports commitments, we came together almost every night for a balanced meal, and lingered in conversation long after we'd taken the last bite. We'd talk about what was going on with us and what was going on in the world. My parents discussed movies and plays, current events and politics with us, and they clarified what terms meant when my older sister, Brigid, or I asked for clarification. We always scored high on vocabulary tests, and I totally credit the family dinner hour for that. In fact, a Harvard study found that eating dinner together as a family aids linguistic development in children, because they're hearing words at the table they don't hear anywhere else.

We might miss a few nights for sports, but eating together was a mainstay. Some nights I'd be at the ice rink, but many more I'd be at home, helping prepare the dinner and then eating with the family. On the mornings I skated for two hours before school, my father would get up with me and we'd share a full breakfast before he dropped me off at the rink and before my mother and Brigid were even up. I remember for a number of years Brigid had a horse show in Santa Barbara (two hours north) over the long Thanksgiving weekend, so my parents created the entire feast on Wednesday night rather than have us miss it.

One of those years, they took her to the horse show and got me all excited about getting to go to a fancy hotel dining room with my grandmother on Thanksgiving. It was fancy, all right, and I remember getting all dressed up in a yellow mohair dress, but it didn't feel like Thanksgiving. I missed the smell of the roasting turkey that would fill the house for hours, setting the table with the special lace tablecloth, the good silver and special china, and being at home with the whole family.

I inherited my family's dining room set, and most nights I share dinner with my husband and kids eating at that same table where all those conversations took place. I tell my kids, "Don't rock on your chair, the legs could break," just like my parents told me. We light candles and put on music and set the atmosphere for pleasure and relaxation. Some nights we may eat at the kitchen counter, but wherever we put our plates, we approach that time as a communal celebration.

I majored in French in college, and through a student exchange program I got to spend a summer living with a French family named the Putods in a tiny village in the Jura region, in the foothills of the French Alps. There I learned to love two-hour meals with free-flowing wine and conversation. My husband spent part of his childhood in Rome, so he, too, knows the joys of family feasting and the central role that family meals have in European culture. After all, everything shuts down for two hours in the middle of the day so everyone can go home and eat together. We go back as a family to visit the Putods every few years and have traveled with our kids in Italy, too, so they are well versed in the European approach to food and dining. We try to recapture the feeling in our own home, especially when we invite friends and family over to share long lunches outside under the apple tree, with Edith Piaf or Charles Trenet cranked up on the CD player.

"I was lucky enough to go to the Slow Food conference in Italy a couple of years ago," says Esther Cook, "and it was so great hitting the streets at midday and watching the kids going home to eat, and those kids were snacking on loaves of fresh bread and fruit, on their own, from school to home. They were not having sodas and chips. Family is such a huge influence on their lives, and I really feel like our kids are on their own."

Cook says she knows how much kids love and crave the experience her students get in The Edible Schoolyard program. "When I ask the kids, 'What is something you do here at King that you don't do at home but you wish you did at home?' they always say, 'Cook together and eat together.'

"But a lot of kids don't have that kind of control in their family, and they can't get their family to eat together. Or somebody is making a meal and everybody is taking their plate into their own room and eating in front of their own TV or their own computer. It's so alarming to hear how many kids are eating alone, even though other family members are home."

Some studies show that half of the families that do eat dinner together always have the TV on in the background, and a third usually eat in front of the TV. Somewhere along the line, those people lost the connection between dining and communication, which is such a key factor in raising children. The kids who learn to communicate with their parents at the table when they're young will tend to continue to communicate with them as adolescents, even as developmentally they begin to separate from their parents. The TV was never on during meals in the home I grew up in, nor is it allowed in my home now, except on rare occasions like the World Series or the Academy Awards. But in general, we all see the dinner hour as a time for eating *and* talking.

Jamie Woolf is a consultant who specializes in leadership coaching and organizational development and is writing a book about how leadership skills can be used in parenting. "There's a chapter in my book called 'Fostering Emotional Connection,' " she tells me. "And it's all about the choices that we make: If they're not about fortifying the emotional connection, we've lost everything. That's the Achilles heel of great leaders who end up losing credibility, and of parents. Being a parent is all about emotional connection. And if you're not eating dinner together, how can you expect to even know what's going on in each other's lives? There has to be a time put aside that shows not only that this is a priority but that also gives the time that it takes to build relationships. That doesn't come automatically, even in a family."

Blaming the Calendar

After a steady decline in family dinners for decades, a 2006 CASA nationwide random survey actually found an increase in the number of kids 12 to 17 who eat with their families five nights a week, to 58 percent, up from 47 percent in 2005. A research project conducted through Harvard's Kennedy School of Government found the low point for families eating dinner together was 2003. So, as Lisa W. Foderaro reported in the *New York Times*, "the trend may have bottomed out or even begun to turn around." Maybe there's hope, although many sports families continue to find making time for the ritual especially challenging. I ask Cook what she'd say to parents who say they can't eat together because of their kids' demanding sports schedules and practices during the dinner hour.

"I would say if you can't eat together at least three nights a week, you need to make some changes. The family has to make that commitment. And three nights is *really* low-balling it. I wouldn't give them a choice," she emphasizes. "I'd say, 'Look, you're a parent. What more important task do you have than nurturing your child?' And eating dinner together is a way to hit all of those bases: to make sure that they're having healthy food, to listen to them and have conversations."

I ask Chelsea Chapman the same question.

"I could say if you're working with your kids and you're all cooking together, you can put a meal together in no time and it can be simple and healthy and fresh. And I could give you quick and simple recipes. But I think there's something going on culturally, in addition to the time crunch that parents are feeling. It's that a lot of the time parents are not so comfortable talking with kids and having that kind of interaction around the table. So that even if you took away the hectic schedule, that underlying factor would still affect the way people are eating. Even if people didn't have sports practice, a lot of families would end up eating in this fragmented way, where the kids are microwaving something and eating it in front of the TV and the mom and dad are eating something else together.

"I think TV often ends up being a parent. If TV's the entity that kids are having dinner with, then that's where they're getting all those big messages they should be getting at the dinner table. I think we put a lot of it on the time crunch, but in fact parents feel really distant from kids. But it's such a valuable experience, it's such a strong community-living thing to do, it needs to be built back in.

"Part of why I think the time-crunch thing is not the root cause—it's part of it but it's not really *it*—is because for a lot of our lower-income students they do have parents who are at home all day, who may not be working for whatever reason or have young kids they're home taking care of, but they're still not eating together. It has a lot to do with the fact that it's so much easier to give the kids two bucks and send them to the fast-food restaurant around the corner.

"I would just say talk to kids, encourage conversation and make eating together a pleasure, and not this angst-ridden experience where you're having uncomfortable interactions with kids. Put out really interesting questions and find out more about what the kids are up to and really focus on the pleasure aspect of it more than anything else."

Magic Can Happen

Parenting author and educator Mike Riera sees how the consistent ritual of the family meal can provide a setting for spontaneity. "If you're eating dinner together every day, a lot of great things happen by accident, just by the intention of this time being carved out: I don't know what we're going to do, but we're going to have fun. And if kids know that, that's when jokes are pulled, that's when pranks happen, that's when you get into laughing fits, that's when a child unloads something that happened at school that's heavy that you had no idea about. But parents and kids shouldn't ever feel the need to be efficient in their communication with one another. It's pretty inefficient. It just sort of comes up as it comes up. If you can perfect the art of hanging out, you hear all sorts of things. And when families are disrupted so there's no regular time to get together, as that gets taken away, I think families slowly start to drift. They need that ritual.

WHY ARE FAMILY MEALTIMES IMPORTANT?*

- Children who do not eat dinner with their families are 61 percent more likely to use alcohol, tobacco or illegal drugs. By contrast, children who eat dinner with their families every night of the week are 20 percent less likely to drink, smoke or use illegal drugs.
- Teens who eat frequent family dinners are less likely than other teens to have sex at young ages, get into fights or be suspended from school, and they are at lower risk for thoughts of suicide.
- If you eat with your children, it is more likely that they will eat healthier foods and more balanced meals.
- Dining together is a chance for parents and children to talk with one another.
- Parental influence and involvement is an important tool in preventing substance abuse. Regularly sitting down for a meal with your children is one way to connect with them and be involved with what is happening in their lives.

*Sources: National Center on Addiction and Substance Abuse (CASA) at Columbia University and American Dietetic Association

"Not every dinner is a great one," he adds. "Not every conversation is scintillating. But when you sit across from each other at the table you look at each other, and I say, 'How are you doing?' And you say, 'Fine.' I get to say, 'You're saying fine, but that's not how you seem to be feeling.' When families create that time just to be with one another, magic can happen. It doesn't always happen. Sometimes it's just a boring meal. But other times, great things happen, and an awkward moment leads to something great happening. And if in that awkward moment, you look at each other and say, 'Dinner's not worth it, let's not do this anymore,' then the magic will never happen."

What puzzles me is that so many sports parents are willing to give up this fundamental part of family life for years at a time.

"Maybe it's parents not believing in themselves enough to insist that time with us as a family is worthwhile, so I'll hand it over to the coach," suggests Riera. "That would be sad."

Esther Cook points out that ever since the 1950s, Americans have gotten the message that cooking is work. Innovations in food products and technology, from TV dinners to instant mashed potatoes to microwave ovens, were all marketed as relieving the homemaker from the time-consuming "drudgery" of cooking. "There was this whole characterization of cooking as taking up our valuable time," she says. "When of course in my view, cooking and eating together create the most memorable kind of time.

"Another factor is that in most cases both parents are working. People are arriving home at 6 o'clock. The last thing they want to do is make a full dinner. The kids have been home. They've already been snacking away on God knows what. It's considered an extra chore. When it would be so easy to pick something up on the way home and everybody can just help themselves. And the schedules are crazy, so the family is not home together every night. It's really piecemeal. And if it's not something that you've done, you don't really miss it. It's really about people's relationship to food, because they're not physically involved in producing it or in cooking it, so it's very detached."

In her book about high-achieving yet troubled affluent teens, *The Price of Privilege*, psychotherapist Madeline Levine underscores how good eating dinner together is for kids. "There are certain aspects of family life that pack a lot of 'bang for the buck' for busy families," she writes. "For example, parents need to remember that kids love rituals and depend on them for a sense of continuity and connection. Perhaps the single most important ritual a family observes is having dinner together."

Levine says in her introduction, "We need to examine our parenting paradigm. Raising children has come to look more and more like a business endeavor and less and less like an endeavor of the heart. We are overly concerned with 'the bottom line,' with how our children 'do' rather than with who our children 'are.' We pour time, attention, and money into ensuring their performance, consistently making it to their soccer game while inconsistently making it to the dinner table."

When I spoke with Dr. Levine, she stressed the significance of the documented evidence that the family meal is beneficial for children. "That happens to be one small fact that we actually know something about. It's not like, clinically, I *think* that it's a better idea. People have been looking at this for a long time. It's one of the things I really push and insist on as a therapist. And no matter what went on with my three kids, we ate dinner together 90 percent of the time.

"I think the dinner experience is sort of a metaphor for family life," she adds. "It's a metaphor for the family itself: Do you take time out to listen to each other? Do you find time for a communal activity? Do you put aside your own needs for the good of the family? I think that's why that keeps popping up as such an important factor, because it probably reflects a whole bunch of other things that go on in the family, like priorities. It's like ritual in religion. I think there's something absolutely critical about having a time set aside that says this is a really important part of your life. And it is more important than a half hour of studying, it is more important than your teams, it's more important than anything that we're a family and we take time on a regular basis to listen to each other. And it's not like brilliant things happen every time, but sometimes brilliant things happen over dinner and you really learn a lot. Sometimes it's just the ritual of spending time together that's salutary and helpful to kids."

I ask her what she says to parents who say they couldn't possibly have regular family dinners because of their work schedules and the kids' sports schedules.

"I always say: 'I'm a writer and a psychologist, my husband's a surgeon, I have three kids, they all were on traveling teams, and we eat dinner together.' And I'll hand them the research. And I'm pretty pushy about saying, 'You're paying me a lot of money to help you with your family, and here's something we know. Here's something that's documented. You want your kids doing better in school? Here's something that helps. You want your kid being more social? Here's something that helps. And if you can't find the time to do it, you really have to do a gut check on what you're doing.' It's like the doctor who says you have to quit smoking because it causes cancer. If you're not doing what he says, you have to check that out and find out why."

"If you want to look at anything that's a predictor of children's well-being, it's family meals," says William J. Doherty, director of the Marriage and Family Therapy Program in the Department of Family Social Science at the University of Minnesota, Twin Cities, co-author with Barbara Z. Carlson of *Putting Family First* and founder of the organization of the same name. "That's far more powerful than sports. So if you want to think about raising good healthy children, it has to start with family, it has to start with kids who have time to hang out. And then we build in other things. If we promote one aspect of a

Oprah Wants You . . . to Eat Together*

In 1993, mega-popular TV talk show host Oprah Winfrey challenged five volunteer families to eat dinner together every night for a month, staying at the table for a half hour each time. As part of the experiment, all family members kept journals to record their feelings about the experience. At first, sharing meals was a chore for many families and the minutes at the table dragged on. But by the end of the month, the families were happy and planned to continue dining together most evenings, if not every night. When the families appeared on *The Oprah Winfrey Show* at the end of the experiment, the greatest surprise to the parents was how much their children treasured the dependable time with their parents at the table.

*Source: Nutritionist Martha Mariano and Nutrition Professor Sue Butkus, on the Washington State University Nutrition Education Network's Web site.

child's life out of proportion to other aspects, and we deny them the core ingredients in a healthy childhood, we have not helped them."

The most convincing research about the positive effects of eating dinner together relates to future drug and alcohol use and abuse. But many parents think they've got that risk covered simply by having their child involved in sports. The athletes and therapists I talked to, however, assure me that's no guarantee.

One high school boy I know who went to a small K-8 parochial school and had never been exposed to illegal drugs got his first offer to smoke pot the day he stepped on the field to begin training with the freshman football team. And some suggest that high-achieving athletes who work hard all week training for the game, striving for excellence, feel they deserve to party hearty on the weekends, because they've earned it. They're essentially mirroring what they see adults do when they work hard at their jobs, then go to a bar on Friday night or have a cocktail when they come home from a stressful day.

Amanda Garcia played elite club soccer and ODP and went on to play for four years at Mills College, in Oakland, a Division III school, where she's finishing her undergraduate degree. She's also assistant coach of the women's varsity soccer team at Head-Royce, an Oakland prep school. Since she has the perspective of both athlete and coach, I ask her about parents' belief that having kids in sports will keep them out of trouble.

"It's a total myth. My brother played baseball at Sacred Heart, and man, those Irish high school boys, they drink. To them it's like holy water. Yes, it has been proven that kids who are involved in sports or really any kind of extracurricular activity, be it theater or band or whatever, are going to be less likely to have time to do that kind of stuff. But you find time, you know what I mean? Until they physically have a hangover and have to go to a game the next day, and they can't play because they feel so sick, that's when they're going to learn that they don't want to be doing this."

FORCES FOR AND AGAINST THE FAMILY DINNER

MICHAEL POLLAN

Michael Pollan is Knight Professor of Journalism at the University of California at Berkeley and the author of the *New York Times* bestsellers *The Botany of Desire: A Plant's-Eye View of the World* and *The Omnivore's Dilemma: A Natural History of Four Meals,* in which he looks at the way Americans eat and why.

How have we gotten to this point where sports comes before eating together?

There are other pressures on the family dinner besides sports. It may well be that the weakening of family dinner has made it less of an issue for people when coaches schedule practices at those times. My son has a 6 o'clock practice—6 to 8 on Thursdays for Little League. If the family dinner were sacrosanct in the culture, as it was when I was a kid, maybe that would affect the way sports gets scheduled and the willingness of people to tolerate that schedule. So whether it's cause or effect, I'm not entirely clear.

But there have been many things working on the family dinner to weaken it. Food marketing is an important one, and the availability of snack food to make it less necessary. Now you can have your PowerBar at practice. It's easier to skip dinner when there's so much convenience food around. And that's the goal of convenience food: to get people away from the dinner table and create eating opportunities 24/7, rather than letting Mom control that time and space at the dinner table.

People eat more if you can market to them individually.

That's a big part of the cause. Certainly people's schedules are a part of the reason. People cite the fact that women work as another reason that there's no time to prepare dinner, although I'm not sure I completely buy that. I just don't find it takes three hours to prepare dinner. You can get a perfectly good dinner on the table in less than a half hour.

It's a complex of things that are involved, but the phenomenon is absolutely true. People are finding other things to do instead of have dinner, or the dinner has been disaggregated, so a couple of members of the family will eat together and then a couple of members will eat later—whatever's left in the pan, or they'll microwave something.

But the fact is that you have the microwave oven, and you have the PowerBar and all the other specifically sports-related products like GU, which is a pure carbohydrate fuel that comes in a little tube and you squeeze it into your mouth when you're exercising. It's food reduced to its absolute most basic function, which is to keep you going, and designed to give you a bunch of calories fast. (It's really designed for bikers and marathoners; you carry it with you.) So all that makes it easier. If you missed dinner, what were you going to do, in the old days? Well, you then had to cook something late at night. Or you had to reheat something in a pan or a pot. But now there's always something in the freezer that you can pop in the microwave. Or you can have all that food designed to be eaten in the car on the way to practice or on the way home from practice.

What changed in the past 20 years to make the food industry accelerate its marketing of individual, prepackaged foods?

I'm not sure of the answer, but my theory is that is has to do with the explosion of cable television channels. It used to be that you couldn't reach individual members of the family as efficiently. Maybe you could reach kids on Saturday morning, but generally there was one TV in the house, maybe two, and you didn't have 24 hours a day of access to children, or males or females or teenagers. So that allows you to take the family apart and market to each one individually in a way that was much harder to do before. So I think that's had something to do with it.

As a culture, can we get back to the dinner table?

I think we can. I think there's so much concern about the obesity epidemic and there's so much concern about diabetes, and there's an increasing understanding that cooking and eating together and rebuilding a culture of food is part of the solution. Like Alice Waters's approach with The Edible Schoolyard.

So there is now a countervailing pressure. There was an article in the *New York Times* recently about how people are starting to have family dinners again. I read that article as kind of funny that now it's news to have family dinners. Can you imagine that being *news* 20 years ago? But there's a consciousness about it in the culture, about its value and importance. And that's the beginning of a change. It's up against a lot. It's up against these schedules that kids have. There's also a sense that kids are overscheduled, and there's a move to simplify kids' lives. There's a move against the massive amounts of homework. I see people choosing to put their kids in schools where it's much less pressured in that way. So I think there may well be a pendulum swing.

So being on a team may not be a guarantee that your kids will keep to the straight and narrow. But we do have research showing that that kids who have been eating with their families, keeping those lines of communication open, feeling loved and listened to, as opposed to isolated and alienated, and having heard their families' values expressed and reinforced nightly will be in better shape to resist temptation and stand up to peer pressure when it comes their way. We can't totally count on sports to keep our kids out of trouble, but we can count on ourselves to nurture their souls and bodies around a communal table. Eating together as a family is too important to just let slip away. It's worth it to find the time, to make the time. It's part of our job as parents.

Rise Up and Revolt: What You Can Do Now

- **Eat dinner together regularly.** Figure out how. With little kids, aim for seven days a week. As sports commitments increase in middle school, see if you can do three to five or more. When teens get busy, try not to dip below three. Remember those dramatic statistics about substance use and abuse increasing as family dinners decrease. Keep in mind that nothing is more important than staying connected to your kids.

- **Eat and talk at the same time.** Good nutrition presented in a convivial atmosphere will guard against obesity, eating disorders and depression. Not to mention the ravages of fast food and junk food. And it will instill a lifelong habit of good eating and conversation. Teach your kids that food is a sensuous pleasure, not just fuel to help you race to the next high-pressured activity.

CHAPTER 8

Are Parents Driving the Craziness?

I had a kindergarten parent say to me, "Are you teaching my son to switch hit?" And I said, "What are you talking about?" And he said, "Well, I want to prepare him for the pros."

—BILL SZYDLO, former head of Northfield Youth Baseball Association, in Northfield, Minnesota

I started playing recreational soccer, and that's where the moms were intense. It's like, "Johnny didn't get enough game time." It was heavy.

—SHAUN WHITE, explaining to the *New York Times*, after he won a gold medal at the Turin Olympics in 2006, why he left organized youth sports to be a snowboarder and skateboarder

Whatever's troubling youth sports, it's not the kids' fault. And it's often not the coaches' fault. Let's see, that leaves . . . uh-oh. That's right: us, the parents. But it's not us loving, well-meaning, self-sacrificing individuals who have our children's best interests at heart who are messing things up. It's those generally positive, sometimes menacing gremlins inside us: parental expectations. When they go haywire, watch out. Because of our expectations, we may push our kids to play sports, to join an elite team, to stay in a sport long after the child has stopped having fun because we're living through the child. Perhaps a parent didn't succeed at sports as a youth and wants a vicarious taste of the glory now. Or maybe the parent was a sports star and wants the child to know what that feels like. Perhaps some parents can't accept that their children are of average ability or are not interested in the sport that the parent had a passion for, or that they're not interested in sports in general. Or maybe the goal is a spot on the high school team or the college team, or even a college scholarship, and so parents start pushing kids from age 5, afraid they'll never meet that goal unless they start high-level training as early as possible.

Regardless of the individual backstory, parental expectations inform everything from decisions about time commitment to sideline behavior. We've all seen parents at our kids' games who shout instructions at their kids during the action of the game, who berate their kids after mistakes, who get overheated by what they see as unfair calls. We have seen or heard of parents who get angry after losses and even violent, hitting other parents in the stands or coaches and referees on the field. There's been a dramatic increase in incidents of violence at sporting events in the past few years. In a 2005 *SportingKid* magazine survey of 3,300 parents, kids and coaches, 84 percent of the kids polled said they had witnessed violent parental behavior toward children, coaches or officials, in the form of shouting, berating or using abuse language. A *Sports Illustrated for Kids* survey found that 74 percent of the kids who responded had observed out-of-control parents at their games. Nationwide, documented incidents of violence among parents involved in youth sports quadrupled between 2000 and 2005.

In August 2005, a parent at a Little League tournament game for 8-year-olds in Carteret, New Jersey, ran onto the field and assaulted a teenage umpire. Police charged the parent with aggravated assault. "I've been doing this a long time and I've never, ever seen anything like this in my life," Greg Nigro, a coach and member of the Carteret Little League executive board, told the *Home News Tribune*. "I've read about it. It happens a lot. And hopefully I'll never see anything like it again. It was the most outrageous and horrendous thing that I've ever dealt with. That's how sickening it was."

Attacks on sports officials and coaches have become so common-place that 21 states have adopted laws to protect them. An Illinois law went into effect January 1, 2005, that gave sports officials the same status as police officers, jail guards and other public employees in cases of assault and battery. The California Penal Code specifies that battery against a sports official carries a maximum punishment of a $2,000 fine and a one-year jail sentence.

Barry Mano, president of the National Association of Sports Of-ficials, told *The Detroit News* in January 2006, "The biggest problem isn't really the coaches or the players, it's really the fans/parents. Over the past five years, there's been almost a sea change in incidents of physical assaults against sports officials."

John Murphy, president of the California Youth Soccer Associa-tion, the largest of the 55 state soccer associations in the country, feels constant pressure from parents he considers overly concerned with what he calls "lowercase winning, meaning winning in athletic competition." He believes his organization, with which 130 leagues comprising almost 222,000 players are affiliated, is about uppercase Winning—by developing the whole child to win in life. CYSA in-cludes elite club teams and the Olympic Development Program, but, says Murphy, "the vast majority—90 plus percent of our players are rec. In fact, if you put that together with our Division III players, it's almost 94 percent of CYSA." Still, he says, parents lobby him to bend league rules governing such things as geographical boundary lines and restrictions on recruiting during a seasonal year. They call to complain about referee calls. And they pressure him to hire personal trainers for the leagues. The common theme to the appeals is parental concern that their child maintain a competitive edge.

Joe Boardwine, assistant director of the National High School Coaches Association, says pushy parent behavior is contributing to a high turnover in coaches at the high school level. "The coaching tenure of high school coaches is getting shorter and shorter," he told

The Detroit News. "There are a lot of reasons for that, but one . . . is meddling parents wanting to control the program."

Murphy recalls, "The only time in my career in soccer management that I was physically confronted and actually threatened was when CYSA's board adopted the position that we wouldn't sanction competitive tournaments for Under 10s. I was walking to my car in the parking lot and I was confronted by a mob of screaming, rabid parents of 6- and 7-year-olds screaming about how I was depriving their children of opportunity. And that's really sick.

"Three years ago, an irate woman phoned me up and wanted me to kill this referee," Murphy recalls. "The referee found out that her daughter was still recovering from surgery and wouldn't let her play. I told her I'm a referee, too, and that's a referee's call. A referee does not have to let an injured player play. And a referee doesn't have to accept the liability exposure of taking that kind of risk, no matter how you feel about it. And she made a statement that almost made me fall out of my chair. She said, 'Well, my daughter's 17 and she has to be seen in this game if she's going to have any chance because she's had five ACL surgeries.' And I said, 'You're going to, if you haven't already, cripple your daughter for the rest of her life.' And she started screaming at me and hung up."

Orthopedists and sports medicine doctors say it's always the parent who balks when a child is ordered to take time off to heal. "When I tell the child he can't play for six weeks," one orthopedist said, "the first thing I hear from the parent is, 'How about four?' "

What astounds me is how parents, who from the moment their baby pops out are concerned first and foremost with maintaining that child's physical well-being, can throw that concern out the window once they enter the arena of sports. Are the glitter of the trophy and the scholarship money obscuring to this most fundamental parental obligation?

"I think parents think that the medical profession can now come in and do arthroscopic surgery and fix it right up, so therefore it's not a problem," Murphy suggests. "But every injury takes its toll."

He stresses that 90 percent of parents are "what I would call normal people, where soccer is not the be-all and end-all, and their kid is no good unless their kid's on an elite team. They're people for whom soccer is just one good thing in their kid's life." But he says it's that other 10 percent, whom he calls over the top, who dominate the teams, run for league positions and go to the meetings and drown out more tempered voices. "We're still talking about a very tiny group, but a lot of these people are like religious fanatics," he says. "You can't talk to them. If you try to reason with them they scream at you. For them, it's literally win at all costs—financial, physical. It's just really sad."

Jim Thompson was so fed up with the win-at-all-costs philosophy in youth sports that he founded the Positive Coaching Alliance (PCA), which works with leagues across the country to combat it. PCA promotes the idea of the Double-Goal Coach, a concept he spelled out in his book of the same name, whereby the coach not only wants to win but also has a second, more important goal: to use sports to teach life lessons and develop players' positive character traits so they can be successful in life. The PCA urges players' moms and dads to be Second-Goal Parents in the same way.

Thompson empathizes with parents who let themselves get out of control in the heat of competition, but in his workshops explains how a change in "the mental model" can lead to a change in behavior.

"I can be sitting in this room saying isn't it crazy how these other parents behave, then the next thing you know I'm at a game and my son just scored a goal and the official was out of position and he calls an offsides and takes the goal away from my son, and all of a sudden I'm going crazy. Having that goal taken away from my son is the worst thing in the world.

"If you're what we call a Second-Goal Parent, the parent should be focusing on what kids learn from sports, not helping them win, unless they're the coach. Then you're looking at that situation as a teachable moment: 'That was unfair. That goal got taken away from you. I know it was a wrong call. Is that ever going to happen to you in life?'

"That's not the kind of conversation you want to have. You want to scream at that official who made the bad call, who's maybe a 16-year-old kid making $5 a game. But it's so much more satisfying to scream at that official and rant and rave about how unfair it was rather than interact with your kid about the lesson to be taken away from that. One of the great things about sports is that sometimes bad things, unfair things happen to you, and that also happens to you in life. And the real key to being a winner in life is how you respond to those unfair moments."

Don't Embarrass Your Child

Trudy Hiraoka, a soccer mom and certified soccer referee, has seen sports parent behavior from all sides. Her daughter, Emily Pankey, plays on an elite club team as well as on her high school team, and Hiraoka refs matches at all levels, from Under 10s to Under 19s, in recreational, Class III and Class I leagues in the Bay Area. "Parents actually feel that they have a right to lose it and become rude and disrespectful and somebody they don't even recognize because, they say, 'I get so emotional and wrapped up in the game.' "

She recalls an incident where a parent was standing directly behind the net and giving constant instructions to the goalie, who was her daughter, which is not allowed. "So I asked her if she wouldn't mind moving from behind the goal. The woman who was with her started walking away, and the woman I had spoken to screamed at me and told me to shut up. Then she said a few other things under her breath and took off in the other direction. Then after the game, she came up to me and said, 'I'm really sorry. And I want to apologize for what I said.' And I said, 'There's pretty much nothing you can say to me that's going to hurt my feelings, because I know more about this game than you do. You don't need to apologize to me, you need to apologize to your daughter, because she heard you and you embarrassed her.' And then I walked away. I just wanted her to learn something: Don't embarrass your kids. This is about your kid. This isn't about me, and it isn't about you."

"The best way to handle those parents who get out of hand," says Amanda Garcia, the assistant women's soccer coach at Oakland's Head-Royce School, "is to say at the beginning of the season, at your team parent meeting, 'This isn't just me as a coach wanting you to stay out of it. It's a safety issue. You will be kicked out by the ref. And you're going to hurt your kids by being out of hand. Your kids don't want to see you get kicked out. I don't want to see you get kicked out. And the refs definitely don't want to have to kick you out. If you have something that you need to say to me as a coach, or to the ref, or to your kids, leave it for halftime. And if you don't have anything nice to say, leave it till the end of the game. Because as badly as you think the ref is calling the game, as badly as you think I'm coaching, you're going to make it worse by being negative. It's not going to help anything.' "

If parents get out of line during the game, Garcia tells them, "it's two strikes and you're out. You get a warning: Please tone it down for now, and if you have a problem, just let's talk about it, but not right now because I'm dealing with your kids, and I'm trying to make this experience good for them. So let's just talk about it later."

Bill Szydlo made waves nationally back in 1996 when, as head of the Northfield Youth Baseball Association, in Northfield, Minnesota, he came up with a system to curb inappropriate parent behavior at games. Northfield is a sleepy college town an hour south of Minneapolis. It's the kind of friendly midwestern community that's full of parks and tree-lined streets where green lawns stretch from house to house without fences to divide them, and driving through it you'd guess that never is heard a discouraging word. Yet even in this Norman Rockwell idyll, Szydlo found parents going nuts over umpire calls, once nearly breaking into a fight, and heard the kind of verbal abuse big-city kids get from their over-amped parents.

Szydlo's solution was to print a little card that said, "We appreciate your attendance at your child's sporting event, but your behavior right now is unacceptable. And if it continues, we're going to stop the game until you leave."

"We didn't want confrontation," he explains. "If fans were unruly or yelling things at players, I had this person called an umpire supervisor, who would just walk around the field. And if we noticed a problem, we would just hand the parent a card.

"At first it was kind of interesting, because all the other parents would say, 'What did you get?' And they'd have to tell them. I think we only ever handed out one, and at that point all our problems stopped. Because the people wanted to be at their child's event more than they wanted to be excluded from it." His system was so revolutionary NPR invited him on the air a couple of times to talk about it—and he wrote a handbook for coaches, parents and players laying out what behavior was acceptable and what was not.

"The problem is not with kids, it's always with adults," says Szydlo. "You have parents who are very well meaning. Everybody involved has an interest in kids. So how do we take that interest in kids and make it constructive instead of destructive? Because a lot of time what these people are doing is repeating what they were taught. The yelling coach, the Bobby Knight syndrome—that's the role model they have. Until you have people who are strong enough to step in and say, 'Wait a second, no. We're not going to tolerate that.'

"What I also found was once you set those lines, you'll find many, many more good people who have the right attitude toward it than the negative ones. Once you stop the negative thing that's being fostered—that sports are everything and I'm going to put you through the rigors of it—you'll find many more good people who are willing to help. But you have to step in, and you have to get people to buy into the theory."

Jim Thompson and his Positive Coaching Alliance are working with leagues across the country to change the culture of youth sports and make it a more fun and valuable experience for kids. Some leagues make attendance at his workshops mandatory for coaches and parents. Maryland hockey mom Nancy Dudley says it made a big difference in her behavior.

"I've had to rein myself in over the years to just be excited on the bench and say, 'Go, team, go! You can do it, you can do it!' " she says. "I've had to train myself to use a certain set of phrases and only those phrases to cheer my child on, because even when my son was 4 years old playing soccer, when they didn't even know what direction they were supposed to run in, I found it was me who had the problem. I was the one who was getting all worked up about the score. And my husband said, 'Honey, these are little kids. This is *youth* sports.' And I think that's what parents forget. What are we doing here, and why are we doing it? So it's really the parents who have to hold it in check."

She went to a required workshop conducted by PCA, and one of the things she learned was how to take a different approach to the post-game chat. "Like when your child gets in the car and you say, 'Well, who won?' or 'What was the score?' or 'Who made the goals?' Those are the first things that come out of your mouth. And they train you to say, 'Hey, how was the game?'—something much more general so that the child can come at it from his or her point of view. 'How was the experience? Was it fun?' So you're reminding them that this is about fun. It sounds silly that you have to be trained to be a positive, responsible parent when it comes to your child's sports. You wouldn't think you'd need a course for it, but it's very illuminating.

Youth Sports and Divorce

Dana Iscoff, MA, MFT

San Francisco psychotherapist Dana Iscoff often serves as a co-parent counselor dealing with divorce custody issues.

It's hard enough when parents in an intact marriage differ on the sports issue. It must be even harder for divorced parents and their kids.

The unfortunate thing for any kid involved in sports is when it's the parents' needs defining things rather than children's needs defining them. The parents become overinvolved in the kids' successes and their failures, and the kids become more of a tool in all these activities rather than a participant who has his or her own feelings about it. The parents are defining the experience, they're defining the expectations, but they're not attuned to what the kid's experiences really are.

You see that a lot in divorced families. The parents are so mad at each other, and everything they do or don't do really has more to do with the other parent than it ever has to do with the kid. So the kid's experience of sports and extracurricular activities, and how much they want to do it and don't want to do it, often becomes another battleground. Like when the father really wants his kid to play on the elite team and the mother doesn't want it. When kids are impacted by divorce and find it hard to let either parent know how they're really feeling, then these issues become even more complex.

For example, I had a 16-year-old boy come in one day, because I was working on a custody arrangement, and he spilled his guts about all sorts of things, including that his father wanted him to be really involved in sports, when the kid was not an athlete at all. His father was completely unattuned.

And in my conversation with him, the boy said, "Do not tell my parents about any of this."

I think this is widespread: that kids feel as if they have to hide their true feelings from their parents, whether their true feelings are about sports or activities or divorce.

The other thing I see is that the kids present one scenario to the mother and one scenario to the father. So they have now internalized the divisiveness that both parents are often experiencing in their marriage and their divorce. It's divisive and they're fighting all the time, and each parent blames the other for all sorts of things, and the kids are a battleground. And so the way these kids resolve this battleground—although it's not much of a resolution—is they become one kid with the father and one kid with the mother. My goal is to get them to work together and to see their kids as they really are, which I find very difficult when the parents are so invested in being adversaries rather than allies. I think for divorce, that's probably the biggest thing regarding anything pertaining to the children.

How does the issue of overscheduling play out in divorced families?

When I work with divorced families, I suggest one activity per parent or per location. So if one parent lives in the East Bay and the other lives in Marin County [the two areas are 30 to 60 minutes apart], the child can have one extracurricular activity in each environment. So then the child and the families get to know both environments, and the parents have to honor both of the kid's environments. Then they can each have an activity in each place, and it also controls it so one parent isn't completely overdoing it and saying, "Johnny can't visit you because he's got this and this on this day and this and this on that day," and it becomes a power struggle.

And it's enough for them. They don't need that many activities. They need some downtime. They need to have their own personal time.

Some kids, due to custody agreements or restraining orders, can't have both their parents at their games at the same time.

And how does that impact the kids? The kids want both their parents to see them play. Some parents fight about "It's my weekend, and you can't come to a game." I never put up with that. I step in and say, "This is about the child. And it means a lot to the child to have both parents at the game."

The research that I rely on says the more divorced parents get along, the better it is for children. They don't have to love each other, they don't have to like each other, but they do have to get along for the sake of the family, for the children. And I think if children can see parents getting along, then somehow they can manage it. It's when they're put in the middle and they have to choose, and they feel they have to ally with one over the other or be one person with one and one person with the other, I think it's so detrimental for these kids. They lose a piece of themselves.

The most important thing is being connected and staying attuned to your children and their needs.

And my husband knows the people who run it, and they are the best. My husband said, 'You have to go to this,' and I grumbled and grumbled and grumbled, yet I was very glad I went. It was extremely worthwhile."

Dudley's husband, former NHL player Mark Heaslip, is a volunteer youth hockey coach, and Dudley says he spends a lot of his time trying to educate the parents that winning isn't everything. She says he "spends hours and hours with parents, counseling them and giving them perspective, and saying, 'This is what I see Johnny doing on the ice.' He's always looking at the child in terms of how can the sport help develop this child? If he's shy, how can it bring him out? If he's uncooperative, how can it help him build some team-building capacities? He's always looking at the sport as a development for the child, the development of his or her potential. And what he often spends time doing is helping these parents see that that's the purpose of the sport. Sometimes he gets exhausted because these parents are so intense with the competitive aspect. And he has to keep saying, 'Well, this is *youth* hockey, they're just little kids,' and he's saying that when they're 16. And my husband is a competitive individual; having played in the NHL he understands the need and the value of competition.

"I've seen many a child in a parking lot on these rigorous, demanding schedules, where the kid is pint-sized, holding a big hockey bag on his shoulder, and his father's yelling at him. And the kid's going, 'I'm trying as hard as I can!' And it's heartbreaking. I have a little six-pound dog that I take with us, and I'm always walking her while the boys are warming up on the ice, so I see these families coming and going in the parking lot and they don't realize they're being observed. And I'll hear these little guys and sometimes older boys having screaming matches with their fathers, very rarely mothers.

"I live in a really affluent town where there's a lot of intensity in sports. But for hockey, I'd say there's probably a tenth of the people involved who are on the wrong track, that it's not a positive experience for their child as a result of the parental intensity. But for everybody else, it's wonderful. It's what they love."

What Makes Parents Lose Control

The two major flashpoints for parents are what they perceive as bad/unfair calls by the official and the amount of playing time their kid is given by the coach. And in rare cases, parents get violent simply over their kid's team losing.

According to the National Alliance for Youth Sports, there were 110 violent incidents in youth sports across the country between 1999 and 2004, including the following:

- An Illinois father, upset that his 6th-grade son was forced to sit out of a baseball game, punched his son's coach and was charged with battery.
- More than 30 adults in Los Angeles got into a brawl at the end of an Under 14 soccer tournament.
- A dozen men charged the field to fight when an argument over an umpire's call erupted after a Miami T-ball game.

The most high-profile case of parent violence in recent years was in 2000, when Thomas Junta beat another hockey dad to death in front of their children after a youth hockey practice in Reading, Massachusetts. The two men had argued over what Junta described as rough play during hockey drills that both men's sons were participating in. Junta was convicted of involuntary manslaughter and sentenced to six to 10 years in state prison.

More recently, in May 2005, a girls' rugby coach was beaten until he was bloody and unconscious during a championship tournament game in Rohnert Park, California. The violence erupted when the coach came to the aid of the referee after a spectator, the brother of the opposing coach, enraged by a call he didn't like, came onto the field and punched the ref. The first coach was holding that man down, waiting for police, when the opposing coach and seven or eight adult men came over and started beating and kicking him, sending him to the hospital for stitches. When the first coach's assistant coach came to his aid he was kicked and punched and got three of his ribs broken. Then the teenage female players started fighting each other, until police arrived to break it up.

In the summer of 2005, an angry father in Connecticut clubbed his daughter's softball coach with an aluminum bat; an irate father in Texas shot his son's football coach in the head; and a youth baseball league in New Bedford, Massachusetts, shut down for five days after a fight between parents and what league officials called "excessive verbal abuse" of the umpires.

And during the 2005–2006 academic year, Seminole County, Florida, ended competitive basketball at middle schools because of hostile behavior by parents. The previous year a shouting match between parents of rival schools had broken out in the stands and continued in the parking lot after the game.

Of course these are the most outrageous incidents, awful or public enough to make headlines. But by all accounts, parental explosions are on the rise nationally at all levels, from the lowliest T-ball games (where officially they're not even keeping score) to the most important championship matches.

W. Robert Nay, a Virginia clinical psychologist and author of *Taking Charge of Anger: How to Resolve Conflict, Sustain Relationships, and Express Yourself without Losing Control*, says there are three triggering factors for parental outbursts at games. The first is alcohol, which was a factor in three incidents of high school parents attacking coaches in Michigan during one month in 2005, all over the issue of playing time. The second is what he calls "unmet expectations."

"These parents are coming in with very, very high expectations about how things ought to go; they're very ego-invested in the child's behavior," Nay told *The Detroit News*. "When anything occurs—when a referee does something they don't agree with, a coach doesn't put their kid in—that's the trigger." The third is stress and arousal. "When you're watching a game like this—and I can remember watching my son, who was a champion wrestler—you get very energized. We call it fight-or-flight adrenaline flow. When something goes wrong, that's when we have this unleashing of emotion. So you put those things together and it's just like striking a match for things to go haywire."

Even if parents are not giving the refs a knuckle sandwich, their investment in their kids' games and sports careers has never been greater. It may affect how their family spends their weekends, whether they eat together, whether siblings get left behind as the focus shifts to the most athletic child. Why are the stakes so high for parents? Psychologists and youth sports experts offer a number of reasons.

1. **Some parents are reliving their childhood experience with sports or working through whatever issues they had around sports when they were growing up.** If they had bad experiences with referees and coaches, then bad calls and denial of playing time are going to trigger their emotions. If they were stars, they may want their kid to be a star and push accordingly. If they were denied opportunity in sports, they may want to give their kid every opportunity—whether the kid likes it or not. A mother I know told me one reason her boys are superinvolved in sports is that her husband was not allowed to play sports when he was a kid because he had to work in the family business, and he was determined his kids would get to do it all. Parents who believe "I coulda been a contender" if only they'd had better training, more supportive parents

or more chances to succeed can remake that missed opportunity through their offspring. Sport psychiatrist Dr. Ronald Kamm told me there's name for it: proxy disorder, "where the parents didn't directly achieve, but the child will be their proxy, and by the child achieving they will have achieved."

2. **The child's athletic success reflects on the parents.** They can brag about it, feel increased worth because of it, and take it as evidence of good parenting. "There are so few tangible things that show you're a good parent, and when your kid excels at sports you can just feel a rush of genetic pride," Jim Thompson told the *Los Angeles Times*. "When a child gets a grade in school, it's private, between him or her and the teacher. But sports is public and dramatic. It's something parents can focus on." Some psychotherapists have suggested that the stay-at-home mom who might otherwise have been able to share some personal achievement in the workplace—a contract she landed or a promotion she got—instead regales her friends with how many goals her daughter scored in the soccer game on Saturday. For many parents, the child's win becomes our win. You can hear it in the way parents talk using the collective pronoun: "We played a tough game. Too bad we lost our best forward in the first half. We've really been hurt this season by injuries."

3. **Parents are anxious in a highly competitive world.** At a time of so much insecurity—economically, with soaring education costs, roller-coaster interest rates and scandals involving financial institutions wiping out life savings; in the job market, with layoffs, union-busting, bankruptcies and merger mania making employees feel that no job is safe; in the neighborhoods, with gang violence and

drugs; and globally, with war and terrorism and mysterious threats to our future from global warming to the bird flu—parents are feeling increasingly vulnerable, which increases their competitiveness. "I don't want my kid to be left behind. I don't want my kid sitting on the bench when the college recruiter comes by. I don't want that call to stand because that's going to affect my kid's stats for the season, or it means his team will lose this playoff game and not move on to the championship." Or, in the beginning, "I have to get my kid on the elite team or in the special program at age 5 so he'll have the best shot at getting a scholarship or a pro career later."

4. **Parents are susceptible to the cult of celebrity.** American society has never been as obsessed with celebrity as it is today. There are more magazines and TV programs and awards shows glorifying young achievers than we have ever seen. *Sports Illustrated* now tells us who the best 6th-grade basketball player in the country is. Youth sports used to be about fun, recreation, learning, development and healthy exercise. Now it's evolved into a star system, modeled on professional sports, which glorifies the stand-out individual, the free agent, rather than the team player. Parents bask in the reflected glory of the superstar, even on the smallest scale. If my kid's a hero, I'm a hero, too.

5. **Parents have gotten hooked on protecting kids from failure or discomfort.** It started with the baby boomers: a new style of parenting in which no opportunity shall be denied my child, and my child shall always have pleasant experiences. The boomers' kids were the first generation to get trophies at the end of the season just for participation. Kids of previous generations learned from losing. Today's kids are under constant pressure to be winners.

And their parents want to help them get there, so every bad call is an affront to their child, a threat to their child's momentary happiness and long-term goal of success.

The Dangers of Being Overinvolved

Parenting is a trendy business. We all run in one direction for a while, then the pendulum swings back and we recalibrate and get centered before we all run off in the next new direction the experts or the masses tell us we should go. The baby boomers' ultra-involvement in their children's lives was a reaction to their parents' underinvolved parenting style.

"Our parents didn't attend our baseball games; they dropped us off at the field and that was that," says psychotherapist Peggy Wynne. "So there's that wanting to have a different experience than what we grew up with. And there's nothing wrong with wanting to be a better parent. We've learned over the years that nurturing children is better than parenting out of fear, which is what the baby boomers grew up with. But it's sort of a rat race in two-income households. You don't really find this in the inner city. The thing is, the poor and working class are very clear about their boundaries, what they can do and what they can't, unlike a lot of the upper-middle-class parents with dual incomes, who are saying, 'I don't want to deprive my child of anything.' Whereas the poor and working class don't have that value. That's not a driving force for them in terms of raising their children."

Annette Lareau, sociology professor at the University of Maryland, spent 1993–95 following 12 families in a study that revealed how child-rearing in middle- and upper-middle-class homes differs from that in poor and working-class homes. She reported her findings in her fascinating 2003 book, *Unequal Childhoods: Class, Race and Family Life.*

"In my book I argue that middle-class parents engage in some-

HEALTHY SPORTS FOR KIDS— TIPS FOR PARENTS*

- Encourage and support your youngster regardless of the degree of success, the level of skill, or playing time.
- Model respect for the coach and highlight the critical nature of contributing to the team and its success.
- Attend and participate in preseason school-sponsored meetings, communicate with coaches and agree to support guidelines for healthy sports.
- Ensure a balance in your student athlete's life, encouraging participation in multiple sports and other activities while placing academics first and foremost.
- Recognize the developmental stages of your youngster, ensuring enjoyment, skill development and team play as cornerstones of sports experiences, with more serious competition left for the varsity level.
- Leave coaching to coaches and avoid placing too much pressure on your youngster about playing time and performance.
- Be realistic about your youngster's future in sports, recognizing that only a select few earn a college scholarship, compete in the Olympics or sign a professional contract.
- Avoid leading your youngster to early specialization, year-long play in one sport and the potential of burnout.
- Understand that today's youngsters strive for excellence, compete to win, but cherish participation most while rejecting "winning at all cost."
- Be there when your child looks to the sidelines for a positive role model.

*Source: Sports Done Right™

thing called concerted cultivation, where they see kids as a project and they develop kids' talents and skills. And working class and poor parents see kids as people they need to take care of and invest scarce resources in, but then they presume that they will spontaneously grow and thrive. The middle-class parents saw them like, 'I don't want him to be Mozart, but I want him to be exposed to music and I want her to have dance,' and they saw it as an ongoing developmental project. And among working-class and poor kids, if they had activities it was more just for fun, and to keep them off the street or to keep them safe.

"I have national data, which I analyzed with Elliot Weinicker, in which we found that kids whose moms have a college degree spend more time in organized activities than kids whose moms are high school graduates or high school dropouts. So clearly there is a difference in number of hours per week that kids are spending in organized activities, and as their moms have more education, they're spending more time. And the parent involvement is a lot higher in middle-class kids' activities than poor and working-class kids' activities. It's not that there aren't athletic activities in poor and working-class neighborhoods; there are. But they tend to take a different structure."

Interestingly enough, Lareau says that when middle-class kids had any free time, even at the end of a day filled with several different fun, exciting activities, they often complained about being bored. "And the working-class and poor kids would have literally no organized activities all weekend, but we didn't hear them complain about being bored. And they certainly didn't think it was their parents' duty to help them be not bored. So there were fewer complaints and the solutions were different."

"Kids definitely need involved parents," says psychotherapist Madeline Levine, the author of *The Price of Privilege*. "Involved parents are shown to raise grades, to raise sociability; it's good to be an involved parent. But then there's the question of: What's the difference between an involved parent and an oveinvolved and an intrusive parent?

"Involved is good. Overinvolved is not so good. And intrusive is damaging," she says. "So the extent to which you're asking, 'How come you didn't get a bigger role in the school play?' or 'How come you're not a starter?' or 'How come you missed that goal?'—you're in not just annoying territory, you're in damaging territory. Because criticism—and I'm not talking about instruction or correction—but criticism is always damaging. So you may say to your kid, 'I don't like the way you did that.' That's OK. But saying, 'What the hell's the matter with you? How could you possibly have missed that layup?' erodes a child's emerging sense of self. And a sense of self is what carries us through life. And to the extent that parents are intrusive and critical, they impair a child's developing sense of self.

"So if you're out there schmoozing on the sidelines while your kid's playing, I think that's fine. If you're out there screaming and yelling, it's not fine. If you're out there feeling anxious or upset or worried, that's not fine, because that's a signal that you're overinvolved. Like if your kid misses the goal and you find yourself really upset about it, that's a signal that you're too involved. These are kids playing games."

Societal factors are at play as well. When youth sports becomes lifestyle, not leisure, it affects how parents relate to each other.

"With the two-income family, there's no social life anymore. Your social life is about going to your child's game and about scheduled events," says Oakland sports mom Jann King, who has also enjoyed a career as a high-powered corporate manager. "So you put your child in all these after-school activities that are not just about having fun, and then you put them in a competitive forum to watch them perform on the weekends, and now it's become a social thing. Because your community is now your sports family community, and there's all this pressure that goes along with that. It's like re-creating your workplace in many ways. And now your workplace is: How good is my child? You go to work and it's all about proving how good you are, and now you've got your child to prove how good you are.

"It's about you needing your child to reinforce who you are. You transfer your issues about self-worth from work into your weekend sport with your child. So your whole self-worth is how many houses I have, how many nice cars I have, and how many children I have in elite club sports. It's about having. It's not about are we having fun, so we have quality time? Americans have become very shallow, and they treat children as commodities, as trophies."

School Just a Tool

Parental anxiety has led an increasing number of parents to micromanage their children's sports careers. Of course there have always been rare sports prodigies whom parents have gone out of their way to give special training, hook up with the best coaches and so on. But now the parent as agent, manager and enforcer from grade school through high school has become so widespread that we're seeing some unfortunate trends in children's academic lives, including:

- starting children in kindergarten a year later to give them greater strength and maturity for high school athletic competition.
- having children repeat 8th grade to give them an edge in high school sports.
- keeping children in prep school an extra year, so that with increased maturity and extra training, these "post-grad" students, as they're called, might have a better shot at a college team.
- transferring children to a different high school when the parents think they're not getting enough playing time.

One mother told me about a boy who had played on her son's high school baseball team for three years, and then his parents transferred him to another school for his senior year in hopes that he'd get more playing time and improve his chances for a college scholarship. Think about what that would be like, to miss senior year with all the kids you've gone to school with since you were a freshman. Think of the social hardship of being the new kid in school at a time when fitting in can be so crucial for adolescents.

Public school districts have tried to thwart the transfer trend with regulations requiring students who switch schools for a reason other than the family's change of address to sit out a year before they can play on the new high school's team. But nationally, school boards and scholastic leagues are being pressured by parents to relax these rules. And many private schools have no such restrictions.

In 2006, eight of the players on the basketball team at Stoneridge Preparatory School, a 50-student school about an hour northwest of Los Angeles, were new arrivals who, six month before, had made up the entire team at Florida Prep in Port Charlotte, Florida. When the Florida Prep coach took a job in California, he brought his players with him, having a private investor foot the bill. "For players at Stoneridge," wrote Eli Saslow in a *Washington Post* story on the phenomenon, "the founding notion of high school sports—that a team represents a school—has been replaced by an altogether different reality. In elite prep basketball, entire squads sometimes change schools. So while much is made of the recent trend of individual players transferring schools . . . Stoneridge represents a new dynamic: the transferring team."

So now the boys ostensibly represent Stoneridge, but the students at the school have never seen them play and have only rarely spotted them in the classroom, since their focus is on a demanding national playing schedule. And how was it that Stoneridge had room for eight new basketball players all at once? Because the former coach took

10 players and went to another private institution, Calvary Christian School, in nearby San Fernando, California.

This is obviously an extreme case, but it's symptomatic of how far families of elite players are willing to go to give their kids what they believe will be the best opportunity in their sport, even if it means altering kids' high school experience and giving up family life.

A trend among East Coast prep school kids is playing in junior hockey leagues, an elite level of competition that 15 years ago was seen as a bridge between high school and NCAA play, where an athlete might hone his already redoubtable skills in preparation for college, but that today is superseding the high school experience. Some athletes are skipping their senior year, and increasingly juniors, sophomores and even freshmen are leaving school to join a rigorous travel team that plays a 60-to-70-game schedule. To do this they often move to a town away from their family and friends, billeted with another family. They attend the high school in that town, where they don't know anyone.

When Nate Frechette, a Winthorp, Maine, senior, played for a junior hockey team in Burlington, Vermont, he told the Portland *Press Herald*, there was a two-month stretch without a home game, and he spent his weekends in motels on his own and eating fast food. "For most kids at 16, 17, it's hard to be away, and away from your family," he said. "You live with a billet family and it's different. You don't have the comforts of home." After 30 games he quit and returned to his high school team, his family and senior year with his friends.

Is It for You or Your Child?

As you look at the landscape of opportunity in youth sports, and as you come to each crossroads—Should he "play up" with older kids? Should she join the travel team? Should I push her harder so she can be a winner? Should I tell him to stick with it when he says he wants to quit?—you have to ask yourself the toughest question: Is this for me or for my child?

"It saddens me to hear parents say 'I'm doing this for my child because the child wants and enjoys it,' or when parents insist 'this heavy schedule is good for the kid,' " says Elayne Savage, PhD, Berkeley psychotherapist and author of *Don't Take It Personally: The Art of Dealing with Rejection*. "But there's another side to consider here. Sometimes it's not in the child's best interest at all. Instead, it's in the best interest of the parents or the coach and can be detrimental to the child."

Savage recently asked her grown daughter about her experience on the high school crew team, "and she said it was the parents' anxiety that was the most harmful. The anxiety about winning, and the parents are so wrapped in their own dreams that they need these triumphs for themselves.

"When I present workshops and work with parent groups and school districts, I use this example: There is frequently massive anxiety around the first day of school. But the anxiety may not actually belong to the child. The child picks it up from the mom or the dad, who is probably reliving their own childhood anxiety about their first day of school. This anxiety also occurs regarding tests and grades. Sometimes parents get desperate and become intrusive, even managing to obtain the number and calling the teacher at home. A similar kind of anxiety happens around their child's sports activities. But there's even more opportunity for anxiety with sports, because children participate in sports so often—once a week or three times a week or even three times a day in some households. All too often, the parents' needs take over. And the child's needs get lost."

So you don't have to be a sideline screamer for your child to feel your anxiety about winning or to detect your desire to have him or her be a success at sports.

"The parents' attitude gets passed down to the child whether something is said verbally or not," says Savage. "Even though many parents will make every effort not to say damaging things to their children, it's the parents' attitude and anxiety that the child picks up. Children of course want to please, and they deeply feel their parents' disappointment. This disappointment feels just like rejection to them. As one teen I know describes it, 'My mother's face turns off whenever I don't play well.' "

In her book, Savage states that "vicariousness is often a form of coercion." "When parents try to live their lives though their children," she writes, "it is a form of exploitation. These parents have some confusion about personal boundaries, they don't know where they stop and where someone else begins. . . . These parents see their children's performance in life as a reflection of their own competence. If the children do well, the parents feel like good parents, successful parents. If the children fall below expectations, the parents feel inadequate and shamed. Then the children are often made to feel inadequate and shamed. The children may lose their sense of self, trading a self for service to the parents."

Savage recalls one of her high school patients who was not athletic, but she thought it would be cool to try out for lacrosse. Her mom was really pushing her to go out for it, but she didn't make the team. "She got cut pretty early, and she was really upset because a girl she was most competitive with at school did make it," says Savage. "At first she was inconsolable, until I asked her, 'What are you the most disappointed about?' She said she just thought it would be so cool to walk around with that lacrosse stick over her shoulder. Once we got to that truth, she was OK with not making the team. Then we had the mom join us for a session so the daughter could tell her she realized she really didn't want to play lacrosse after all. Once mom heard her say that, she, too, could let go of her own dream about having a sports star in the family. I know this may sound a little different from kids who are really good at sports and have a passion for it. However, the point is that it may not be the passion of the child as much as it is the zeal of the parents."

A lot of parents' pushing comes down to the fear that their child will be left behind. "Feeling left out is such a basic, primitive feeling for so many of us, arising from our childhood experiences," Savage says. "That's where much of today's urgency around competition comes from. It's not just that you have to be the best or No. 1. The biggest fear seems to be if the child doesn't do it all now they'll get left in the dust."

"I see families that are so obsessed with their kids being the best that they do more than is healthy," says Andy Bonchonsky, director of coaching for Bay Oaks, an elite soccer club in Oakland. Bonchonsky coached at the college level for 12 years, including eight years for the UC Berkeley women's team, as well as ODP, and now is the coach of the Under 17 Pacific Regional Team. "I've had teams that would win the State Cup in January, win throughout the whole spring and then Regionals in June, and the families would put pressure on our coaches to go to these tournaments two or three weeks after going to the Regionals, when at that point the players needed a break. I remember sitting in a parent group and talking to a parent who wanted their kid to go to a three-day tournament in Sacramento in 100-degree weather three weeks after the Regionals. I said, 'These kids need a break.' And the parent was like, 'No, we've got to keep playing.' "

So sometimes it's the parents who are pushing kids in unhealthy ways. But sometimes, as we'll explore next, it's the coaches.

Rise Up and Revolt: What You Can Do Now

- **Establish a code of conduct and a code of ethics for the parents on you child's team.** And don't tolerate violators. Have parents attend workshops by the Positive Coaching

Alliance or sign up for an online program from the National Alliance for Youth Sports. Adopt guidelines laid out by Sports Done Right or the Partnership for Youth Development Through Sports.

- **Speak up!** You're the only one who knows what's best for your child and your family. Even if you've joined an elite team and know going into it that the time and travel commitment is high, when there is a team meeting, don't keep mum if you have something to say. Bill Doherty notes, "Parents nowadays are not afraid of the traditional authority figures. They're not afraid of the teacher—teachers are their employees. They're not afraid of physicians—physicians are now employees of big HMOs. But they're afraid of coaches. Because coaches control playing time, coaches control whether kids will make the team. Any number of parents have told me that either they felt intimidated to speak up at the meeting where the schedule was set, or when they spoke up, nobody supported them. For instance, someone said, 'I don't think we should play every three- and four-day weekend of the year.' And the coach said, 'Yeah, but these are chances to improve because we play a higher level of competition.' And all the other parents sat on their hands. And then when they left the meeting the other parents said, 'I was with you there. Glad you spoke up.'"

FAMILY PROFILE

JANN KING

What's a parent to do when her child shows exceptional talent? I asked Jann King, a mother in Oakland whose two sons are successful multi-sport athletes six and a half years apart. Her eldest, Michael, has played CYO and MVP basketball, rec soccer, and has been an all-star Little League player for years. Now he's a sophomore on his junior varsity high school baseball team and has been recruited for an elite summer travel team. His younger brother, Devin, a 4th grader, is widely viewed as a prodigy, someone with extraordinary talent on the baseball field, though he also plays rec soccer and CYO basketball. Jann and her husband, John King, a physical therapist who specializes in sports medicine, are two of the sanest, most reasonable parents I've seen in how they guide and support their boys' athletic development. They recognize their sons' gifts, but they also keep their personal and family values in the forefront of their decision-making. I think it's particularly instructive to hear the story of how they've nurtured Devin, a pint-sized leftie with a mean fastball and a killer smile.

How did you know that Devin was a gifted athlete?

From the time that Devin was 18 months old, when Michael was already playing baseball—he was about 6 years old—Devin was insisting that he was going to play baseball, and he was going to play it "the right way." He was very observant, and he had already made the observation that he was not going to use the T-ball. So from the time he was 18 months old, when I came home from work every day, he would request/demand that I go change my clothes and come out in the backyard and pitch to him. He had to swing a live bat and hit a live ball, no T-ball. And what I found fascinating at that age was his incredible attention span. He would swing at a pitched ball for literally 30 minutes or so, which is quite a long time for an 18-month-old.

It was around that time that I read the Tiger Woods book [*Training a Tiger: A Father's Guide to Raising a Winner in Both Golf and Life*, by his father Earl Woods], where it said that he was swinging the golf club and making these incredible shots when he was 2½ years old. And so I could see that, with special athletes, the passion is within them, that it's not necessarily parental pressure. Because we certainly had never encouraged or forced Devin to swing the bat. Not to say that he's a Tiger, but to say that many times in these special children there's an innate desire to do it themselves. In raising children over the past 15 years, I've seen that there certainly is a clear population of parents who do push their kids, but then there are also kids who succeed probably because they have that innate passion and desire to do so.

Did you put him in regular rec league or what?

Well, because he was such a special case—he was already throwing strikes, really hard strikes, from 20 to 30 feet when he was 4 years old—and Peanut League would not allow him to start till he was 7, we went to the Babe Ruth League. There are a couple of different leagues in Oakland, so we found a league where they were willing to take someone who was just under 5, and the other players were 5- and 6-year-olds. He played two years in Babe Ruth, which is out of our district. So he started very early, and we found forums for him to play and enjoy his sport.

At what point did he go to a club team?

When he was 9, so he had played three or four years of regular league play. After we'd played Babe Ruth for a while we switched to Little League so we could play in our community. And then he "played up" a couple of years, meaning that there were kids on his team that were two or three years older than he was. We didn't go out looking for other opportunities, but his reputation preceded him, so eventually he was recruited by a coach out of our district who was looking for players for a traveling team.

It's a challenge trying to find a nurturing, developing environment in a highly competitive team. While most parents would like that, it's still very hard to find. If you find it, you're blessed. But I think many coaches are driven by the need to win at all costs. That's very commonplace.

Was it hard to tell, going in, how it would be?

When he got on his first traveling team, we were excited that they wanted him, and we had some reservations, but it's your first time, so you kind of ignore them. But it became very clear that this coach was inept and all he cared about was his son, and whether his son was qualified or not, he was going to play his son at the most vulnerable position. A number of us realized that immediately and we quit within two months of being with that team.

Through that team, I connected with a parent who wanted to start a traveling team, and two or three months later we joined that team, which he played on for another year and a half. And during that time, the coach had recruited some of the most talented players, but ultimately it ended up being such a competitive, vicious group of parents and parent-coaches—each of the four coaches had sons on the team—that even though the level of play was so exciting, it made being on that team and getting through it on a daily level just not fun anymore.

Was it the parents' behavior on the sidelines? Or were they criticizing your kid or jostling for playing time?

All of the above. And eventually a number of parents conspired against the head coach who had started the team and mutinied against him and shut down his own Web site. At that point I realized I didn't want to be with any of these parents. To me it was not a place for any kind of role modeling that I wanted my child to be exposed to. And it was agonizing, because these kids were good.

What do you think was going on with those parents?

I think the behavior has to do with being self-absorbed. They no longer practice anything close to being a team. It was about *my* child and what's the most I can get for *my* child. That team got so bad that we stepped away from high-level play because it was just too contentious for us to deal with.

So where is Devin playing now?

He's back in the Babe Ruth League, which has restructured the teams this year, so he's playing on a pretty highly select team. One of our concerns about league play was that that it hasn't been competitive enough. So now they've done the schedules so certain teams can go off and play tournaments. So you can play with these tournament teams that we were with before. So that's something we're willing to try at least for this year.

So Devin has options, and now that we've seen what kind of skill and talent can make it onto a high school team, we feel a little more confident that Devin will have a good chance in high school, and that he doesn't have to kill himself in hyper-competitive teams as long as he maintains his skills and his passion. We're still talking about a long road—four or five years from now, before high school is a consideration. But we're not as panic-stricken. We'll see. But I think he'll do fine.

CHAPTER 9

When Coaches Have All the Power

As I say to the families and the children, which they all agree with, there's about an 8- or 9-year window when their lives are put on hold, so to speak. All their vacations, all of their free time is spent with the sport that they have chosen.

—BRIAN DOYLE, director of coaching for the elite Michigan Wolves-Hawks Soccer Club for kids 8 to 18

If someone had told me three years ago that you're going to have a T-ball coach who's going to have a kid try to harm another kid on the same team so you can win a T-ball game, I would have said, "No. That's beyond the pale."

—JIM THOMPSON, founder and leader of the Positive Coaching Alliance

It sounded almost unbelievable when it hit the news in late June of 2005: A Little League coach named Mark Downs, of suburban Pittsburgh, allegedly paid one of his 8-year-old players $25 to assault a fellow teammate, a 9-year-old autistic boy, so he wouldn't have to let him play the league-mandated three innings in a playoff game. According to court testimony, Downs told Keith Reese two different times to hit Harry Bowers, Jr., during warm-ups, first in the groin and then in the side of the head, so he would be too sore to play.

Downs was charged with criminal solicitation to commit aggravated assault, corruption of minors, conspiracy to commit simple assault and recklessly endangering another person. The story made many a year-end list of worst sports events of 2005. Downs was convicted of corruption of minors and conspiracy to commit simple assault and sentenced in October 2006 to one to six years in prison.

While this story is shocking, and especially poignant given that it was an attack on a disabled child who was the coach's own player, it is unfortunately one egregious example among many that show where a win-at-all-costs mentality can take you if you let it. Acts of violence by coaches—against officials, opposing coaches and parents—is a growing trend indicative of a values crisis in youth sports. And the age of the participants doesn't seem to matter. In November 2004, a soccer referee was attacked by a youth coach at halftime in a match between 8- and 9-year-olds in Albany, California.

Acts of violence by coaches are occurring with alarming regularity. In just a few months of 2005, we saw the following stories:

- In May, a Pop Warner flag football coach in Freehold, New Jersey, ran onto the field and threw a 16-year-old referee to the ground as he was speaking to the coach's son and a player from the opposing team during the game.
- In June, a 41-year-old youth soccer coach head-butted a 16-year-old opposing coach in Marlboro, Massachusetts, during a game of Under 10 boys.
- In July, a youth baseball coach in Cuyahoga Falls, Ohio, south of Akron, allegedly caused the death of a concession worker at a baseball tournament in a dispute over a $5 parking fee. The 40-year-old grocer, who also ran a concession stand at the tournament to raise money for the high school team, died of blunt force trauma to the head. Local Police Chief Kenny Ray said the dispute stemmed from the parking, but that the coach may have also been upset because his team had just lost a game in the tournament. The coach was convicted of assault in May 2006 and sen-

tenced to one year's probation, after a six-month jail sentence was suspended.

- In September, at a football game for 5th and 6th graders in Newcastle, Pennsylvania, three coaches of the losing team shouted obscenities at three referees over what they perceived was a bad call, leading the refs to end the game with a little under six minutes left. One of the coaches threw a football at the refs as they left the field. The coaches were arrested outside the stadium, where angry fans had gathered and the police had to break up the crowd.

- In October, a YMCA Pee Wee football coach in Montgomery, Alabama, was accused of shooting the boyfriend of his star player's mother after she pulled the 12-year-old running back from the team as a punishment for having gotten into trouble.

Again, these are a few headline-grabbing incidents out of the thousands of youth sports games that were played that year, but the root of the violence is the same among many coaches and parents who care so much about winning that they let their anger get the best of them. The fact that these are kids, and this is only youth sports, makes no difference. For them, it might as well be the World Series or the Super Bowl.

And it's not just violence that's infecting youth sports but its corollary, bad sportsmanship. In San Francisco, the traditional post-soccer game ritual of having teams line up and walk by each other giving high fives and saying "good game" to each player you pass was banned for a time because some girls' teams, instead of hitting the hand, would slap their opponents in the face. What kind of coach would let players do that? The Positive Coaching Alliance ended up working with the San Francisco School District sports teams to get them back on track.

Soccer ref Trudy Hiraoka says she's seen losing teams eschew the post-game ritual of shaking hands and acknowledging the refs. Instead, "They turn their backs. They're so invested in it that they were wronged, they were cheated, that they don't have the decency to learn—and neither does the coach insist—to be a good sport."

"One thing I have noticed is as the coach goes, so goes the team," says Vermont hockey referee Rick Sullivan. "So if you have a coach who's kind of out of control, the players generally will be out of control. A couple of years ago I experienced a remarkable switch on that: The coach was out of control, but the captain of the team was a 16-year-old kid who was the most mature and respectful person in the building. That's the one time I had to throw a coach out of the game—he was yelling and swearing and just wouldn't calm down—but the kid was amazingly respectful."

Playing to Hurt

Sullivan has watched the game he played in prep school become increasingly violent, and says there's currently a controversy in youth hockey about checking (knocking into another player). "In youth hockey, there's no body checking allowed until you're up at the Pee Wee level, which is 11 and 12 years old. There's a movement to delay it even further, but they haven't been successful in doing that. Some leagues have recently been formed with no checking. Girls' teams have body contact but no checking. And a lot of kids have been turned off by hockey because of the violence and the checking. And they've started to form these leagues in Minnesota where there's no checking, to keep kids interested in playing, because they're just too scared of the violence, which I think unfortunately filtered down from the NHL.

"There's a really specific reason to body check, and it's defined in the rule book: to remove the player from the puck. But unfortunately it has morphed into intimidation. It's used as intimidation, not to gain an advantage other than to make somebody scared, or scared to do a particular thing. It's a real problem. And it really comes from the coaches and, I believe, the commentators on TV. There are terms that are used that have no meaning, like 'Finish your check.' What does that mean? If the player doesn't have the puck, you're not supposed to hit him. But he had the puck a second ago, so I'm going to keep going and I'm going to smash him. And in a fast game, it's a hard call for an official to make; it's not as cut-and-dried as all the other penalties. But you can tell when it's happening. I can tell when the teams are out there to intimidate each other.

"When I do Juniors (16 and up) and Midgets (15- and 16-year-olds) and high school games, they are really out there to hurt each other. And some of it is so ferocious. And it wasn't like that when I played in 1970. I think part of it is because when I played, we didn't have a full face mask. That didn't come till after I played. The college game became as ferocious as it did after that. With a face mask on, you don't have to worry about catching a stick in the face and getting cut. They've become fearless. And that's not a good thing.

"But it's intimidation, that's what we're talking about. And I find it despicable. It's not part of the game. I always tell the kids, 'We're not going to turn this into the World Wrestling Federation on ice.' I had something happen at the game I refereed today. There was a big pileup at the net and then everybody came in and started throwing punches. There was a big melee all over the place. We threw a few of the kids out of the game, but fortunately in this game that was all it was and they finished the game and there wasn't any more stuff. But you can get games where it's just awful, and they act like they want to kill each other. I tell them, 'You don't have to like your opponent, but you have to respect him.' During the late teenage years, the language and everything is so bad. I just want to say to them, 'If you put as much energy into working with your teammates and coming up with a plan and putting the puck in the net as you do yelling at the other team or yelling at us and swearing and everything, you'd score 100 goals.' "

Hiraoka has seen how playing dirty can take the fun out of the game and change the athletes themselves. She's observed this from her unique vantage point as both soccer ref and mother of an elite female soccer player.

"The saddest thing is when you see kids who are maybe 12 or 13 and have no joy," she says. "They are serious, they work hard, they even learn how to do dirty playing, because they're taught to by the coach that they follow almost blindly. And all of a sudden these girls who were two years before giggling and laughing and looking forward to the post-game snack are now these hardened girls who have bought into the notion that 'I'm good, dammit, and I'm gonna show you.' So there's no openness about them, they're really shut down, there's no joy in them. It's really kind of ugly. They're not just disappointed if they lose; they're *mad*. And they're not mad because despite their best efforts it didn't work out that way. That's disappointment. They're mad because the ref made a bad call. It's always something external. It's not, 'Hey, sometimes you win, sometimes you lose.' It's, 'Oh, that girl did this to me and I'm gonna get her back.' It becomes a personal thing and it stops being a sport and it stops being a game.

"And it stops being a learning tool. Because what sports is really is a slice of life. You learn how to cope with things, you learn how to struggle when things aren't going well. You learn how to be elated if something turns out just terrific. But they don't even take advantage of all it has to offer. It's all, sadly, about winning. And I see these young girls lose a lot of their spirit and their joy and their appreciation of life because all of a sudden it's all about the score. And they sometimes don't care how they get it. If it's playing dirty, then that's how it goes. So they lose a lot of who they are all to be the winner of that game on that day."

Many people point to the influence of professional sports, with all its arrogance, bravado and disrespectful behavior, as the culprit when considering this aspect of the evolution of youth sports. "I think humans by nature are imitators," says Jim Thompson. "If we see Michael Jordan do something and we're on the high school basketball court, we try to do it, too. So what we're imitating is the model that the professional entertainment business of sports has put out there. That's what we [PCA] see as our enemy: It's not competition, it's not trying to win, it's a win-at-all-costs mentality, so that we're at the point of that T-ball game incident.

"What we're trying to do is say you can't change what's happening in professional sports. You can't change what's happening in the media, but you can change what happens in your league. That's why our customers are the leaders of organizations. We do coaches' workshops and parents' workshops, but it's really the people who are running youth sports organizations who we're here to serve and encourage to do what we think is the right thing. And clearly, when you walk into a gymnasium or a baseball field or a soccer field with an organization that is working to develop a strong organizational culture of positive coaching and honoring the game, you can tell the difference. You can tell the difference in how the parents are behaving on the sidelines."

As of May 2006, PCA had 120 certified trainers, and more than 180,000 coaches, parents and administrators had participated in its workshops, of which it was conducting 1,300 to 1,500 a year. Its National Advisory Board includes sports luminaries NBA coach Phil Jackson (PCA's national spokesperson), basketball great and former senator Bill Bradley, Olympic gymnast Nadia Comaneci, Women's World Cup winner Joy Fawcett, former NFL quarterback and U.S. Representative Jack Kemp, former NFL coach Bill Walsh and Oakland A's pitcher Barry Zito, among many other athletes, coaches, educators and business leaders.

Hiraoka thinks a lot of the problem in soccer is volunteer coaches who in the younger age groups are usually players' fathers, most of whom have never played the sport. "They learned it in a class, and they're trying to teach these young kids a sport that they don't know much about," she says. "And so almost from the beginning, they don't teach them the right stuff. And then, because they don't know the rules, they'll say something like that was a bad call from the ref, and you really should have gotten that goal. Well, what does that make the kid believe? That the people wearing the funny-looking uniform are doofuses and they're always going to make mistakes, 'but I'm the coach and I'm always right no matter what.' I can't tell you how many times a coach has no idea, from his perspective standing at the center line, what's going on at the opposite corner. There's just no way you can see everything. It's a fluid sport with nonstop movement by 22 people; fewer at the younger level. It's a very complicated game.

"There are some recreation coaches who are even more serious than the club coaches. Serious in the way that they are nonstop riding their kids: 'Get over there. Do this. What are you doing? Move this way.' It is just a running commentary. They will not stop.

"A lot of it is the personal investment coaches and parents have in it," she adds. "And I don't know it for a fact, but there's an appearance that there are many coaches who do it just so their kids get to play. And then there's probably as many or more coaches who do it for all the right reasons."

Fred Engh, the author of *Why Johnny Hates Sports: Why Organized Youth Sports Are Failing Our Children and What We Can Do About It* and the founder of the National Alliance for Youth Sports, thinks educating coaches is key. He says we don't let uncertified teachers teach our kids, so why do we let uncertified volunteer coaches teach our kids?

"We build a school, and we would never dare think of letting volunteers be in charge and run the school," he says. "We build an athletic facility and we say, 'Go ahead, you run it.' You know why? We look at the academic development of children and place that on a high pedestal. We look at the life development of children, and we don't care. We don't care because we let anybody get these facilities, run the leagues, yell and scream at kids, telling them they're stupid idiots because they strike out, telling them at 5 years old, 'You are a great disappointment to your mother and me because you didn't hustle today.' And so we destroy their self-esteem. We embarrass and humiliate them. We destroy the opportunity to teach good techniques of teamwork and discipline and training, and all the things that sports can provide, which are what we need to have for good, working citizens in our society to get along with people.

"So we have programs that are run by a group of volunteers who create chaos, who create kids playing an enormous number of games per season. We have overuse injuries in sports because the coach says you've got to play because we've got to win the championship. All of these problems that are out there are the result of us not getting strong in the beginning and saying, 'We're not going to let you use this facility because all these people don't know what they're doing, so they'll do anything that they want.'

"The reason that we have the problem is our fault," Engh stresses. "It's our fault the leaders in America in the field of recreation never stopped to require these people to be educated, so that they know from the get-go that this is improper."

Engh's West Palm Beach, Florida–based National Alliance for Youth Sports (NAYS) has worked since 1981 to make sports safe and positive for kids. The organization has developed National Standards for Youth Sports, covering such issues as equal opportunity, minimum playing time in games, age-appropriate participation, safe conditions, rejection of the star-system professional model for youth sports, focus on maximum participation, understanding kids' physical and emotional development, sportsmanship, positive role modeling of coaches and providing a drug-, alcohol- and tobacco-free environment. Coaches are trained for NAYS membership in the National Youth Sports Coaches Association in on-site clinics around the country or in an online program, followed by a sport-specific online clinic. Since 1981, more than 2 million coaches have become trained members of the NYSCA.

Coaches' New Role

As youth sports has changed, the role of the coach has changed, says my old sociology professor, 49ers consultant Harry Edwards. The evolution toward specialization of the athlete and the increased emphasis on productivity mean coaches are more interested in winning and churning out specialists in one sport or one position, as opposed to developing a well-rounded athlete and human being. To help me understand, he contrasts his own experience with that of the kids he sees rising today:

"When I played football in elementary school," says Edwards, "by the time the average kid left elementary school he had already been spotted as an *athlete*. In junior high school, he played basketball, football, baseball or he ran track and field. He would begin to take on the identity of a *football player* who's playing basketball, or of a basketball player who's running track. By the time you got into high school, and into your junior and senior year, you were not just a football player, you were a *linebacker* and were being recruited as such by some college. So that evolution from 'He's really a nice athlete' to 'He's a football player playing basketball and baseball' to 'He's a linebacker in high school' took a period from when that kid was 6 or 7 up until that kid was 17 or 18.

"Now, by the time he gets into junior high school, because he's been to all of these Pop Warner camps and everything else, not only is he a football player, it's 'That kid's going to make a great tight end.'

And from that point on, his body, his mind and the vision that other people have of him are choreographed around that identity. If the decision is that that kid is going to make a great defensive tackle, from that point on, he begins to do weight training that the defensive tackles do. He begins to do agility drills that the defensive tackles do. I would talk to kids in junior high in 1975–76 and ask someone, 'What are you?' and he'd say, 'I'm a football player.' I go out there now and ask, and I'll hear, 'I'm a linebacker.' It's already in his mind.

"When I go to the Combine [before the NFL draft, where prospective players show their skills to the NFL scouts] to interview guys we're looking at beginning here [the 49ers], I'll ask them, 'Have you ever played any other sports?' 'Yes, I played basketball' or 'I ran track.' I ask them when. That period has been moving further and further back over the 20 years I've been here. Twenty years ago I'd hear, 'I played my freshman and sophomore year in college.' Ten or 12 years ago, I'd hear, 'I played in high school, but I didn't play in college.' Now, last year, they're saying 'I played in junior high school.'

"I ask them about their position: 'You're a linebacker. Have you ever played any other position?' Years ago the answer was, 'I played tight end when I first came to college.' Then it was, 'I played fullback in high school.' Now, it's, 'Yeah, I played tackle in junior high.'

"So not only has the youth sports culture changed, and not only has it changed the way athletes evolve, but it has changed the way that evolution takes place. It's younger and younger, and it's focused on productivity: They spot him early, they get him trained, they get him choreographed mentally, physically, in terms of expectations of him and the way other people see him, and they start him on that road toward productivity.

"So this whole thing has changed and evolved from 30 years ago. The other side of it is that the expectations of him from the outside have brought tremendous pressures. The coach is no longer the teacher/mentor coach. He's the entrepreneurial coach today. Thirty years ago the coach was a father figure, mentor, teacher on the football field. But that assumed an evolution of the player from young man to football player to a great athlete. Today, that coach has productivity expectations of that kid when he gets there. Father figure? Teacher? Mentor? Give me a break. It's winning, production, and this has turned the coach into an entrepreneur, because the more productive he is, the more he is paid where he is and the greater likelihood he's going to move to the next level.

"The parents are now looking toward not the development of their child as an athlete among all of the different realms and aspects that they expect him to develop—as a student; as a wholesome, decent, responsible human being; as a caring person; and oh yeah, by the way, he also plays a nice game of football. All the rest of that stuff has gone out the window. They're looking to him to be the linebacker, the all-star, the productive, highly recruited linebacker who's going to eventually end up in the NFL, the Pro Bowl, the Hall of Fame and the rest of that stuff. And that pressure starts from the time they become involved in these camps.

"Because that's what the camps are for. They're not trying to make the kid the best football player he can be along with being the best student and best human being, etc. They have to sort out and cull the very best. And as you evolve through that system, the expectations of the coaches in terms of what you're bringing to the table when you get to them, and the expectations of your parents in terms of what you're going to do with that coach all escalate to the point that the kid, the youth, gets left behind. The youth is simply the vehicle that all of these hopes and expectations and aspirations and choreography is riding on. All this stuff is riding on this kid. And the kids feel the pressure. They feel it not right up *to* but right up *through* the professional career. That 2 percent who are lucky enough to get there."

Of course there are many coaches who still try to develop the whole child and to rein in coaches who are abusive to kids. Bill

Szydlo, who reformed his local baseball club in Northfield, Minnesota, says his guiding philosophy was that "our goal is not to turn out superstar players. If a child develops that kind of an interest, that's something he develops on his own. But our goal was to make these kids good members of the community. And by doing that we were going to model appropriate behavior for them, because we could have more of an impact on them and get them involved in the community and show our support, because a lot of kids did not have a supportive, solid home life. So that was my focus: How we were going to treat them as kids? We dealt with things like playing time. My philosophy was every kid should play equally. They're on the team and they deserve that."

Even on the travel team? I ask.

"Basically at any tryout, you're looking at two or three standout kids. And the rest go in about the same bracket; there's not a whole lot of difference in them," he explains. "And you need more than nine players to support the team, because you can't make it on nine alone. But those other kids shouldn't be sacrificing for those top nine. In other words, they should all get to play. And that was a real uphill struggle."

If one of the coaches in his club didn't share his positive philosophy, Szydlo wasn't afraid to relieve him of his duties.

"Like I told a guy one time, 'Look, I think you know baseball, you have an interest in kids, but the way you're approaching them is completely wrong. So you have one of two choices. Either you do it my way, or you're gone. It's your call. I'm happy to work with you, but those are your two choices.' And he said, 'Well, I can't change.' And I said, 'Then thanks.' And there were no hard feelings about it.

"But until you get people who are strong enough to say, 'These are your choices, and this is what we're going to tolerate' . . . I looked at it as a way of educating the parent as much as the kid. Because, basically, we're talking parenting. There are very few places where you have a number of adult males willing to work with kids in the community. So that was my philosophy: Now we have these people who want to work with kids, let's teach them how to. Because you usually don't get fathers at PTA or any other venue. But this is one you could: sports. Now you've got to teach them how to do it."

Szydlo, a former high school band director, says he got involved in the Northfield program not because he loved baseball so much, but because "I think it's a wonderful vehicle to teach kids, if done well, that you're going to fail more than you're going to succeed. What other profession if you bat .300 are you considered good? Not in mine!" Szydlo is an air-traffic controller.

"So if you have a game where you're going to fail more than you're going to succeed, that's a perfect opportunity to teach kids and not to emphasize the times you failed. That's why I got involved with it."

Athletic Arms Race

On highly competitive teams, a coach's demands on an athlete's time can be astounding. I've often wondered why the number of tournaments for the travel teams or games and practices for other teams must keep escalating, with little regard to family life. I ask Jim Thompson why the coaches have to grab so much of kids' time, and wouldn't it be possible, for example, to have fewer practices?

"Yes," he says emphatically. "How about two nights a week instead of five nights? It's a culture of excess. I remember when I was coaching grade school kids in sports (Cupertino Hoops, a league I helped start many years ago), and we'd have a two-hour practice in the week and then a game on Saturday. So I kept thinking, if we could have practice every day, just think how great we'd be. Then I became the girls' basketball coach at Fremont High School in Sunnyvale, and we practiced every day and sometimes also on Saturdays, and we practiced two and a half hours, and still I'd think, 'Oh, I just need a little more time,' " he says, breaking into laughter. "Once you're on that treadmill of 'winning is so important, we've got to do everything we can to win,' then you're never going to have enough time to practice.

"The question I would ask is, do you really get that much of an advantage by doing it more and more and more? You can kill the creativity and the freshness. I run pretty much every day. And every once in a while I take a day off, and when I go back the next day, I just feel so great, having that ability to step back."

The trouble is, coaches tell me, if the other teams are practicing that much, they need to as well to stay competitive. That's what's led to this arms race of practices, games and tournaments.

Another thing to take into account, says Bishop O'Dowd High School women's varsity soccer coach J. T. Hanley, is that youth coaches, especially in California, were volunteers until recently. "I didn't get my first paycheck as a club coach, even at the highest premier level, until about six years ago," he says. "So you could have a national license, you could have coached for years, you could have no affiliation with any particular kid, you were just coaching, but you were still doing it as a volunteer.

"Now, people make a living being club coaches, training maybe two or three teams, or being a director or an assistant director of a club, and maybe running a side training business, and make $50,000, $60,000, $75,000, $80,000 or more. When your mortgage is dependent on that, it changes the equation. Because now it's no longer about the love or the game or working with kids, it's a job. And part of your job is winning. Part of your job is getting kids noticed, getting them recruited. And so those pressures are all there, they're just not articulated as openly and honestly as they should be. But there's a lot of pressure there."

The Tournament Tango

Coaches' insatiable appetite for athletes' time can be seen most dramatically among elite travel teams, in the demands they make on families and in the way they have eroded or superseded high school programs. Hanley notes how despite the Interscholastic Association's mandate that the club team season not overlap the high school season in California, late season tournament play keeps encroaching on high school soccer's start-up schedule. "This year we're going to have 15 girls who are not eligible to play in the high school season until after Thanksgiving," he says, "even though the high school season begins on the seventh of November. They're all going to tournaments through Thanksgiving weekend. The year before, there were eight. The year before that, there were four. And the year before that, there was one. And prior to that, there was never a conflict. So just in the past four or five years, the intensity of that competition and pressure has gone way up. And a lot of it comes down to pressure to go to a tournament where they're told there's going to be a lot of people looking at them, with the opportunity to go to college. And that's what sells the players, but more the parents.

"Then also, a lot of the club coaches have competing interests, in that there are a fair number of club coaches who are also college coaches. So if you're a college coach and you're coaching a high-level club team, and you go to one of these blue-chip tournaments, certainly it's an opportunity for your players to show, but it also gives you the rest of the tournament to walk around from field to field and recruit. It's not acknowledged out loud, but it's part of the program."

The parents I talked to who have kids on elite travel teams said how much they travel depends either on the coach or on the team parents, if they get to vote on which tournaments to participate in. So there's a variety of experience. When told that a team goes to eight tournaments a year, a parent on another team told me, "Oh, our coach would never make us go to that many." Another parent said that the parents vote on which ones to go to, but that a dissenting parent might feel intimidated into compliance. Another explained that the coach might say at the beginning of the season that there will be six tournaments, then along the way he'll receive and accept invitations to additional ones, so the parent ends up feeling trapped into a more intense schedule than she bargained for at the outset.

Of course, the experience of those around me who play outdoor sports in California is affected by our mild climate. We play more because we can. A local elite soccer club competes up to 40 weekends a year.

Brian Doyle, director of coaching for the Michigan Wolves-Hawks Soccer Club in Livonia, an affluent suburb of Detroit, which includes 25 teams and is one of the top clubs in the country, thinks that's way too much. He says his club plays at such a high level—his girls' program, the Hawks, was ranked fourth in the country by *Soccer America* magazine in 2006, and the club has had teams in the national finals for the past four years and won national championships in '89, '91, '92, '01 and '03—that it gets invited to everything. But his teams go to only a few tournaments because they don't want the kids to get burned out and don't want the parents to have to spend so much money. "We travel as little as possible," he says. "We pick and choose our traveling options because of the expense for the families."

The parents vote on how many tournaments they go to, but he recommends only two, three at the most. "We can get good competition within the three states—Illinois, Michigan and Wisconsin. And we go to Canada to get games if we want something new. You go through the bridge in Detroit and you're in Windsor, Ontario. So we're right there." Doyle says that on average, his teams will be out of town six to eight times a year.

His club participates in two out of the three possible national soccer championships: the Stickers USYSA, featuring teams that have won their regional championships, and the Super Y League National Championship, for an invitation-only league the Wolves-Hawks' home page describes as "the most competitive and exclusive league in the country."

His teams play one game per weekend and practice twice a week, except in preparation for State Cup (for the 13-to-18-year-olds), when it goes up to three, and in winter, when it goes down to once a week, because of the weather. That is to say, families get a break driving in bad weather at night. The kids would have no trouble playing at the fabulous practice facility they use: Total Sports Complex, an enormous, state-of-the-art indoor sports center in Wixom, Michigan, that includes two full-size soccer fields with the finest artificial turf, which really looks like grass, in addition to hockey and roller rinks, fields for football and baseball, batting cages, a full-time weight room and exercise room.

So somehow, without practicing as much and without going to as many tournaments as the West Coast kids, they're still managing to be top national players.

"The most important thing is that the athlete is doing what they truly want to do," says Monica Mertle, the St. Mary's basketball player. "And that can be difficult when parents are pressuring you, especially in high school, when there are the big viewing tournaments. You could be going all summer with an AAU team. My dad [who was also her AAU coach] would let me go to three tournaments. It's about a 30-day period, and you could play straight for those 30 days. And I was not allowed to do that. He said you don't need to go out and do 50,000 tournaments, because what you really should be doing is getting to the gym and working on your skills. Those tournament games aren't going to help you with that. And if you're good, they're going to see you in those three tournaments, and if you play in all of them, you're going to get burned out."

I guess Monica's dad was right, since she got a scholarship to a Division I university.

Dean Koski, the Lehigh University soccer coach, agrees that repetition is the key to maintaining and improving skills, not membership on an elite team and constant travel.

"There's such a rush to get kids to play organized sport at young age because the parents want these kids to learn skill sets. And my argument is that they don't learn skill sets, because they don't get repetition. And you know to get good at something you have to practice it over and over and over again. I can watch an Under 8 soccer practice and see a line of 15 kids and one soccer ball and a goalie, and for an hour they each take a turn and take a shot, so during that course of the hour a kid touches the ball five times. They're not developing a skill set at that age. And that's a great age to get kids at least introduced to a skill set through repetition. You go watch a Little League practice, and in an hour and a half, each kid's going to get five swings at the bat, maybe eight if they're lucky. I'll take my son out in the backyard and toss him 100 tennis balls in 15 minutes, and it's not surprising that he's doing well with those skills because he's getting repetition without the pressure of everybody watching him. He's having a good time. The easiest thing for a kid to learn is how to be a part of a team. The hardest thing for kids to learn is a skill. So that's why so many great athletes came out of our generation, because they played all the time. Season after season, we were outside playing, getting repetition.

"Look at inner-city basketball. These kids are out in schoolyards playing all the time. And that's why we're developing so many great basketball players, and some of our best athletes in the country are coming out of the inner cities."

Summer Sacrifice

An unfortunate aspect of year-round play is kids' not getting summers off, and coaches telling families if or when they can take a summer vacation. For soccer teams, it's usually within a specified two-week period. For Extreme Baseball, forget about it. The player has to be available throughout the entire summer. Sixth-grade girls in my daughter's class who joined an elite volleyball club this year found they couldn't go away for spring break, as they have every other year with their families, because they would miss three scheduled practices. Would the girls really fall that far behind if they missed those three to have a once-a-year experience with their parents and siblings? Do the coaches not own a calendar and see it coming? I guess the message is: Volleyball is more important than family.

Parenting author Mike Riera says, "I think it's nuts that a 15-year-old or a 13-year-old playing on a club team can dictate the whole family's vacation. I remember as a kid when we went on vacation and I had to miss games, I thought it was awful. I'd say, 'My friends are counting on me.' And I remember my dad saying, 'We're going away for the weekend and you're coming with us, and that's all there is to it.' And I would bitch and complain all the way, but I'd get there and have a great time with the family. I would never say to my dad on the way back, 'Dad, that was good. I'm glad you made me come,' because teenagers have too much pride. But I was appreciative that he did that, because otherwise I would have missed those experiences with my family. And those are what I remember as an adult, not if I'd won two games that weekend."

Riera says parents face the grown-up version of peer pressure when it comes to "making the decision to stand up to their kids and stand up to the other parents who say, 'Your son or your daughter is a really important player, and they have to be here this weekend and your family needs to cancel its trip to wherever you're going.' "

In her book *The Price of Privilege*, psychotherapist Madeline Levine relates a story of basketball great and vice president of the Golden State Warriors Chris Mullin facing the same issue with his 10-year-old son who was on a select soccer team. The Mullins have four children and traditionally spend every summer on the East Coast visiting family and old friends. "When the family announced their plans," Levine writes, "their son's coach gave them an ultimatum: if he missed summer practice he would be cut from the select team. The parents of every other child on the team changed their summer plans to accommodate the coach's demand. It took Chris and his wife, Liz, a 'nanosecond' to make their decision. They went back east; his son was cut, but continues to play on the local soccer team, and the world goes on."

Of course some might say that since membership on a club team is voluntary, and you've chosen a highly competitive team with a demanding schedule, you get what you pay for.

Bill Doherty of Putting Family First puts that notion in perspective. "This rhetoric is the same rhetoric that used to be used only about professional teams: 'You married a professional baseball player, he's gone six months of the year. It comes with the territory. You knew that when you got into it.' We now are applying the 'gut it out and make all necessary sacrifices' to 9- and 10- and 11-year-olds. That's what's crazy."

Club Versus High School

Ceding decisions about family and school life to the club coach has all kinds of consequences for young athletes. One of the most wrenching ones is over playing for the high school team in your club sport or a different sport. As we explored in Chapter 3, many club coaches prevent or discourage their players from playing for their school teams, accounting for the brawn drain that is threatening high school programs across the country.

Elite Michigan soccer club coach Brian Doyle says, "We do not deter them from playing for their high school," but says that when they return to the club after playing the high school season, "we find the girls come back to us much worse and out of shape than when they leave us every year.' He also thinks it's in the athletes' best interest to focus on their primary sport if they have aspirations to play in college, rather than play a different team sport for their school. A lot of his female players enjoy playing basketball with their schoolmates in their fall season, in addition to playing the club soccer schedule, and Doyle, who coached at the college level for 22 years and is well versed in the recruiting process, makes it clear how he feels about it.

"Let me give you an example," he says. "One of our very best players on the Under 17 Hawks—this girl is going to get a scholarship to one of the top 10 schools in the country; she's an outstanding player—she just blew out her ACL last fall going in for a layup or a rebound or whatever. And I said to her, 'Let me ask you a question: Did that high school coach just give you $125,000? Because that's how much college scholarship money you might have thrown away just now.' And that's the way it is. And I said, 'They all love you there. But are they all chipping in to pay for your school? So if you want to throw a hundred and fifty thou down the tubes, you go right ahead playing for your girlfriends who want you to play basketball.' We don't stop them, but that's the case I make to them, a bit sarcastically."

Alexi Pappas is a super-talented athlete in Alameda, California, who had done cross-country in junior high and wanted to try out for her high school cross-country team the fall of her freshman year, in 2004. Her club soccer coach was not too happy about it, she says, "but in the end I think he tried to understand. I tried to explain it to him that I can't just not try out a different sport that I think I have a lot of potential in. He told me the possible negative aspects of me doing it. Obviously missing practice would affect my playing time. But I understood that. And that's fair, as long as he's consistent—if somebody else misses a practice, then they don't play, either."

So Alexi tried out and was so good, she made the varsity cross-country team, which went on to win second in the state at the California Interscholastic Federation Championships, where Alexi got third place in her Division IV race. She did cross-country again as a sophomore and, though the challenge was greater since her school, Bishop O'Dowd, got bumped up to Division III, she still finished fourth in her race, made the 2005 California All-State Sophomore Girls Cross-Country Squad and is now getting approached by college recruiters. Wouldn't it have been a shame if her club soccer coach had kept her from those freshman tryouts?

One way club coaches undercut high school participation is to not allow their players to participate in camps the high school holds during the summer. One mother told me her daughter's club soccer coach forbade the girls on his Under 15 team from attending the school's soccer camp, because "he didn't want somebody else coaching them," even though some of the girls were sophomores who had attended the camp the year before under a different club coach. It was also a strength and conditioning camp, where the incoming freshmen would have gotten to know the coaches and been introduced to the team's athletic trainer and learned stretches and drills to prevent ACL injuries. Still, they were denied, and not going may have hurt their chances of making the team come tryout time. Maybe that was what the club coach intended all along.

Total Control

The unwavering commitment to the coach has led to unfortunate consequences in the rare cases where a coach takes advantage of players. When incidents of sexual assault or giving alcohol or drugs to underage players come to light, parents, players, school and league administrators all feel sick about having had their trust violated.

Incidents in 2005 included the following:

- In September, a 33-year-old former high school girls' basketball coach in Des Arc, Arkansas, pleaded guilty to watching girls undress in the locker room and to inappropriate sexual contact with two female students.
- In October, a 32-year-old former club soccer coach in Bushnell, Florida, was arrested on charges that he sexually abused two of his teenage players at his home for almost a year. The girls were 14 at the time of his arrest.
- Also that month, a 33-year-old Pee Wee football coach in Dayton, Ohio, was accused of drugging and raping a 14-year-old boy several times at his home.
- In December, a 47-year-old youth basketball coach was arrested in Milford, Connecticut, on charges he had a long-term sexual relationship with a teenage player that started when he seduced the then-16-year-old at a sleepover party at his home in August 2003. The victim became pregnant during their affair and had an abortion.

"Coaches wield considerable influence in their athletes' lives because they are most often the conduit through whom players are exposed to college coaches and scholarship money," wrote San Francisco *Chronicle* reporter Michelle Smith in an August 2005 story about two male AAU basketball coaches who had sexually assaulted female players. One of the coaches, Rick Lopez, had coached the Colorado Hoopsters to national prominence. He was accused of having had sexual relationships with three former players, was arrested and hanged himself in jail in December 2004. The other, Sean-Alan Dulan, had coached his Berkeley Under 14 team, the East Bay Xplosion, to a third-place finish in the 2003 national championships. Dulan was arrested in October 2004 for having had a sexual relationship with a player, starting when she was 14 and lasting more than a year. He was sentenced to 12 months in county jail.

"Most AAU coaches sincerely want to help the girls on their team and do the best they can," Clay Kallam, a high school coach and editor for the women's basketball Web site Full Court Press, told Smith. "There have been big problems with this in soccer, in volleyball, in swimming. It's an issue when you have young girls being coached by men." At least some of the contact with each girl in the Lopez case, Smith reported, took place while the team was on the road playing in tournaments.

"Maybe Rick did have a little bit too much control," Stanford player Cissy Pierce, who had played for Lopez's Hoopsters, told Smith. "When we traveled, it always seemed like he was in control of everything. There were never any parents watching over him on the road. He was the only one who knew where every girl was staying, what room they were in. Even though we played a lot of games, there was a lot of downtime, and stuff could easily happen, and we know now that it did happen. Yeah, I can see now that he just had too much control."

Coaches who commit criminal offenses against kids are thankfully quite rare. But tyrannical coaches who use humiliation and intimidation as the tricks of their trade are more common than we'd like. When I was very young, I had a German figure skating coach I was terrified of, who would reduce me to tears when I couldn't perform to her satisfaction. And the summer I was 13, I had a coach who would weigh all of us teen girls weekly and publicly in a sort of group shaming that sends shivers down my spine all these decades later as I remember it.

As my *Chronicle* colleague Joan Ryan pointed out in her powerful book *Little Girls in Pretty Boxes: The Making and Breaking of*

THE PRIORITY LADDER
OF COMMITMENTS

J. T. Hanley, women's varsity soccer coach at Bishop O'Dowd High School, in Oakland, California, distributes this to his players each year, with this note at the top: "*ALL* players in the Women's Soccer Program are expected to both understand and choose to conform to the following list."

1. Family
2. School
3. This Program
4. Everything Else!

Below the list he writes: "If we strive to keep this list in order, we will achieve great things together. If at any time this list does not match your own, you should be prepared to remove soccer from the list. It is only through a shared understanding of and commitment to this ladder by each of us, players, parents and coaches, that we can reach our goals as individuals, a team and a program."

Elite Gymnasts and Figure Skaters, coaches have driven girls in those sports to eating disorders, depression, amenorrhea and even suicide. She explains that young girls who starve themselves to please their coaches end up delaying puberty, which has serious long-term health consequences:

"In staving off puberty to maintain the 'ideal' body shape, girls risk their health in ways their male counterparts never do," writes Ryan. "They starve themselves, for one, often in response to their coaches' belittling insults about their bodies. Starving shuts down the menstrual cycle—the starving body knows it cannot support a fetus—and thus blocks the onset of puberty. It's a dangerous strategy to save a career. If a girl isn't menstruating, she isn't producing estrogen. Without estrogen, her bones weaken. She risks stunting her growth. She risks premature osteoporosis. She risks fractures in all bones, including her vertebrae, and she risks curvature of the spine. In several studies over the last decade, young female athletes who didn't menstruate were found to have the bone densities of postmenopausal women in their fifties, sixties and seventies. Most elite gymnasts don't begin to menstruate until they retire. Kathy Johnson, a medalist in the 1984 Olympics, didn't begin until she quit the sport at age twenty-five."

Coaches' insistence on maintaining a sport-specific physique has led athletes in track and field, baseball, football and other sports to take a shortcut and use steroids or other performance-enhancing drugs to meet that demand.

Of course the degrading coach, the unscrupulous coach, the sexually transgressive coach are ugly exceptions in a field filled with admirable men and women, volunteer and paid, who devote their lives to helping, educating, training and inspiring children in sports at all levels. I mention the dark side only in its relation to parents' entrusting their child to someone in a role more powerful than it has ever been. If coaches are seen as holding the key to college scholarships, it may affect parents' judgment when their gut tells them something seems fishy. If the coach holds the child's future in his hands, parents may not want to rock the boat. Luckily, leagues, schools and sports organizations are becoming increasingly vigilant as incidents of abuse have become more prevalent. They are instituting background checks, stressing training in positive coaching principles and making sure safeguards are in place during road trips.

But frankly, I'm more concerned with the win-at-all-costs coach than the sex offender. The latter affects a handful of athletes nationwide. The former type affects millions, from tiny tots tripping over their cleats on dewy fields every Saturday morning to college hopefuls training hard after school each afternoon. I'm more wary of the coach who insists we play an optional tournament Thanksgiving weekend or makes a player miss her 8th-grade graduation dance—a once-in-a-lifetime event in a brief childhood—because of a game than I am afraid of criminal behavior. The coach who demands the team be No. 1 in a kid's life is vastly more common that an adult who would harm a child.

The important thing is for parents to seek and find a coach who can be their partner in developing their child's skills and character. And to find a coach or a league or a level of play that matches their family's needs and shares—or at least does not oppose—their family's values. We need to be on guard not only for tyrants and abusers, but for those who would put the team above all else, including family.

Rise Up and Revolt: What You Can Do Now

- **Establish a code of conduct and a code of ethics for coaches.** Have coaches attend workshops by the Positive Coaching Alliance or a training clinic or on-site or online program from the National Alliance for Youth Sports. Have your league and/or team adopt coaching guidelines laid out by PCA, NAYS, Sports Done Right or the Partnership for Youth Development Through Sports.

- **Find the coach who is right for your child.** Kids thrive under a coach who is encouraging, supportive, gives positive feedback and constructive criticism and who doesn't let frustration get the better of him or her in the heat of competition. You might think it's hard to find a perfect coach, but you can seek out coaches who have those qualities. And you can avoid or quit playing for coaches who display negative behavior or promote values you don't endorse. Listen to your child. If you hear, "Coach is always yelling at the guys," or "I feel humiliated every time he yells at me for striking out," it may be time to take action. At the rec level, your kid may just get placed on a team and have to make the best of it for a while. But players at the elite level make choices about which top team to try out for. A team may have a stunning win-loss record, but do some research into how the coach treats the players. Style matters. If the coach has a style that works for your child, you'll see the best results.

- **Don't discount playing for the high school team.** If your child's club coach discourages him from playing for his high school, consider all that he'll miss: representing his school, bonding with his schoolmates, playing for something larger than himself—an institution with a history, a legacy. If he's really good, the college recruiters will hear about him. If he's not truly scholarship material, why deny him the unique experience of playing for his school and the memories that will last a lifetime? And he still might make the college team as a walk-on.

CHAPTER 10

Start a Revolution

You, as the parent, are the gatekeeper. Ultimately it is up to me where my kid is going to put his energies and his time, and how much of it he needs to spend with his family. I don't think there's anything more important than solidifying that family foundation. Nothing, nothing, nothing is more important than that. So sports fits into that rather than the other way around, I think.

—JOAN RYAN, San Francisco *Chronicle* writer and author of *Little Girls in Pretty Boxes: The Making and Breaking of Elite Gymnasts and Figure Skaters*

I think there's a confluence of voices on this and we have to keep it going. You don't reverse something like this overnight. It's a big issue. It's huge. It really may be the parents of the young ones who turn this around.

—BILL DOHERTY, University of Minnesota professor and co-founder of Putting Family First

Now that we've examined the various forces that have driven up the intensity of youth sports and changed the patterns of family life, what are we going to do about it? It can be overwhelming to think about changing the system, much less bucking the entrenched culture. I'm only one person! We're only one family! But these are my kids, and your kids, whose childhoods are at stake. What's more important than that? It may seem daunting to revolt against the status quo, but I've found in my research that change is afoot across the land. Rebels are springing into action from Maine to California.

A few years ago, when Madeline Levine's youngest son was 11, he was on an elite soccer club team in Marin County. His two older brothers had been on elite travel teams as well, and one of his brothers played on both the varsity basketball and varsity soccer teams. So Dr. Levine was no stranger to youth sports or the demands of highly competitive play. But something just didn't feel right. She hated how the parents were carrying on along the sidelines, and she didn't like the coach's disingenuous point of view. "The coach would tell the kids before a game, 'There's a college coach here today and he's watching you,' even when there wasn't," she recalls. "It psyched up the kids, and it made it much more stressful. And the way you play at 10 or 11 may or may not say anything about the way you're going to play at 15 or 16."

She also was concerned about the nature of highly competitive play for kids that young, how it was affecting them developmentally.

"There are certain tasks that kids have to accomplish during their childhood. One of them is learning how to study, one of them is figuring out how to make friends and get along with people, another one is figuring out what they're interested in. And if you constantly have kids in competition with each other, they basically learn competition as opposed to cooperation. And because this was a high-level soccer team, they were always playing against each other for their positions, and it was clear that it's either you or your buddy. And I think it's a very destructive thing to do to middle-grade children. Because they're supposed to be learning how to be friends with people, not to constantly be in competition. There's plenty of time as they get older, in high school and college, for competition to become more intense."

Her son's team had won the county championship two years in a row, and the third year she pulled him, and so did three or four other parents. But Levine didn't stop there. She helped form a lacrosse league for her son and others to play in as an alternative. She says she hooked up with "these soccer dropout parents who were sick and tired of the pressure of soccer" and started a league "with very clear commitments and boundaries about what would be acceptable and not acceptable. And that turned out to be a real pleasure, and now my child plays lacrosse in high school."

Levine remembers feeling trapped and isolated while her son was on that soccer team, but it turns out she wasn't as alone as she thought.

"You don't have to capitulate to the culture," she stresses. "And you really have to think about whether this is a culture that makes sense to you, whether it makes sense to your child's health. And there are other people out there who are like-minded. I remember in the days I was in the middle of it that it felt like there were no options. But that's not true. And when we opted out of certain things, we found lots of people who felt the same way.

"It takes some work to go out and find some people who feel the same way you do," she says, "and you may get some resistance from your kid. But my experience is much more often you get relief from your kid." She says that most of the teens she sees in her psychotherapy practice who are pushed and whose parents are overinvolved "are just beside themselves when I can get the parents to back off and give them back their childhood. I mean, this isn't childhood. This is like professional sports. Those guys get paid $8 million to be examined and yelled at and screamed at. And these are children playing a game."

A few years later and 2,000 miles away, in a small midwestern community south of Minneapolis, a group of parents formed an organization called Balance4Success and, in the fall of 2005, announced a boycott of Sunday youth sports games and practices to begin June 1, 2006. Concerned that youth sports was taking up too much of their lives and eating up too much of their kids' childhoods, they came up with the Taking Back Sundays initiative. They didn't ask the coaches to change their game and practice schedules. They asked only that their children not be penalized for not participating on Sundays.

"We're not trying to change sports per se," Balance4Success leader Andrea Grazzini Walstrom told the Minneapolis *Star Tribune*. "We just want to help parents take back one day a week."

"That got the attention of the community and the sports leaders more than anything else," says Bill Doherty, who inspired the creation of Balance4Success. "Once you've named a problem—and locally this problem has been named; in the Twin Cities the conversation is well under way—you have to do something more radical than keep talking about the problem.

"So the first community was the Putting Family First group. Those are the ones who named it and got a lot of national attention. Then the next two communities I worked with did family dinner initiatives, where they had pledge drives for family dinners, and the mayor of Minneapolis and his wife were the first ones to do it. And that got a lot of attention. But what I noticed was that big youth sports stayed on the sideline all the time. So when I was approached by Andrea Grazzini Walstrom about facilitating an initiative in the Apple Valley-Eagan-Rosemount area, I said the next group I want to work with is going to have to be willing to be edgier and take on youth sports. And they said they were, and the boycott came out of that. It's a strong word. And feelings were hurt. You should have seen the letters! The leagues were hurt that we didn't come to them first. They had to read about it in the paper."

Actually, it's not such a wacky idea, or unprecedented. The high school league in Grazzini Walstrom's area, as in many parts of the country, does not schedule games on Sundays, nor does much of the NCAA. CYO makes sure the Sunday mornings are free so families can go to church. In fact, for 4,000 years, the Sabbath has been off-limits, reserved as a day of rest. Just in the past 20, youth sports leagues have overturned a policy in place since biblical times.

A few months before the June 1 boycott deadline, I snag Grazzini Walstrom for a talk, interrupted intermittently by her 4-year-old and 7-year-old, who've just come home and occasionally squeal for Mom's attention. I ask her what kind of feedback she's getting from the community. "There are those parents who have signed on absolutely. Then there are other parents who have said we totally buy into the principles, we're already doing it, it validates what we've done. And what we're seeing more of—and this is the real cultural shift—is parents saying, 'We're making small changes. We're not quite ready to leap off into the abyss. But we're looking very closely. We're not signing up for the spring league for hockey. We still might do winter and might even do a summer camp.'

"As exciting as it is to hear people say, 'We're taking back Sundays,' what's more exciting is to see the second wave of parents saying, 'We're making changes. We're trying to scale back on Sundays, but maybe we're not doing it 100 percent, or maybe we're scaling back on a different day.' Because we're not so interested in Sunday being this magic day. It was simply a day of scheduling balance and allowing the community to kind of get their arms around one focus, one day. So I think what's really exciting is that second wave of parents saying 'We're getting there. We're not making extremely dramatic changes, but we're really thinking about what we're signing our kids up for.' "

Wayzata, Minnesota, just north of Minneapolis and home of Putting Family First, is another hotbed of change. The community there decided a long time ago to resist overscheduling children, make time for family and scale back the intensity of youth sports. David Gaither, head of the Wayzata Plymouth Youth Football League, who is also a former state senator and current chief of staff for Governor Tim Pawlenty, restricts his traveling league of 4th through 8th graders to five hours of practice a week, with no games on Wednesdays, Sundays or Jewish holidays. He also addressed the issue of playing time and opportunity: There are no A or B teams, kids of different athletic ability are mixed equally among teams, and every participant plays 50 percent of the time. Turning away from the professional model, there are no playoffs, no championships, no off-season training and no traveling tournaments. He rejects the idea that more training, more games, more tournaments and more travel are necessary to produce competitive athletes. He notes that the Wayzata High School football team has made it to the state championship game more than half a dozen times in the past 20 years with players who came up through his program. "We're leading by example even if we are just one candle in the darkness," he told the *Star Tribune*.

On the East Coast, Dr. Bruce Svare, a psychology professor at the State University of New York at Albany, agrees that what's needed is a fundamental change in the way youth sports are structured. As founder and director of the National Institute for Sports Reform, he's developing a different play model from the predominant one. Svare has coached basketball from the youth to the elite amateur level and has coached Little League and Babe Ruth baseball, Pop Warner football and youth soccer. He is also the author of the books *Crisis on Our Playing Fields: What Everyone Should Know About Our Out of Control Sports Culture and What We Can Do to Change It* and *Reforming Sports Before the Clock Runs Out: One Man's Journey Through Our Runaway Sports Culture*.

"Right now it's all about the professional model," he says. "We're mimicking at the youth level what we see with high school sports and college sports and pro sports. And we should be much more concerned with development of skills, development of a love for the game, fun, participation—everything that our elite teams are not doing.

"So the play models that I recommend, and the one I'm working with a group on, are based on, for lack of a better word, the recess model, where kids are more involved in determining their teams, they're more involved with who participates and at what times, and it's more about the kids directing the practices and the games, as opposed to mom and dad and coach doing it. It's a return to the way things used to be. And kids survived very well in that kind of an at-mosphere and loved sports. You didn't get the 70 percent dropout rate by the age of 13 that we now experience now because there's way too much pressure on winning and the professional model."

Svare is developing his model with the Partnership for Youth Development Through Sports, working closely with Bob Bigelow, former NBA player for the Kansas City Kings, Boston Celtics and San Diego Clippers and co-author of *Just Let the Kids Play: How to Stop Other Adults from Ruining Your Child's Fun and Success in Youth Sports.*

"It's not unlike Sports Done Right in Maine," says Svare, "but it's focusing on the youth level outside the school system."

Robert Cobb, the University of Maine education professor who created the Sports Done Right initiative, figured the way to recast youth sports as a vehicle for fun and learning and encourage a life-long love of sports was to reconfigure it according to the education model rather than the professional sports model. Once you do that, it's standards-based rather than scoreboard-based. It's about skill de-velopment, good sportsmanship and ethics rather than winning at all costs. Cobb and his select panel developed standards of excellence, as well as coach, athlete and parent behavior, and published them in a report issued in January 2005 titled "Sports Done Right," which serves as a blueprint for schools to reorient and improve their existing sports programs. Then he got an initial two-year federal grant to im-plement the standards at 12 pilot sites representing 29 Maine schools (15 middle and 14 high schools). Like schools monitored and evalu-ated for academic accreditation, coaches will be held to the standards. Cobb also worked to develop assessment tools, again following the academic model. As of spring 2006, two additional school districts (not pilot sites) had officially begun the implementation process, and more were expected to sign on after Cobb sent an invitation in June 2006 to all of Maine's school districts to implement the program.

There are a lot of people working to reform youth sports team by team or league by league. Cobb has been able to do it statewide.

"Of course Maine is a lot different from many states in that we only have about 1.3 million people in the whole state, so it's a much more manageable total population," says the ever-humble, avuncular Cobb. "But the unit of change that we're focusing on is the school and the community. And we're hoping that by getting school boards and their communities on board with these standards and devising the ability for them to self-assess against the standards, then that will be in some ways a self-starter, and beyond that, something that enables them to keep revisiting how they're doing against those standards. So it's a standards-based approach to programming in youth sports and school sports. And we're trying to get youth sports on the same page as the interscholastic sports programs are in their community. That's the goal. And so it becomes more of a systemic or a holistic approach."

Has it made a difference? "Absolutely," says Cobb. "Some of the officials organizations, like the basketball referees, are our biggest boosters. They want to wear our Sports Done Right logo as a patch on their uniforms. It is really beginning to acquire momentum of its own and requiring less stimulation or support from us and becoming more self-sustaining and self-generating. So I'm thinking in Maine, we're going to have this done right in about five years. I know these agreements can lose their impact on us in the heat of competition. But I really think there are going to be so many people who know what the standards are for good behavior, good performance and high performance that you're always under the looking glass. And it isn't a matter of just one person judging whether this is being done right; it's the whole community. So I'm thinking we're going to do it in Maine. Whether people will continue to pay attention to what we're doing and be able to adapt it to their far larger population centers, I honestly don't know. I know there's a desire to."

Cobb's message is reaching well beyond Maine's borders. By spring of 2006, 39 states had contacted him, wanting to learn how they could bring Sports Done Right to their communities, and the initiative's Web site was getting 200 visitors a day. The National Interscholastic Athletic Administrators Association distributed copies of the Sports Done Right report to the board of directors and the executive director of each state association at the 2005 National Athletic Directors Conference in Orlando, Florida, with the hope that its recommendations eventually will be adopted in every state.

"In a lot of ways we're on the same page with Sports Done Right," says Svare. "And I applaud them. Boy, is that a breath of fresh air. It's great that they can do it statewide. It's a small enough state with small enough school districts where you can really get a coalescing of people with a common cause to get together and say enough is enough. Achieving that kind of cultural change, where people are used to doing things a certain way and have been doing them forever in that fashion—it's a hard nut to crack. But one of the ways in which it can be done in communities, and this is what I would urge parents to work for more actively, is what's called the power of the permit."

If parents find that a youth sports program in their town is not benefiting all the kids, and instead is benefiting just a small portion of the kids, Svare believes that's the time to take it up with the recreation director or the athletic director in the school who issues permits to the leagues to use their facilities. Taxpayers pay for the gyms and fields in the city and the public schools. They have a right to protest and demand change if they don't feel their money is being spent properly.

"A youth sports program should be judged on the basis of how it treats its least talented kids in terms of athletic ability, not on how it treats its most talented kids," says Svare. "It's got to be more about participation, more about teaching skills, and less about winning, less about going for championships, less about the coach drafting kids in order to have a good team. We've got to take the ego of coaches out of this completely.

"When you see a dropout rate of 70 percent, to me that suggests something," Svare adds. "If you or I were running a business and we had a 70 percent failure rate, we'd be out of business pretty soon. And I think that's happening with sports. Kids aren't having fun at the lower levels. They're sitting on the bench most of the time. You've got mom or dad or coach caring more about winning and strategizing and standings, and the kids just want to play and have a good time. And the kids quickly learn that the agenda and needs of mom and dad are much more important than theirs. That whole thing's got to change."

So people all over the country are taking matters into their own hands. Whether it's leaving a competitive soccer team to start your own lacrosse league, taking back one day out of seven for the family, transforming school sports for a whole state or designing a new way to play youth sports that's more like recess than the Super Bowl, parents and sports reformers are looking for another way, because the one we've got isn't working well for everyone. People looking for more balance in their lives, fairness on the field and a better experience for kids and families are saying enough is enough and too much is too much. If the pendulum hasn't started to swing back, at least some people are standing up to give it a yank.

Is Change Really Possible?

When I spoke with 49ers consultant Harry Edwards about youth sports, he said he didn't see it changing because the people involved don't want it to change, because there's big money at stake, and "everybody's pursuing their own little part of it, whether it's the leagues at the pro level and the teams at the collegiate level pursuing the money—the national championship, which they finally got, paid $14 million to each team! Television is pursuing the money. The camps are pursuing the money. The parents are pursuing the vicarious experience, the celebrity, the stardom and ultimately *the money*. The kids want to be like Michael Jordan not just because of all the great things he did on the court but because, 'Hey, I can get that money, I can get that car, I can get those ladies, I can live that life.'

"How does one extract that which is well worth salvaging from that tangled mess of factors and influences? Especially under circumstances where nobody wants it extracted, nobody wants the change? Parents don't want the change. Coaches don't want the change. People who run the camps and clubs don't want the change. The media doesn't want the change. Not even the sportswriters. They revel in Michelle Wie, who's 16 years old and playing pro golf, and LeBron James [who got an NBA contract straight out of high school at 18, and before he'd played a single NBA game had signed a shoe deal with Nike for $90 million] and Freddy Adu [who at age 14 got a six-year contract to play in Major League Soccer for $500,000 a year]. The NCAA and the colleges don't want the change. They're feeding on it—these are their farm clubs. The pros don't want the change because the colleges are *their* farm clubs. Not even the athletes want the change."

When our interview is over, Edwards walks me to the parking lot and sends me off with a lot to think about. I get in my minivan, strewn with my kids' bats, balls, gloves, cleats, shin guards and basketball shoes, and ponder his conclusion on the drive home.

I later take up the issue with Bill Doherty, who rejects Edwards' gloomy assessment. "I always tell people I inherited the optimistic Irish genes, not the depressive ones. I'm hopeful. This group of parents and I started this six years ago in Wayzata, Minnesota, developed the term 'overscheduled kids,' and now we are having a national conversation about a problem. And even many of the coaches and the athletic leaders in the school district where Balance4Success is located are admitting that there is a problem of kids being overscheduled, but it's not in their own particular sport, thank you. It's hockey if you're soccer. Or it's baseball. So what I'm seeing is a growing consensus that there is a cultural problem. That did not exist six years ago.

"Now the debate is not whether there is a problem," he continues. "The debate is what are the sources of it, and are particular activities contributing to it or not, of course with everyone denying that they are part of the problem. The major debate now is about the solutions. The athletic leaders' response to the boycott of Sunday participation is: If there's a problem—and maybe there is—it's an individual parent and family solution. In other words, just say no. Decide for your own child. And this is of course the great American way. Smoking, alcohol abuse, obesity, anything you can name comes down to a problem of an individual. The fact that there's a multibillion-dollar advertising industry marketing to 3-year-olds has nothing to do with anything," he adds sarcastically.

"So that's the rhetoric now, that yes, there may be a problem, but it's just up to individual parents to do the right thing. And what I'm arguing, what we're arguing, is that yes, that's true, but this is also a community problem and we have to also address it at the community level."

The Tide Is Turning

Doherty says Edwards is wrong about parents not wanting change. "I've spoken to thousands of parents who are upset about this," he says. "They've not had a name for this, they've not had a way to talk about it. But these talks I give are like revival meetings. Parents are very astute on this, but they are isolated. They call it organized sports for a reason: It's organized. Parents are not organized. And that's why this group Balance4Success is so into organizing."

Parents are no longer taking it for granted that they will push and overschedule their kids just because everyone else is, he says, and the promise of more is better is being scrutinized now in a way it wasn't before. Parents are seeing that each of these apparent gains comes at a cost. "People are pausing," he says. "I can tell you that the athletic leaders in this school district where we're organizing the boycott, they are afraid not that they're going to lose the parents that they currently have. They're afraid that they're going to lose the next generation. They're afraid of the parents with the preschoolers now, because we're making inroads there. They're not afraid that kids on the elite teams are going to quit, but that they won't be able to fill their elite teams."

Madeline Levine senses a sea change as she sits in her therapist's chair. "I think it's reached a kind of critical mass, where enough people are feeling overwhelmed and enough kids are turning up in psychologists' offices with all kinds of symptoms," she says. "It's like taking back your life."

She says she's hearing different things from parents these days regarding how much they'll push their agenda for success on their kids. "It used to be the standard line from parents was 'I know what this can do for her. I know it'll help for college applications. I know it'll help her for the Olympic Development team.' Now I'm hearing more, 'It's up to her.' That may be because I beat people over the head with what the needs of children actually are. I mean, the kid doesn't need to be trained like a professional athlete. And there's a body of knowledge that's emerging now about this, and it needs to reach the public."

Annette Lareau, the sociologist who followed families of con-trasting economic status for her book *Unequal Childhoods,* says she's noticed a cultural shift beginning. "What's interesting is there's an evolving movement against having kids overscheduled, so now parents literally schedule unscheduled time. Someone told me she heard somebody yelling at their kid, 'Come on, you're gonna be late for unscheduled time!'

"I did my research in '93 to '95, and while I was doing my research the term 'soccer mom' came into the common language; it wasn't there when I started. In the revised edition of my book [published in the fall of 2006], which has a new chapter where I follow the 12 kids 10 years later at age 20 and 21, I include a *Doonesbury* cartoon from that time that has this woman saying, 'Oh, I'm so busy, it's the first day of school,' and she describes all the things kids are doing. And then she asks, 'What is your kid doing?' And the other mom says, 'Nothing.' And the first mom is stunned, and then says, 'Well, I guess technically that's not child abuse.' Whereas now physicians are sending home notes saying don't overschedule your kid, there's that book *The Over-Scheduled Child* and there are these groups springing up. I wouldn't say it's a mass movement, but it certainly didn't exist in 1993."

Leadership coach Jamie Woolf ran up against peer pressure to sign her 11-year-old daughter, Anna, up for a travel team but resisted when she considered what it would do to her family of four (her other daughter is 7), and whether Anna really needed it. "We have a friend who's a college professor and coaches both of his kids' soccer teams, and one is on an elite club team. And he asked me, 'Why isn't Anna going out for the Class III or Class I team? She's good enough to compete at that level, so why don't you have her doing that?' And I said, 'Because she's having fun on this low-key recreational league, where they never win much but they love each other. And I don't want to travel. I don't want to schlep her around more than I already am. I'm already giving up the season's worth of Saturdays. Why would we want to change what we're doing?' And he looked at me like I was insane, like I was a neglectful mom. And this is a smart guy and in other ways I feel like we have similar values. But he could not understand why I wouldn't take it to the next level simply because Anna showed such capability on the soccer field. As if that were the only prerequisite to make the decision to go on."

Sick and Tired of Being Sick and Tired

I keep thinking that things will change because it's just too stressful to maintain this pace. It causes frayed nerves and burnout in both children and parents.

In observing middle- and upper-middle-class families, Lareau recalls, "we saw 10-year-olds look exhausted and fall asleep often. And we saw parents seeming exhausted from racing from event to event. I had this phrase in my book that if the 19th-century center of the house is the hearth, the 21st century's is the calendar. Because the calendar was really the matrix of life. A 5-year-old gets an invitation to a birthday party and really wants to go and the mom checks the calendar and says, 'You're in luck, we're home that weekend,' because it depends on his older brother's sports schedule."

That reminds me of the epiphany I had when I flipped over the old month on the kitchen calendar only to reveal a new month where all the squares were already filled in. That was the moment I realized that our lives were on overload.

"The kids like the activities," says Lareau. "The people who were busiest weren't the kids, it was the moms. We followed these kids in their daily lives, and we'd see them get changed and have a little snack and then they'd sit. And then the mom would come home, change her clothes, answer the phone, put out the dog, get the chairs, get the ice chest, fill it with drinks, find her keys, get her sunglasses, yell at the kids to get in the car and get them on the road. So it was the moms who were busy. And some of the dads, but the moms especially. And these were moms who worked outside the home, and worked a lot.

"So the exhaustion and the invisible labor—there's all this coordinating work, you have figure out how to get everyone everywhere. Arlie Hochschild, who wrote *The Second Shift*, talks about women's work having deadlines. You know it doesn't really matter if you have dinner at 7 or 7:15, but if a kid is done with an activity at 5 o'clock, parents have to be there basically by 5:03 or they are late; 5:08 is really late and 5:15 is wildly late. So it's much more regulated for sports than it is for housework. Those activities create a lot of deadlines for parents.

"I don't think the kids were exhausted so much—sometimes they were—but it was the parents who were exhausted. Especially the parents who have the travel team schedule."

Search Your Soul

Even if you're not ready to change the system or revamp the youth league, there are things you can do right away—all those "What You Can Do Now" suggestions at the end of the previous chapters—in your own family and on your kid's team to gain balance in your life, let your kids experience more childhood and less pressure, and promote a vibrant, enriching family life.

The most important thing to do is examine the motivation for your decisions regarding your child's sports involvement. Is it for my child or for me? And what is the goal—a scholarship? Fun? Healthy exercise? A positive social environment? Knowing the joys of the game? Learning a skill set? Discovering a passion? Many believe that sports at the youth level should be about the three F's: fun, fitness and friends. There's plenty of time to get serious later, like in middle school or high school.

If the desire for a scholarship is driving your decision-making, be realistic. Every college coach I talked to said starting your kid in a sport at 5, training on an elite travel team from age 8 and specializing in one sport early do not guarantee a scholarship or even a place on a college team. A walk-on with exceptional talent could ace your kid out of a slot in a heartbeat. As football coaches often say, "You can't coach in what God left out." Talent, not training, is the definitive factor in star athletes. What muddles the equation at the youth elite level is the pay-to-play system, where kids who can afford it can play with the best, even if they're not the best.

Another thing to look at is the child's level of passion and ambition. "You can't teach a kid to love sports, and you can't teach them to be competitive," National Alliance for Youth Sports founder Fred Engh told me. "They either have it or they don't at every level. Not just a child level of competitiveness, but as you get higher, at every step of the way, competition eats at you. That's how you find out whether you are really this super athlete. And if you don't have love, and you don't have a fierce competitive attitude, you can have all the running, catching, throwing, kicking skills that someone can teach, and you won't be."

College coaches also told me that if parents really want their kids to have a free ride at a university, they should push them to get good grades, because there are many more academic scholarships than there are for athletics. "I think there's a mass delusion going on about the end point of athletics for kids," says Madeline Levine. "Your kid's likelihood of getting a college scholarship is infinitesimal. I'm in Marin County, two of my sons have played a lot of sports, and the number of kids who went on to D-1 scholarships is absolutely a handful in the 20 years that I've lived here."

"It gets back to what the scholarship means," says Robert Cobb, "and it's not so much the money, because if you were to save the money you spent for sports equipment and what you've paid on for these elite teams, you could probably have the equivalent or probably even more than a college scholarship. But it's the prestige of being able to say my son or my daughter is a scholarship athlete. That's a big deal for people. If they had invested that money in some kind of non-taxable education fund they certainly would have realized more than what the scholarship provided. But it's the prestige that goes with it. There are kids who get partial scholarships that amount to maybe one-tenth or one-fifteenth of the annual cost of going to college, but they're able to say I received a college athletic scholarship, and that is a badge of honor in many quarters."

By the time our kids are teenagers, they are in a better position to decide to go all out for a sport. Practices are every day in high school. It's a big commitment, but it's age-appropriate. When our kids are little, it's up to us to decide what level of involvement is appropriate or desirable for them and for us. Do we value balance in our home life? In our kids' childhood? Is athletic excellence our No. 1 family value, or is it somewhere in the middle? As parenting author and educator Mike Riera says, "I think parents have to look in the mirror and decide: Is this the way I want my children to spend their youth?

"I think the intention is good, but here's the part that unnerves me," says Riera. "A lot of these decisions are usually based on fear: If I don't get my kid into this now, then they won't be able to play in high school or they won't be able to play in college or maybe they'll miss out on a career as a pro. That may be true, but I think it's more false than true. Great athletes tend to rise to the surface one way or another. Adonal Foyle, the center on the Golden State Warriors, didn't start playing basketball till he was in 10th grade. So I guess I just don't buy it that our kids need to be that invested in it."

Bill Doherty also recommends some soul-searching. "We have to ask ourselves: What are the essentials in child development and what are the electives?" he says. "The essentials are spending weekends together, doing things as a family and having fun—the close family life, which requires a good amount of time. So it's really a question of putting what's first first. It's just that our priorities are out of whack."

My colleague Joan Ryan, longtime sportswriter, columnist and now feature writer for the San Francisco *Chronicle,* who is married to FOX News sportscaster Barry Tompkins, with whom she has a 15-year-old son, says, "As a parent, you should never forget why your child is playing sports. They're not playing sports so they can throw a better curveball or hit the ball farther or score more goals in soccer. They're not doing it to build a good sports résumé. Because the likelihood that they're even going to play high school sports is fairly low. And 90 percent of the kids if not more are never going to play in college. And it's extremely unlikely that they're going to play as their profession. So why are they participating in this at all? Well, it's to build better human beings, to learn values and teamwork and self-discipline and goal-setting and all of those great things that you learn from sports that are going to then translate into making them good workers, good fathers and mothers and neighbors and citizens. That's the whole point of it. And I think we forget that way, way, way too much. Certainly coaches and league administrators forget why they're there. But that's the core of youth sports.

"So, given that, you have to integrate it into the rest of your life. It's not separate from the values you're trying to instill at home and around the dinner table and at school. So sports should never take priority, because it's just one of many ways in which you as a parent are trying to build a better human being. If you always remember that, then hopefully you'll always be guided. You'll make the right decision."

Unfortunately, she says, parents are always looking over their shoulder, struggling to do what our competitive culture tells us we must to keep up. "I'm not a good parent if I don't get my kid into the right preschool. I'm not a good parent if they're not keyboarding by the time they're 6 and they're not reading novels by the time they're 7. That's how we think of being a good parent. I'm sucked right into it like everybody else. There's that constant anxiety that your kid is going to be left behind, and it's going to be your fault if he's left behind. I think what we need to do—and you can only do on an in-dividual level, because the culture doesn't reinforce it—is redefine for yourself what it is to be a good parent. And ask yourself what kind of person you want your child to be 20 years from now, not what kind of child you want your kid to be next year."

So there are your marching orders, fellow revolutionaries. Stay focused on the kid, not the scholarship. Keep your child's needs, not yours, in mind. And remember, not so long ago it was common for childhood to be filled with a variety of experiences, plenty of downtime, lazy summers, dinners and hang-out time with the family. Today's children deserve all that as much as yesterday's.

The world may have changed and gotten more competitive and speeded up, but kids should still get to be kids. Don't push them toward college and a career so fast. They'll be gone before you know it. I know we do what we do out of love. But we can lighten up a little on the throttle. They'll still get there.

Acknowledgments

I'd like to begin by thanking for their inspiration my two journalism heroes: R. Edward Jackson, whose brilliant, open mind and insatiable curiosity took him around the world; and Harold Gilliam, who proved you can make a difference with the words you write.

There are many colleagues and friends who helped me on this journey from idea to the printed page. MVP goes to Joe Di Prisco, wise counselor and first reader, who understood what I was talking about from the get-go, brainstormed with me for my original article on this subject, gave me contacts and pep talks as needed and feedback every step of the way. And I thank Alix Madrigal, my colleague, friend and cosmic adviser, who was also there for me chapter by chapter, and whose enthusiastic cell phone commentaries buoyed me throughout the writing process. And thanks to Heidi Benson, whose wit and unflagging emotional support get me through every workday at the paper, and whose confidence in my ability to do this helped give me the energy to go home and work all night.

Special thanks goes to Alison Biggar, editor of the *San Francisco Chronicle Magazine*, whose decision to publish my article in March 2005 led to my book deal. And enormous gratitude to my agent, Betsy Lerner, for getting me that deal, and for being so sure from the start. Eternal thanks to Joan Ryan for steering me to Betsy, and to Ken Conner for pointing me toward Joan. Applause to my editor, Erin Moore, for her savvy guidance, eagle eye and steady hand, and to Paula Reedy for her precise and judicious copyediting.

A mega-*merci* to Jerry Hinek, my dear friend and computer wizard, who responded to every panicked call, day or night, saving my files as well as my sanity.

A tip of the cap to Kathleen Beakley, who shares my belief that the world would be a better place if copy editors were in charge. And thanks to my parents for teaching me the value of eating dinner together, to my boss, Oscar Villalon, for his encouragement and freewheeling football opinions, and to Heidi Swillinger for always urging me to write.

Invaluable players in this project were all the people who led me to the people I interviewed: Carol Gould, who knows everybody, and in the rare case where she doesn't, she'll post a message on the Web and find 'em, Heather Maddan, who never misses or forgets anything, Brigid McMahon, whose love and generosity sustain me, Jane Applegate, the first journalist in my life, Roger Jackson, Pam Percy, Jeanine Lim, Randi Protopappas, Daphne Bogart, Lacy Metcalfe, Linda Harbrecht, Arlie Hochschild, Marlene Bjornsrud, Rosemary Graham, Bob Asklof, Michael Bauer, Carol Ness, Sylvan Brackett, Michelle Smith, Mark Smoyer, David Dayton and wonderful Tom Fitzgerald, who unstintingly opened his Rolodex to me. Go, Bears!

I will be forever grateful to those who shared their thoughts and experiences in interviews: Brandi Chastain, Caitlin Meyer, Alexi Pappas, Monica Mertle, Kaitlyn Moore, Louie Reed, Christina Humphrey, Eric Jaffe, Adrian Strait, Margo Freistadt, Linda Safir, Nancy Dudley, Jamie Woolf, Joan Ryan, Mike Riera, J. T. Hanley, Jeff Green, Jim Thompson, Fred Engh, Bruce Svare, Robert Cobb, Bob Tewksbury, Bill Doherty, Andrea Grazzini Walstrom, Bill Szydlo, Dr. Ronald Kamm, Michael Thompson, Annette Lareau, Michael Pollan, Marion Nestle, Esther Cook, Chelsea Chapman, Carlos Arreaga, Anne Van Dine, Trudy Hiraoka, Karen Beato, Dennis Reichert, Al Vanegas, Jann King, John King, Harry Edwards, Richard Louv, Dean

Koski, Greg Strobel, John Murphy, Brian Doyle, Rick Sullivan, Tess Amato, Leslie Olney, Amanda Garcia, Shawn Perry, Dana Iscoff, Diane Ehrensaft, Madeleine Levine, Peggy Wynne, Elayne Savage, Cathy O'Keefe, Seth Familian, Lance Williams, Mark Fainaru-Wada, Andy Bonchonsky, John McMannis, Steve Pezzola, Barbara Irias, Anu Raud, Sharon Kappleman, Diane Del Signore, Sandra Esteves-Guidi and Lauren Shaughnessy.

And while I spoke to people all over the country, I had particularly good access to athletes and parents in my own backyard: at Bishop O'Dowd High School, which my son attends, although he is not on any of its sports teams; and at Redwood Day School, an independent K-8 school. During my research it was challenging to find kids or parents who would speak on the record—many feared something they said might hurt the child's athletic career—so I am extremely appreciative of the openness and candor of the folks from these two Oakland schools who shared their stories and feelings with me. Thanks to O'Dowd's Steven Phelps and Lisa Mahoney, and Redwood Day's Kathleen Duhl for helping me gain access to families at their schools. Go, Dragons! Go, Cougars!

Kudos to Susan Faust, Pat Holt, Terry Ryan, Elissa Rabellino, Meredith White, Narda Zacchino, Rico Mendez, Johnny Miller, John Leopold, Mary Eisenhart, Andrea Beach, Travis Jack, Maureen Bogues, Joe Kane, Fi Li Tjioe, Steve Berta, Carly Howie, Karen Bovarnick, Jessica Sindler and Lisa Richardson for their support and assistance. Blessings to Dr. Rae Lynn Winblad and Jennifer Prongos, who helped maintain my physical well-being during a year of increased stress. Humble appreciation to Brooke Warner, who was the first person to see the potential for a book in my original article.

Finally, thanks to my children, Kyle and Hayley, who gracefully tolerated many months of my working nights and weekends, and who challenged me with their own thoughts and opinions about the state of youth sports. And to my loving husband, Blair Jackson, who always does more than half, who stepped in to make dinner when I was glued to my computer even though he had his own book to write, who edited my manuscript with care and alacrity, and who recounted what I missed on *The Daily Show* when I worked too late. You knock it out of the park every day, and you make it look easy.

Resources

Balance4Success
www.balance4success.org

Bay Area Women's Sports Initiative
www.bawsi.org

Center for Sports Parenting
www.sportsparenting.org

The Edible Schoolyard
www.edibleschoolyard.org

National Alliance for Youth Sports
www.nays.org

National Institute for Sports Reform
www.nisr.org

Partnership for Youth Development Through Sports
www.yes-for-kids.com

Positive Coaching Alliance
www.positivecoach.org

Putting Family First
www.puttingfamilyfirst.org

Rescuing Recess
www.rescuingrecess.com

Sports Done Right
www.sportsdonerightmaine.org

Taylor Hooton Foundation: Fighting Steroid Abuse
www.taylorhooton.org

Youth Sports Parenting Information for Sports Moms
www.momsteam.com

Bibliography

Blumenthal, Karen. *Let Me Play: The Story of Title IX, the Law That Changed the Future of Girls in America*. New York: Atheneum, 2005.

Chastain, Brandi, with Gloria Averbuch. *It's Not About the Bra: Play Hard, Play Fair, and Put the Fun Back into Competitive Sports*. New York: HarperResource, 2004.

Doherty, William J., and Barbara Z. Carlson. *Putting Family First: Successful Strategies for Reclaiming Family Life in a Hurry-Up World*. New York: Henry Holt/Owl Books, 2002.

Engh, Fred. *Why Johnny Hates Sports: Why Organized Youth Sports Are Failing Our Children and What We Can Do About It*. Garden City Park, NY: Square One Publishers, 2002.

Fainaru-Wada, Mark, and Lance Williams. *Game of Shadows: Barry Bonds, BALCO, and the Steroids Scandal That Rocked Professional Sports*. New York: Gotham Books, 2006.

Ginsburg, Richard D., and Stephen Durant, with Amy Baltzell. *Whose Game Is It, Anyway? A Guide to Helping Your Child Get the Most from Sports, Organized by Age and Stage*. New York: Houghton Mifflin, 2006.

Haner, Jim. *Soccerhead: An Accidental Journey into the Heart of the American Game*. New York: Farrar, Straus & Giroux, 2006.

Honoré, Carl. *In Praise of Slowness: How a Worldwide Movement Is Challenging the Cult of Speed*. New York: HarperSanFrancisco, 2004.

Lancaster, Scott B. *Fair Play: Making Organized Sports a Great Experience for Your Kids*. New York: Prentice Hall, 2002.

Lareau, Annette. *Unequal Childhoods: Class, Race, and Family Life.* Berkeley, CA: University of California Press, 2003. Revised edition, 2006.

Levine, Madeline. *The Price of Privilege: How Parental Pressure and Material Advantage Are Creating a Generation of Disconnected and Unhappy Kids.* New York: HarperCollins, 2006.

Louv, Richard. *Last Child in the Woods: Saving Our Children from Nature-Deficit Disorder.* Chapel Hill, NC: Algonquin Books of Chapel Hill, 2005.

Pollan, Michael. *The Omnivore's Dilemma: A Natural History of Four Meals.* New York: The Penguin Press, 2006.

Ryan, Joan. *Little Girls in Pretty Boxes: The Making and Breaking of Elite Gymnasts and Figure Skaters.* New York: Doubleday, 1995.

Thompson, Jim. *The Double-Goal Coach: Positive Coaching Tools for Honoring the Game and Developing Winners in Sports and Life.* New York: Quill/HarperResource, 2003.

Index

abductions, 2, 111
abuse of athletes, 232–37
academics
  and burnout, 140
  and club sports, 57–58
  of coaches, 217–18
  and competition, 196
  and family dinners, 158, 159, 162,
    170
  homework, 51, 65, 140, 151, 175
  and overscheduling, 64–65, 132
  and parents, 197, 199–201, 222–23
  and physical education, 27
  and repeating grades, 199
  and scholarships, 18, 255
  study time, 125
ACL injuries, 73, 231
adolescence, 58, 92
Adu, Freddy, 249
advertising, 250
age of athletes, 22, 26, 58, 72–73, 136
Akers, Michelle, 11
alcohol abuse, 155, 159, 167, 172, 191,
    219
Amateur Athletic Union (AAU)
  and coaches, 37, 233
  competition levels in, 72
  and injuries, 70
  recruitment, 25
  shortcomings of, 48–54
  and soccer, 33
  and summer schedules, 227
Amato, Ashley, 20–21
Amato, Jamen, 20
Amato, Mary, 20

Amato, Tess, 20, 154
American Academy of Pediatrics, 45, 96
American College of Sports Medicine,
    92
American Heart Association, 124
American Media, Inc., 94
American Obesity Association, 109
American Sports Data, Inc., 101
American Youth Soccer Organization
    (AYSO), 23
anabolic steroids, 86–94
Andrews, James, 67, 68, 97
anxiety. *See* fear and anxiety
aptitude for sports
  and balance, 45
  and off time, 77
  and overscheduling, 131, 136
  and parents, 15, 178, 186–87
  and practice styles, 228
  and school teams, 27
  and training, 254–55, 256
Archives of Family Medicine, 157
Arreaga, Carlos, 44, 71, 141
arthroscopic surgery, 181
Atlanta, Georgia, 9–10, 108
Atlantic Youth Hockey League (AYHL),
    50
Averbuch, Gloria, 12

Babe Ruth Baseball, 59, 207–8, 209,
    244
baby boomers, 127
background checks, 237
balance, xii, 44, 196, 241–42. *See also*
    prioritizing sports

Balance4Success, 241–42, 249–50,
        250–51
ballet, 151–52
Bandura, Albert, 105
Batson, John, 78
Bay Area Laboratory Co-Operative
        (BALCO), 88–91
Bay Area Women's Sports Initiative
        (BAWSI), 12, 15, 17
behavioral issues, 121. *See also* substance
        abuse
benefits of sport
    child development, 189
    coping with failure, 194–95
    empowerment, 17
    and family life, 185
    and girls, 20–21
    and parental motivations, 254
    values and teamwork, 257
    weight control, 14
Bicycle Industry and Retailer News, 101
bicycles, 101
Bigelow, Bob, 245
Bills, Doug, 80
Bishop O'Dowd High School, 3, 38, 44,
        70, 224, 232, 235
Bjornsrud, Marlene, 12, 14
Blumenthal, Karen, 8
Boardwine, Joe, 179
body weight, 79–86, 90, 109
Bonchonsky, Andy, 204
Bonds, Barry, 15
boredom, 112, 155–56, 197
The Botany of Desire (Pollan), 173
Bowden, Blake S., 156
Bowers, Harry, Jr., 210
boycotts, 241–42, 250
Boyer, Stephen, 68
Boys and Girls Clubs, 25, 32
Bradley, Bill, 216
Breuer, Joe, xiii
Brown University, 9
burnout, 49, 67, 137–42, 147–48,
        226–27
Bush, George W., 10

California, 94, 179, 226
California Interscholastic Federation,
        94, 232
California Interscholastic League, 46
California Youth Soccer Association
        (CYSA), 179–80
camaraderie, 53. *See also* socialization
camps, 38–40, 62–63, 133
Canada, 226
Cardozo, Roy, xiii
Carlos, John, 114
Carlson, Barbara Z., 170
Carter, Jimmy, 8
Carteret Little League, 178
Cartoon Network, 123
Catholic Youth Organization (CYO), xi,
        131–32, 242
Cavalry Christian School, 201
celebrity, 194. *See also* media
        professional sports role models
Centers for Disease Control and Preven-
        tion, 79, 87, 109, 123
certification for coaches, 217–18
Cesano, Fred, xiii
changing sports, 141. *See also* multi-
        sport athletes
Chapman, Chelsea, 160, 165
character development, 51, 222
Chastain, Brandi, 9, 11, 12–17
cheating, 90
checking (hockey), 213–14
Chez Panisse Foundation, 157–58
Children's Hospital Boston, 74
City Block Sports, 24
civic purpose of sports, 222
Civil Rights Act (1964), 2–3, 3–4
Clarke, Arthur C., 112
Class III soccer, 59
class issues
    and cost of club sports, 55, 255
    and family dinners, 166
    and immigrant communities, 22
    and the media, 115–16
    and parental education, 197
    and parenting challenges, 195

and scholarships, 63
and the suburbs, 25–30
club sports. *See* elite clubs
  travel teams
coaches
  and competition, 223–24
  control exercised by, 232–37
  and ego, 248
  and ethics, 237–38, 240
  and financial incentives, 224
  influence on young athletes, 210–13
  new role of, 219–23
  and parental involvement, 196
  parents as, 139–40
  and performance-enhancing drugs,
    89, 90
  private coaching, 64
  respect for, 196
  as role models, 213
  and schedules, 128, 148, 149–50,
    225–28
  selecting, 238
  and sportsmanship, 215
  and standards-based sports, 245–46
  and travel teams, 57
  turnover among, 179–80
  and violent incidents, 190–91
  volunteer coaches, 217–18
Cobb, Robert, 36, 142, 245–46, 255
codes of conduct and ethics, 204–5,
  237–38
Codey, Richard J., 93
Cohen, Amy, 9
College of Education and Human Development, 36
college sports. *See also* National Colle-
    giate Athletic Association (NCAA)
    scholarships
  and the economics of sports, 248–49
  football programs, 10
  recruiters, 33, 42, 47, 54
  resistance to change, 249
  and specialization, 231
  summer camps, 62–63
Comaneci, Nadia, 216

communication, 161, 164, 166–76,
  196
competition
  and age of athletes, 179–80
  and child development, 240–41
  and coaches, 223–24
  culture of, 257
  and free time, 148
  and natural talent, 255
  overemphasis on, 196
  and parents, 179, 193–94
  and reforms in youth sports, 244
  and steroids, 90
  and stress, 127–30, 142
  and tournaments, 226
  and violence, 210–12
conflict resolution, 104, 189
convenience foods, 173–74
conversation, 161, 176
Cook, Esther, 161, 168
Cooper Aerobics Center, 92
cooperation, 240, 257
Cooperman, Cory, 81–82
cost of sports. *See also* economics of
      sports
  college football programs, 10
  and elite clubs, 33–34, 37, 53, 54–55
  and injuries, 74–75
  and school budgets, 27
  and steroids, 88–89
  and stress, 142–43
  and travel teams, 16, 42–44
  various expenses, 60–65
  volleyball clubs, 60
crash exercise programs, 80
creativity, 104, 113–18, 120
crime, 2, 210–11, 232–34
Crisis on Our Playing Fields (Svare), 244
criticism, 130, 145, 198
cultural issues
  changing priorities, 251
  and competition, 257
  culture of youth sports, 219–20, 250
  and family dinners, 163, 174–75
  organizational culture in sports, 216

cultural issues *cont.*
  and overscheduling, 137
  and peer pressure, 130–31
  and stress, 129
curriculums, 160
custody battles, 186–88
cycling, 101

dance, 151–52
danger, 2, 94–95, 122. *See also* health
  issues; safety issues
DaSilva, Robbie, 67, 77
daydreaming, 112
De Paul University, 156
decision-making skills, 121, 133–34,
  201–2
depression, 89–90, 130, 140, 144, 236
deprivation, 195
development rates of adolescents, 46, 71,
  96, 105–6, 117–18, 196
Di Prisco, Joe, 47, 118
diabetes, 86, 124, 175
diet and nutrition
  documentary on, 81–84
  and family dinners, 156–57, 157–60,
    167, 173–75
  and gender issues, 236
  nutritionists, 64
  and obesity, 109, 123–24, 154, 175
  and weight management, 79–86
Dietz, Bill, 79
DiFiori, John P., 77
dinners
  benefits of family dinners, 154–57,
    166–76
  and Edible Schoolyard program,
    157–60
  frequency of, 159
  and overscheduling, 145, 147,
    164–66
  and socialization, 160–64
  support for family dinners, 242
  trends in, 164–66
disabled children, 105, 211
disappointment, 203, 215

discrimination, 3–4
dispute resolution, 120
diversity, 160
divorce, 135–36, 186–87
Doherty, William J.
  on family dinners, 170
  on power of coaches, 205
  on priorities of sports, 230
  on purpose of sports, 256
  on reforms in youth sports, 239, 242,
    249, 250
Don't Take It Personally (Savage), 202
Doonesbury (Trudeau), 252
Double-Goal Coaches, 181–82
Downs, Mark, 210–11
downtime
  and burnout, 140
  and coaches, 210, 229–30
  and creativity, 120–21
  devaluation of, 136–37
  and divorced families, 188
  and elite teams, 52
  and family, 51
  importance of, 112, 117
  off-season, 34
  and reforms in youth sports, 242–43
  and sports schedules, 39–41, 98, 145,
    147, 153
  summers off, 28–29
  and travel teams, 234
  trends, 125
  vs. competition, 148
Doyle, Brian, 58, 100, 210, 226–27,
  231
drinking, 155, 167
dropout rates, 245, 248
drug abuse, 155, 159, 167, 172, 176,
  191, 219
Dudley, Nancy, 50–53, 144, 185, 189
Dulan, Sean-Alan, 233–34

eating disorders, 85, 236
economics of sports. *See also* cost of
  sports
  and coaches, 219–20, 224

economic impact of sports, 44
economic impact of tournaments, 42–44
incentives for status quo, 248–49
professional athlete salaries, 15
profit motive, 37, 44
and soccer leagues, 55
The Edible Schoolyard, 158–60, 160–61, 163, 175
Edison, Thomas, 112
education. *See* academics
Education Amendment, 2–3, 4
Edwards, Harry, 113–14, 219, 248, 249, 250
ego, 192, 248, 255–56
Ehrensaft, Diane, 135, 137
Eliot, T. S., 112
elite clubs. *See also* travel teams
    and coaches, 210, 238
    and competition, 18–19
    cost of, 142
    and downtime, 52
    and family life, 50–51, 55–59, 156
    and fear of being left behind, 35–43
    future of, 251
    and high school sports, 54
    and injuries, 66–71, 78
    and overscheduling, 134
    and parents, 179, 182, 186–87
    rise of, 23
    and scholarships, 46
    and Title IX, 11
    and tournaments, 225–28
Engh, Fred, 217, 255
enthusiasm for sports. *See* passion for sports
equity issues, 218, 247. *See also* class issues
    playing time
errors, 24
ESPN magazine, 44
exhaustion, 144, 253–54
expectations, parental, 135–37, 177, 189, 191–94
Extreme Baseball, 54, 229
facilities, 2, 227, 247

Fainaru-Wada, Mark, 87
Fair Play
    Making Organized Sports a Great Experience for Your Kids (Lancaster), 24
family life
    and downtime, 117
    importance of, 239
    missing practice, 35
    and peer pressure, 121
    prioritizing, 41
    and sports schedules, 119, 126, 145, 149, 210
    stresses of, 147
    and summer camps, 229
    support of family, 63
    and travel teams, 50–51, 55–59, 60–65, 143, 201, 252
    "unplugged nights," 147
    and vacations, 62, 102, 122–23, 127, 136, 137, 145, 229
Favre, Brett, 70
Fawcett, Joy, 216
fear and anxiety
    anxiety disorders, 137
    of being left behind, 35–43, 204, 257
    and burnout, 140
    and child safety, 2, 27–30, 110, 111, 122
    of coaches' powers, 205
    and competition, 128
    decisions based upon, 256
    health consequences, 143–44
    parental anxieties, 193–94
Ferrari, Cynthia, 85
Field Guide to the American Teenager (Riera and Di Prisco), 47, 118
Florida, 93, 191
Florida Prep, 200
Foderaro, Lisa W., 165
football, 10, 80, 86, 94–95, 119, 244
Ford, Gerald, 8
Foudy, Julie, 9, 10
FOX Soccer Channel, 54–55
Foyle, Adonal, 256

fractures, 74–77, 109, 236
Frechette, Nate, 201
free play, 99, 112, 122
free time. *See* downtime
Freeman, Joe, 55
Freistadt, Margo 5–7
Full Court Press (Web site), 234
fun
    and competitiveness, 137, 215
    and family time, 123
    and overscheduling, 98
    and parents, 185
    and recreational leagues, 252
    and self-worth, 199
    and specialization, 31, 73
funding for sporting activities, 4, 42–43.
        See also cost of sports

Gaither, David, 243
Game of Shadows (Fainaru-Wada and
        Williams), 87, 88–91
Garcia, Amanda, 172, 183
Garciaparra, Nomar, 70
Garibaldi, Ray, 87
Garibaldi, Rob, 87
gender issues in sports
    and benefits of sports, 20–21
    generational differences, 22
    and parents, 130, 253–54
    and soccer, 1, 11–19
    and Title IX, 2–3, 3–11
    and weight management, 85
    and youth soccer, 23
Gibbons, Larry W., 92
Girls Athletic Association (GAA), 6
goals of sports, 254. *See also* benefits of
        sport
GoGirl!Go!, 12–13, 15
Golden Bear, 60
Golden State Warriors, 114
Goodall, Jane, 112
Gordon, Paul, xiii
Gorman, Christine, 73
Graeve, Katie, 70
Grazzini Walstrom, Andrea, 242–43

Great Depression, 22
greed, 44
Green, Daniel, 73
Green, Jeff, 98
Groeschen, Tom, 74
growth hormone, 88–89

Hamm, Mia, 9, 11, 24
Haner, Jim, 22, 36, 235
Hanley, J. T., 3, 10–11, 19–20, 25,
        224–25
Harvard University, 165
Head-Royce School, 172, 183
health issues. *See also* injuries
    and burnout, 140
    and coaches' influence, 236
    crash exercise programs, 80
    heatstroke, 94–95
    illnesses, 71, 143–44
    overscheduling, 143–44
    somatic symptoms, 143–44
    and steroids, 86–94
    and weight management, 79–86
Health MPowers, 123
Heaslip, Mark, 50, 189
Heaslip, Sean, 50, 144
heatstroke, 94–95
heel injuries, 74–77
Herrion, Thomas, 86
high school sports
    and coaches, 238
    decline of, 32–33, 46–47, 201
    and overscheduling, 119
    participation rates, 257
    and repeating grades, 199–200
    skill levels, 209
    vs. club sports, 230–32
    and weight management, 84
Hill, Gordon, 54
Hiraoka, Trudy, 182, 213, 215,
        216–17
hobbies, 145
Hochschild, Arlie, 253
hockey, 1, 144, 201, 213–19
holidays, 149

Holleman, Joey, 67, 78
Holperin, Jim, 102
homework, 51, 65, 140, 151, 175
Honoré, Carl, 118, 126, 128
Hooton, Don, 92–93
Hooton, Taylor, 92
hospitality industry, 42–44
Humphrey, Christina, 28–29

identity issues. See self-image
Illinois, 226
illness, 71, 143–44
"I'm on a Diet" (documentary), 81
image issues. See self-image
imagination, 106–7, 112, 120–21
immigrant communities, 22, 160
In Praise of Slowness (Honoré), 118, 126, 128
independence of children, 101, 102–7, 122, 139
individual sports, 1, 32
injuries. See also health issues
    ACL injuries, 73, 231
    and burnout, 141–42
    cost of, 64, 74–75
    heel injuries, 74–77
    and hypercompetitiveness, 218
    knee injuries, 73, 74–77, 231
    Little Leaguer's elbow, 74–77
    overuse injuries, 66, 67–71, 72, 74–75, 78, 96–97, 144, 218
    and parental obligations, 180–81
    preventive measures, 67
    rates of, 74–79
    rehabilitation, 77
    and specialization, 49, 66–71, 72–73
inner-city athletes, 228
Institute for Social Research Center, 125
International Labour Organization (ILO), 102
Interscholastic Association, 225
intramural sports, 124
Iscoff, Dana, 133–34, 186–88
It's Not About the Bra

Play Hard, Play Fair, and Put the Fun Back into Competitive Sports (Chastain), 11

Jackson, Hayley, xi, 132
Jackson, Kyle, xi, 131
Jackson, Phil, 216
James, LeBron, 249
Japan, 137
Johnson, Kathy, 236
Jordan, Michael, 216, 249
Junta, Thomas, 190
Just Let the Kids Play (Bigelow), 245

Kaiser Family Foundation, 100
Kallam, Clay, 234
Kamm, Ronald, 66–67, 106, 193
Kemp, Jack, 216
Kennedy School of Government, 165
kidnappings, 2, 111
Kindlon, Dan, 117
King, Billie Jean, 15
King, Devin, 206–9
King, Jann, 66, 78, 198, 206–9
King, John, 206
King, Michael, 206
knee injuries, 73, 74–77, 231
Knight, Bobby, 184
Knudstorp, Jorgen Vig, 99
Koski, Dean, 18, 30, 103, 137, 149, 154, 228
Kremchek, Timothy, 68, 77

Ladouceur, Bob, 118–19
Lancaster, Scott B., 24
language, 212, 214
Lareau, Annette, 195–96, 197, 251, 253
Last Child in the Woods
    Saving Our Children from Nature-Deficit Disorder (Louv), 107
lawsuits, 6
leadership skills, 104
legislation, 93–94, 108
Lego Corporation, 99
Lehigh University, 30, 81–84, 137, 149

Let Me Play (Blumenthal), 8
Levine, Madeline, 130, 169, 197, 230, 239–40, 251, 255
Lewis, Harry, 118
liability, 110
Lilly, Christine, 11
Lipinski, Tara, 67
Little Girls in Pretty Boxes (Ryan), 234–36, 239
Little League Baseball, 1, 42, 59, 78, 100–101, 178, 228, 244
Little League International, 70
Little Leaguer's elbow, 74–77
locations for sporting activities. *See* facilities
Lopez, Rick, 233
Lott, Ronnie, 114
Louv, Richard, 107, 110–13
low income families, 166. *See also* class issues
Lowell High School, 5
Ludlow, Kenny, 5

Maddux, Greg, 77
Major League Baseball, 90
Major League Soccer, 17
Manchester United, 54
Mano, Barry, 179
marketing, 173–74, 250
Marriage and Family Therapy Program, 170
Martin Luther King, Jr. Middle School, 158
maturity, 45–46. *See also* development rates of adolescents
Mavericks (training facility), 64
McGuine, Tim, 86
McMahon, Brigid, 162
media
  and cost of sports, 54–55
  coverage of sports, 30
  and the cult of celebrity, 194
  and professional athletes, 15
  resistance to change, 249
  and role models, 114–16

and violence in sports, 214
Meehan, Brian, 95
Mertle, Monica, 37, 72, 227
Meyer, Caitlin, 35, 38–41, 70, 98, 138–39
Micheli, Lyle, 74, 78–79
Michigan, 226
Michigan State University, 137
Mills College, 172
mistakes, 17, 24
Montana, Joe, 114
Moore, Kaitlyn, 151–53
Moore, Marianne, 118
Moore Orthopaedic Clinic, 78
Mullin, Chris, 230
multi-sport athletes, 31, 34, 72, 96, 206–9, 231–32
Murphy, John, 179

Nakahara, Stan, 64
National Alliance for Youth Sports (NAYS), 190, 205, 217–19, 237–38, 255
National Association for Sport and Physical Education (NAPSE), 123, 124
National Association of Sports Officials, 179
National Athletic Directors Conference, 247
National Basketball Association (NBA), 115
National Center on Addiction and Substance Abuse (CASA), 155, 164
National Collegiate Athletic Association (NCAA), 4, 11, 80, 83, 84, 242, 249
National Federation of State High School Associations, 80
National Football League (NFL), 115
National Football League Youth Program, 24
National High School Coaches Association, 179
National Hockey League (NHL), 213
National Incidence Studies of Missing,

Abducted, Runaway or Thrown Away Children (NISMART-2), 111
National Institute on Drug Abuse, 87
National Interscholastic Athletic Administrators Association, 247
National PTA, 123
National Public Radio (NPR), 99, 184
National Sporting Goods Association (NSGA), 100–101
National Wrestling Coaches Association, 10
National Youth Sports Coaches Association, 219
nature, 107–13
Nay, W. Robert, 191–92
Nelson, Robert, 70
New Jersey, 93
New Leaders for New Schools, 123
New Mexico, 93
Nigro, Greg, 178
No Child Left Behind Act, 108
Northern California Volleyball Association (NCVA), 62
Northfield Youth Baseball Association, 183–84
nutritionists, 64. See also diet and nutrition

Oakland, California, 114
Oberlin College, 5
obesity, 109, 123–24, 154, 175
obscenity, 212, 214
officials, 178–79, 190, 246
O'Keefe, Cathy, 105–6, 122, 127
Olney, Leslie, 66
Olympic Development Program (ODP), 10, 38, 40, 179, 251
Olympic Games, 9–10, 12, 30, 114, 196
Olympic Project for Human Rights, 114
O'Meara, Mike, 93–94
The Omnivore's Dilemma (Pollan), 173
Oprah Winfrey Show, 47, 171
Oregon School Activities Athletic Association (OSAA), 94–95, 119
Osgood-Schlatter disease (OSD), 74

outdoor activities, 100, 101–2, 107–13
The Over-Scheduled Child (Rosenfeld), 116, 252

Paige, Rod, 10
Pankey, Emily, 182
Pappas, Alexi, 231–32
parents
    anxieties and stress, 129, 199–201, 202
    behaviors of, 177–82, 182–90, 204–5, 209
    and coaching, 139–41, 222–23
    and divorce, 186–88
    and education, 199–201
    expectations of, 135–37, 177, 189, 191–94
    and family dinners, 168–70
    as gatekeepers, 239
    and injuries, 78, 180–81
    involvement levels, 2, 167, 192, 195–99, 226
    motivations of, 201–4
    and multi-sport athletes, 206–9
    organization of, 250–51
    and scheduling issues, 126, 134–35, 152
    and scholarships, 14
    and self-control, 190–95
    and the soccer craze, 30
    and Title IX, 2–3
Partnership for Youth Development Through Sports, 205, 238, 245
Pasadena, California, 101
passion for sports, 27, 131, 137–38, 204, 207
Pawlenty, Tim, 243
pay-to-play system, 255
Peanut League baseball, 207–8
Pee Wee football, 212
peer pressure, 121, 229, 252
performance-enhancing drugs, 86–94, 236
Perry, William "Refrigerator," 85–86
personal life, 39–41, 48, 203. See also downtime

perspective in sports, 257–58
physical education, 13, 108, 123–24
pickup games, 103–4, 105
Pierce, Cissy, 234
pitching, 66, 68–69, 78
Plano West High School, 92
play, 31, 122, 125, 244
playing time, 63, 190, 199–200, 205,
    218, 222, 243
Police Activities League, 32
Pollan, Michael, 173–75
Pony League, 66
Pop Warner football, 1, 6, 156, 211,
    219–20, 244
Positive Coaching Alliance (PCA)
    and coaching ethics, 237–38
    and Double-Goal Coaches, 181–82
    founder, 43
    and hypercompetitiveness, 210, 212,
        216
    and overscheduling, 156
    and parents, 204–5
    and the purpose of sports, 185–89
premier teams, 19. See also elite clubs
prep schools, 132, 172, 183, 199–201
President's Council on Fitness and
    Sports, 123
pressure, 24, 142–47. See also stress
The Pressured Child (Thompson), 56,
    116–17
prestige, 255–56
The Price of Privilege (Levine), 130, 169,
    197, 230
prioritizing sports, 133–34, 169–70,
    235, 257
private coaching, 64
private schools, 200
professional sports
    and competition, 196
    cult of celebrity, 194
    impact on youth, 114–15
    as model for youth sports, 243–44, 249
    professionalization of youth sports, 47
    and role models, 213, 216
    scouting, 69

and weight management, 85–86
proxy disorder, 193
psychological issues
    benefits of sports, 120–21
    and parental stress, 129
    proxy disorder, 193
    and steroids, 89–90, 92
    and unstructured play, 105–6
puberty, 96
Putting Family First (Doherty and
    Carlson), 170
Putting Family First (organization), 230,
    239, 242, 243

quitting sports, 137, 245, 248

Raising Cain (Thompson and Kindlon),
    56, 117
Ray, Kenny, 211
recess, 6, 108, 123, 244–45
recovery, 77, 78, 96–97, 136, 204
recreational sports, 59, 252
recruitment
    and club coaches, 224, 225
    as goal of youth sports, 47
    and multi-sport athletes, 231, 232
    professional scouts, 69
    and specialization, 219
    and tournaments, 42
    for travel teams, 208
Reed, Louie, 144
Reese, Keith, 210
Reforming Sports Before the Clock Runs
    Out (Svare), 244
reforms, 239–48, 248–50
Reichert, Dennis, 42
repeating grades, 199
repetition, 73, 96, 109, 228
Rescue Recess, 123
rest, 77, 78, 96–97, 136–37, 204
Riera, Mike, 47, 73, 103, 112, 166, 229,
    256
Right from Wrong
    Instilling a Sense of Integrity in Your
        Child (Riera and Di Prisco), 118

Robbins, Jeff, 42
Rodriguez, Alex, 15
role models
  coaches as, 213, 219–20
  and competitiveness, 209
  and the cult of celebrity, 194
  and media coverage, 114–16, 249
  and professional athletes, 194, 213,
    216
  and steroids, 88
  and weight management, 85–86
Roosevelt, Eleanor, 112
Rosenfeld, Alvin, 116
Ryan, Joan, 234–35, 239, 256

safety issues. *See also* health issues
  injuries
  and abuse of athletes, 232–37
  and checking, 213–14
  and child abductions, 2, 111
  and coaches, 218–19
  and daycare centers, 27–30
  obsession with, 105
  and parental behaviors, 183
Safir family, 60–65
salaries, 15, 114–15
San Francisco Ballet Company, 151
San Francisco School District, 212
San Jose CyberRays, 12
Santa Clara University, 13
Saslow, Eli, 200
Savage, Elayne, 202
schedules
  and academics, 151
  and burnout, 137–42
  changes in, 125
  and cultural shifts, 251
  and divorced families, 187
  and elite clubs, 35
  and family, 126–27, 143, 156, 176
  and health issues, 69–70, 71, 78,
    143–46
  and high school teams, 46
  limiting obligations, 148
  practice frequency, 223–24

and stress, 142–43
and summer camps, 38–41
and team conflicts, 29, 149–50
and tournaments, 225–28
and travel teams, 28–29, 52
trends in, 116
variety of activities, 130, 131–34
Schilling, Curt, 70
Schneider, Tim, 42
scholarships
  academic vs. athletic, 95
  and age of athletes, 31
  availability of, 35–36
  and club players, 63
  and coaches, 228, 233, 236
  competition for, 90, 95, 128, 196
  and cost of sports programs, 37
  and ego, 255–56
  and high school sports, 33
  likelihood of, 254
  and overuse injuries, 72
  and parents, 138, 180
  and specialization, 231
  and Title IX, 3, 11–18, 19
Schwarzenegger, Arnold, 94
scouts, 69. *See also* recruitment
Scripps Ranch, California, 107
The Second Shift (Hochschild), 253
Second-Goal Parents, 181–82
security, 112
self-control, 190–95
self-image, 21, 130, 199, 218, 220
Seminole County, Florida, 191
Semrau, Dennis, 86
Sever's disease, 74
sexual abuse, 232–34
Shape of the Nation Report (NAPSE),
  124
shin splints, 74–77
siblings, 56
skipping practice, 140
sleep, 144–45
"Slow Down" (Lewis), 118
Slow Food conference, 163
Smith, Jaden Chastain, 13

Smith, Jerry, 13
Smith, Michelle, 12, 233–34
Smith, Tommy, 114
smoking, 155, 159, 167, 219
Smythe, Tom, 119
soccer
    camps, 38–40
    impact on youth sports, 22–31
    player profiles, 28–29
    and the scholarship craze, 19
    "soccer moms," 252
    social aspects of, 132
    and suburbia, 25–30
    and Title IX, 11–19
    and volunteer coaches, 217–18
Soccer America, 226
Soccerhead (Haner), 22, 36
socialization
    as benefit of sports, 72, 130, 222
    and elite teams, 52–53
    and mealtimes, 160–64, 170
    and overscheduling, 152
    and pickup games, 103
    and social clubs, 22
    and social pressures, 27, 198
    and travel teams, 48, 57
    and unstructured play, 103–4
sociology of sports, 113, 219
somatic symptoms, 143–44
specialization
    and age of athletes, 31
    and coaches, 34, 219–21
    and competition, 196
    and injuries, 49, 66–71, 96, 231
    recommendations against, 45–46,
        72–73
    and soccer, 26
    and Title IX, 14
Spoiling Childhood (Ehrensaft), 135
SportingKid, 178
Sports Done Right, 36, 49, 142, 205,
    238, 245–47
Sports from a Different Perspective
    (Tewksbury), 45
Sports Illustrated, 12, 194

Sports Illustrated for Kids, 178
Sports Psychiatry Association, 66–67
sports psychology, 45
Sports Travel, 42
sportsmanship, 103, 118–19, 212, 214,
    215, 240, 257
spring break, 229
standards-based sports, 245–46
Stans, Anthony, 68
State Cup (Michigan), 227
Staying Connected to Your Teenager
    (Riera), 47
steroids, 85, 86–94, 236
Stickers USYSA, 227
Stoneridge Preparatory School, 200
stress
    addressing, 142–47, 147–50, 253
    and burnout, 137–42
    and family life, 129, 147, 155–56
    monitoring, 133
    and obligations, 131–35
    and overscheduling, 126–31, 135–37,
        151
    and scholarships, 138
    signs of, 140
Strobel, Greg, 81–84
structure in sports, 25–26
substance abuse, 155, 159, 167, 172,
    176, 191, 219
suicide, 92–93, 236
Sullivan, Rick, 146, 213
summers. *See also* vacations
    and family time, 149
    and free time, 28, 153
    and heatstroke, 94–95
    and sports schedules, 229–30
    summer camps, 34, 117
    variety of activities, 133
Sundays, 241–43
Super Y League National Champion-
    ship, 227
supplements, 85, 86–94
Surf Cup, 42
surgeries, 68–69, 95, 181
Svare, Bruce, 244–48

switching sports, 141. *See also* multi-
    sport athletes
Szydlo, Bill, 177, 183–84, 221–23

"Take Me Ouch to the Ballgame" (Hol-
    leman), 67
Taking Back Sundays initiative, 241–43
Taking Charge of Anger (Nay), 191–92
talent. *See* aptitude for sports
taxpayers, 247
Taylor Hooton Foundation, 93
team selection, 102–3
team sports, xv
teamwork, 257
television, 147, 164, 165, 174, 214
Tewksbury, Bob, 45, 48–49, 49–54, 69
therapy, 122, 129
Thompson, Jim
    on balance, 43–47
    on coaching, 181, 210
    on fun in sports, 185
    on hypercompetitiveness, 223
    on media coverage, 216
    on overscheduling, 156
    on parental expectations, 193
Thompson, Michael, 56, 116–17
Title IX, 2–3, 5–7, 8, 11–19
Tittle, Y. A., 114
tobacco use, 155, 159, 167, 219
Tommy John surgery, 68–69, 95
Tompkins, Barry, 256
Toole, Susan, 143
Total Sports Complex, 227
tourism, 42–44, 102
tournaments
    and coaches, 225–28, 237
    and competition, 224
    economic impact of, 42–44
    frequency of, 37–42
    limiting number of, 148, 149
    missing, 41
    and overscheduling, 152
    and travel, 61–62, 146
toys, 99
trainers, 33–34, 44, 64

Training a Tiger (Woods), 207
travel teams
    and educational opportunities, 54
    expenses, 61–65
    and family life, 60–65, 156, 163
    and number of tournaments, 148
    and overuse injuries, 78
    and peer pressure, 252
    and playing time, 222
    pressures of, 16, 65, 142–43
    recruitment for, 208
    and schedules, 28, 47–55, 201,
        225–28
    and tourism industry, 42–44
    and tournaments, 39, 225–28
Trecker, James, 54
True Life, 81
tutors, 64
Twain, Mark, 112

Ueberroth, Peter, 114
Unequal Childhoods (Lareau), 195–96,
    251
United Nations, 102
United States Olympic Committee, 114
United States Soccer Federation, 24
United States Youth Soccer Association
    (USYSA), 23
University of Maine, 36, 142
University of Michigan, 125
University of Minnesota, 157, 170
University of South Alabama, 127
unstructured play, 26, 99, 100–103,
    125
U.S. Consumer Product Safety Commis-
    sion, 74
U.S. Department of Education, 108,
    123–24
U.S. Department of Justice, 111
U.S. Supreme Court, 9
U.S. Women's National Soccer Team,
    9, 24
USA Volleyball, 62
USDA Nutrition Connections Confer-
    ence, 157

Utah Football Coaches Association, 80

Utah High School Activities Association, 96

Utah Sports Commission, 42

vacations
  and coaches, 229
  importance of, 122–23
  and overscheduling, 145, 210
  reduction of, 102, 127, 137
  and travel teams, 62
Van Auken, Lance, 70
Van Dine, Anne, 32, 35, 139–41, 142–43
Van Dine, Ginny, 32
Vanden Broeder, Ryen, 79
Vander Schilden, Jack, 79
variety in sports, 31, 67, 129–32. *See also* multi-sport athletes
Varona, Donna de, 10
Velocity Sports Performance, 34
Verstegan, Robert, 70
violence, 178, 190–91, 210–12, 213–14
volleyball, 60
volunteers, 217–18, 224

walk-ons, 19
Walsh, Bill, 216
Waters, Alice, 157, 175
Wayzata, Minnesota, 243–44, 249
weekends, 127, 152

weight management, 79–86, 90, 109
Weinberger, Caspar, 4
Weinicker, Elliott, 197
Welter, Tim, 95
White, Shaun, 177
Why Johnny Hates Sports (Engh), 217
Wide World of Sports, 116
Wie, Michelle, 249
Williams, Lance, 87, 88–91
Winfrey, Oprah, 171
winning, 196, 212, 215, 218, 219, 237
Wisconsin, 93–94, 226
Wolves-Hawks Soccer Club, 58, 100, 210, 226
Women's Sports Foundation, 12–13
Women's United Soccer Association (WUSA), 12
Women's World Cup, 9–10
Woods, Earl, 207
Woods, Tiger, 67, 207
Woolf, Jamie, 164, 252
work schedules, 126, 168, 170
World Cup, 30
wrestling, 79–85
Wright Institute, 135
Wynne, Peggy, 120–21, 126, 129, 195

Young Men's Christian Association (YMCA), 32, 72, 212

Zeisz, Jennifer, 156
Zito, Barry, 216

796.083   McMahon, Regan.
M
          Revolution in the
          bleachers.

$25.00

DATE			

e kept
only
ewed

BAKER & TAYLOR